Creating the Dynamic Classroom

A Handbook for Teachers

Susan Schwartz

Mindy Pollishuke

PEARSON

Education
Canada

Edited by Kate Revington
Designed by Fortunato Design Inc.
Cover Photo: Bruce Ayres/Stone

1 2 3 4 5   08 07 06 05 04

Printed and bound in Canada

Table of Contents

Foreword

In this useful and practical teaching handbook, Susan Schwartz and Mindy Pollishuke have developed a wonderful resource package for beginning teachers and for teachers who want to rework and rethink their classroom programs and environments. This book is filled with helpful and pertinent information for organizing, planning, and implementing a dynamic classroom. As well, the authors, as experienced educators, provide a philosophical underpinning for why good teaching requires such a carefully considered approach to the set-up and the running of an effective classroom. An understanding of the nuts and bolts of how a classroom works best is exactly what teachers require if they want to focus their teaching time on the children and their different needs. By building a cooperative, collaborative, and safe place called school, we can ensure that we offer a program so professional that parents will recognize, value, and support our contributions to the education of their children. And, of course, the children will want to be there, secure in their knowledge of the way the classroom functions, of the schedule of activities, and of their own responsibilities. They will feel the satisfaction of being in a professional educator's classroom.

Someone just visiting a classroom would not necessarily understand the preplanning and preparation that go into the running of an effective learning environment for 25 or so young people. Fortunately, since Susan and Mindy have read, researched, and reflected on their own educational experiences and observations as teachers, consultants, administrators, and university instructors, they are able to present us with this wide-ranging guide to creating a dynamic classroom, a distillation of the complexities of setting up and maintaining a teaching/learning environment that functions as contemporary educational theories would suggest.

This book offers organizational strategies, teaching techniques, options for helping with management and discipline, designs and diagrams for classroom set-ups, assessment and evaluation checklists, book lists for curriculum connections, and forms for recording and communicating, many of which appear on the accompanying CD. These features address the concerns of the teachers with whom I work, and I know that *Creating the Dynamic Classroom* will help them to develop a thoughtful and practical approach to creating an effective classroom with the children at the centre.

Children are, by definition, spontaneous creatures, and for teachers, this reality poses particular challenges. How can we set up school experiences that promote learning while at the same time allowing for the developmental and explorative nature of childhood? One suggestion would be to organize the place of learning so that both our time and strength, and their energies, somehow coalesce. *That is the hallmark of a dynamic classroom,* and this book offers us both careful direction and concrete help in achieving that aim. We are fortunate indeed to have Susan Schwartz and Mindy Pollishuke providing us with support in our determination to be true professionals in our classrooms.

David Booth
Professor of Education
Ontario Institute for Studies in Education
at the University of Toronto

Preface

Welcome to the wonderful world of teaching! Beginning a career in education is a most exciting prospect but one that may be viewed with some trepidation. As you embark on creating a special environment for your students, you will have many things to consider. *Creating the Dynamic Classroom: A Handbook for Teachers* is our attempt to help you to develop and refine your practice. This book grew out of our profound interest in continuing to help teachers, both new and experienced, navigate their journeys through the multitude of theories and philosophies about teaching and learning and the many rules, regulations, and guidelines confronting them in education today.

Over ten years have passed since we wrote *Creating the Child-centred Classroom*, which was designed as a practical tool to help teachers create active, holistic classroom environments and programs. Educators at all levels have repeatedly told us how much they have benefitted from the knowledge and practical understandings our book has given them. In 1990 when the book first came out, we were thrilled to receive the Excellence in Writing Award from the Federation of Women Teachers' Associations of Ontario, acknowledging our efforts and the quality of the resource for new and experienced educators alike.

During the past decade, we have continued our pursuits and educational endeavours, continuously striving to bring theory and practice together in a manageable way. Both of us have experienced the joy of working with enthusiastic teacher candidates in preservice teacher education programs — Mindy as course director at York University's Faculty of Education Concurrent program and Susan currently as instructor and coordinator at the Ontario Institute for Studies in Education, University of Toronto. Both of us have also enjoyed working with teachers new to the profession — Mindy currently working with new teachers in her role as educational consultant with the Toronto District School Board, and Susan working with new teachers in her past roles as principal and vice-principal in both the elementary and secondary panels. These experiences have helped us realize just how useful a text such as *Creating the Child-centred Classroom* has been to new teachers and to experienced and seasoned educators, as well as to course directors at the university and college level. This thinking led us, with enthusiasm and with fresh eyes and vision, to revisit *Creating the Child-centred Classroom*.

We hope you will find our new book, *Creating the Dynamic Classroom: A Handbook for Teachers,* to be just as useful as our original resource. We use a similar format that highlights important understandings about teaching and learning, and include practical and easy-to-follow classroom-tested strategies and sample tasks. We continue to provide bibliographies of our favourite children's literature and professional resources, organized in an accessible and reader-friendly format. Useful blackline masters for student and teacher use can now be found on the accompanying CD-ROM.

Although this book focuses on elementary classroom experiences, secondary educators may find much of value here. School principals, mentors, consultants, and university faculty can use this handbook to facilitate their work with new and experienced teachers. Parents, too, may find this book helpful in providing them with a clearer understanding of what the classrooms of today and tomorrow are all about.

Like *Creating the Child-centred Classroom*, our new book offers a variety of recommended strategies for you to sample and implement. Please look carefully at what works and what does not work based on your ongoing experiences, readings, and conversations. We ask you to reflect upon your own teaching and learning needs and interests, and upon those of your students, ensuring that these are uppermost in your mind as you go about creating your own dynamic classroom.

Creating the Dynamic Classroom: A Handbook for Teachers strives to meet today's greater demands for accountability. As we experienced new political initiatives in education, we saw the evolution of clearly delineated learning expectations at each grade level, new units and resources produced to meet the needs of the curriculum, a focus on information and content learning, and a growing emphasis on standardized testing and evaluation. These changes also brought forth many budget cuts across all areas of education, a rethinking of special programs, a revamping of the role of administration, and a new look at how we go about the business of education. They also produced an increase in parental involvement and awareness. To deal with this new world, we encourage you to continue to think about and value your own personal beliefs and understandings about how children learn and how teachers teach. Your philosophy about teaching and learning directly influences what and how you teach, so it is important that you know yourself and your beliefs. You can then program effectively and appropriately for your class of learners.

With these underlying beliefs, we write and present this book. We highlight our philosophy and understandings and then provide possible learning experiences, strategies, and techniques based on these understandings. We begin by examining your classroom environment as an instructional strategy that plays a major role in what happens in your room. We look at establishing routines and classroom atmosphere as a way of instilling respect, cooperation, and collaboration, as well as valuing each person's contributions and backgrounds. We

share our views on literacy and language learning and introduce ideas for creating a balanced and effective literacy program. Technology is highlighted as we acknowledge the increased role of computers in today's society. We share ideas on planning an integrated curriculum, while at the same time, we encourage you, as the teacher, to bring your own background knowledge and interests into the classroom. We take a comprehensive look at assessment and evaluation in light of the strong emphasis on accountability today, and we share ideas on how to establish strong partnerships with parents and community, realizing that these partnerships benefit both students and the wider educational community.

In *Creating the Dynamic Classroom: A Handbook for Teachers*, we feature important information on homework as a window into your classroom. We emphasize the importance of different types of homework and of involving parents as active participants in the learning process. We also highlight the need for relevant out-of-classroom learning experiences to enrich the classroom program. We provide handy tips for new teachers as well as reminders for experienced teachers about what to do when beginning the year in a new school. Finally, we include a CD for you to personalize the letters and forms that appear throughout the book. Our hope is that you will use this CD to make our examples reflect your own personal needs and interests.

We wish you well on your continuing journey to create stimulating teaching and learning environments for your students. As you create a dynamic classroom, we encourage you to work at developing your personal philosophy of teaching and learning. We hope that you will find this text a supportive partner in your quest to bring theory and practice together in meaningful, productive, and exciting ways!

NOTE: *For the purposes of this publication the word "parents" is meant to represent parents, guardians, and other essential caregivers.*

Acknowledgements

As we collaborated during many weekend, summer, and vacation hours to produce this book, we were influenced and supported by so many wonderful people. A great big thank-you to the friends and colleagues who have inspired us with many conversations about teaching and learning.

To David Booth: We thank you for your wonderful sense of humour, your continuous encouragement, and for inspiring us to pursue our professional writing. We are truly honoured to have you write the Foreword to this book and acknowledge our work in such a public way.

To Gillda Leitenberg: A big thank you for your expertise and enthusiasm throughout this process. It is a pleasure working with you!

To Maxine Bone: Thank you for your wisdom, good advice, and friendship. We appreciate your passion for the teaching/learning process.

To Elizabeth Hartman: You continue to inspire us with your joy for teaching and your love of children. We wish you well in your retirement as you embark on new adventures.

To Kim Gordon: Your positive attitude and continuing friendship always help to remind us about the importance of collaboration and support.

To Carol Rolheiser: Special thanks for your energy, enthusiasm, guidance, and continuous modelling of the teaching/learning process.

To Barbara Goldenberg: Your enthusiasm and passion for teaching and learning help to remind all of us about the joys of being a professional.

To Ron Benson: Your continued mentorship has always been a guiding light when times were unsure. You have given us good advice, good laughs, and great ideas!

To Julia Arnold and Roz Doctorow: You have both always given of yourselves, personally and professionally, and we appreciate your sound judgment and good advice.

To the English Literacy Team at the Toronto District School Board. You have all been so supportive and encouraging over these past years.

To Larry Swartz: We value your friendship, energy, and thoughtful, caring approach to life.

Warm thanks to *Anne Marie Chudleigh, Doug McDougall, Steve Anderson, and the North Option Learning Community team at OISE/UT.* Your support over the past few years has been much appreciated.

To the rest of our colleagues across the Toronto District School Board, York Region District School Board, at OISE/UT, and at York University: Our sincere appreciation for your insights, professional dialogue, and ongoing encouragement as we embark on new and exciting initiatives.

A special thank you to the many *teacher candidates* that we have worked with at OISE/UT and York University. Your zest for learning and enthusiasm for the teaching profession have given us the impetus to write this book in order to guide you in your journey into the world of education.

Acknowledgments to the *staff, students, and parents* of Arbor Glen Public School, Earl Haig Secondary School, Harrison Public School, and Firgrove Public School in the Toronto District School Board, and at Upper Canada College

Preparatory School and to all the new and experienced teachers we have worked with over the years. Our work with you has helped us to conceptualize and crystallize some of the ideas in this book.

To our husbands Saul and Stephen: We are grateful for your continuous patience, encouragement, and support of our efforts every step of the way. You have always been there for us and with us!

To Marnie, Rena, Kimberly, Michael, and Matthew, our loving children: You continue to teach us about the true meaning of lifelong learning and education. You are our touchstones, always bringing us back to reality and the importance of family. We are pleased with your every achievement and anticipate your future successes with much joy. We are especially proud of our daughters, Marnie, Rena, and Kimberly, who are embarking on their own careers in education. Knowing that they have been surrounded by "teacher talk" all of their lives, we are not surprised at their calling in life. Our sons, Michael and Matthew, continue to help us in many ways, including coming to our rescue when our writing demands call for greater understanding of technology.

And finally, a warm and loving thanks to all of our family and friends: We value you for supporting our efforts and achievements, and for always being there for us and listening when we needed an ear. We are grateful for your love.

1 Philosophical Understandings

Welcome to our vision of the wonderful world of education! Come along with us as we take you on an exciting journey down many paths and around many corners.

As we began to map out this journey, we wanted to show you, in a concrete and visual way, the philosophical underpinnings for this book. As we talked, wrote, drew, and experimented with a number of ideas, the image of a wheel surfaced repeatedly. A wheel can move constantly, just as education changes, adapts, and evolves to meet the needs of this day and age. As an educator, you need to have a sound philosophical and theoretical foundation in this era of rapid change. You also need to know yourself well in order to adapt to these changes in a positive way.

The Momentum of a Wheel

Just as the spokes on the wheels of a bicycle move together in order to work effectively, so, too, do the components that create a dynamic classroom need to work together to make an effective learning environment. The spokes of the wheel represent the many components that are necessary in creating effective classrooms. These components support the wheel and help to keep it moving towards the ultimate goal of lifelong learning.

The components are highlighted and explained in each of the chapters in this book. The physical set-up, the classroom atmosphere, and the timetabling possibilities all work towards establishing effective learning environments. When you plan an integrated curriculum, you create environments for literacy, incorporate technology into aspects of your curriculum, include homework as a window into your classrooms, provide out-of-classroom excursions to complement and reinforce your units of study, and use a learning centre approach to encourage interaction, collaboration, and active learning. Throughout this process, you need to maintain records and assess and evaluate your learners constantly. You also need to remember that ongoing communication with parents and involvement of parents are vital aspects of the process.

The centre of the wheel, or the axle, represents the partners in the educational process — the students, the educators, and the parents — all of whom need to work together to keep the wheel moving forward.

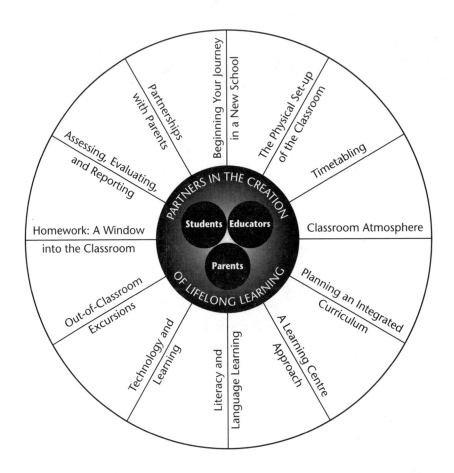

Figure 1.1 *Moving towards creating the dynamic classroom*

The wheel is surrounded by the sturdy outer rim, which, for our analogy, represents the basic conditions required for successful learning. These conditions, first outlined by Dr. Brian Cambourne, head of the Centre for Studies in Literacy at Wollongong University in Australia, are not linear or sequential, but interconnected and interwoven. They can be summarized as immersion, demonstration, expectations, responsibility, approximations, practice, and feedback. Just as the wheel is circular, so, too, are the conditions of learning. They interact dynamically and in complex ways with one another.

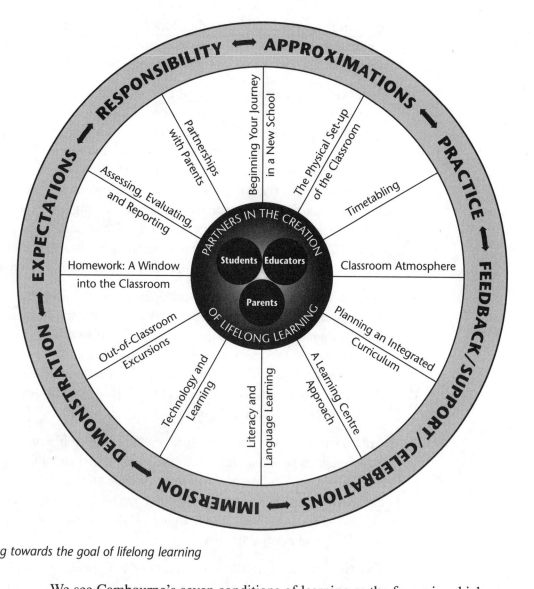

Figure 1.2 *Moving towards the goal of lifelong learning*

We see Cambourne's seven conditions of learning as the frame in which learning occurs. Each of these conditions is outlined below.

Immersion: When you are learning something new, you need to be immersed in the content and context of that new learning. The more you are immersed, the more you internalize the new learning and it becomes a part of you. As a teacher, you need to provide environments and learning experiences that immerse learners in the sights, sounds, and content of the curriculum. Students need to be saturated with meaningful and relevant content and contexts in order to make sense of the new learning.

Demonstration: Demonstrations provide practical and concrete models for learners. These can be planned or spontaneous, but always require an explicit action that provides learners with a visual or auditory representation of the new learning. Demonstrations are the artifacts shared, the read-aloud opportunities, the words used in a think-aloud experience, the examples you present, and the exemplary samples of student work. Demonstrations are the models of the process and products that you want students to emulate.

Expectations: Expectations are the knowledge, skills, and attitudes that you expect your students to know, be able to do, and value. These need to be developmentally appropriate and geared to the age and stage of the specific learners. As a teacher, you need to ensure that realistic and achievable expectations are clearly understood by students. Expectations can be developed in collaboration with students and parents in order to increase ownership and understanding. Always encourage your students to reach for the highest expectations while still allowing them to make mistakes and to learn from them. Above all else, ensure that you create a supportive environment where students will feel valued and motivated to achieve the desired goals and to reach their potential.

Responsibility: When students take part in problem-solving experiences and have opportunities for choice, they make decisions and become more accountable for their own actions. They become more responsible. As a teacher, you need to ensure that students have many opportunities for leadership experiences in order to feel responsibility for and take ownership of their own learning. Providing opportunities for students to take responsibility should be a key aspect of your program and practice.

Approximations: Approximations are the cornerstones of learning as students explore and experiment, take risks, make mistakes, and ultimately learn from their mistakes. As a teacher, you must provide your students with an environment that promotes risk taking so that they feel free to make approximations, to "have-a-go," to try out new learnings as they move along the continuum towards lifelong learning.

Practice: Students need many opportunities to practise and use their knowledge, skills, and attitudes in authentic ways. You need to provide time for students to practise in large and small groups, and individually. Practice becomes an integral part of the teaching/learning process when students are given the time to refine, synthesize, and integrate their learning.

Feedback/Support/Celebrations: Feedback should occur continuously and in a variety of ways. As you provide feedback to your students, you are responding to their learning in a supportive and encouraging way. You need to celebrate all successes and encourage students to meet new challenges by providing them with concrete and realistic feedback that helps them to set goals, plan their next steps, and move towards positive outcomes. Value all attempts at learning as you provide feedback that will nudge your students towards reaching positive goals.

Final Thoughts

If you are a beginning teacher, you have a unique journey ahead of you. You will acquire new knowledge, experience, and support as you pedal and steer towards creating a dynamic learning environment. This support can be represented by the training wheels on a bicycle. These extra wheels provide the necessary balance to keep you from falling. Experienced teachers, consultants, and administrators will act as mentors, providing the necessary support through collaboration, ongoing feedback, and coaching. As you internalize the skills, knowledge, and values of effective teaching, you will be able to shed the training wheels and travel the path of professional growth and lifelong learning with a greater sense of confidence. You will continue your journey as you read professionally, take courses, attend workshops, collaborate with your peers, take on leadership roles, and ultimately become a mentor to someone else beginning their journey. If you are an experienced teacher, our hope is that this book will also provide support for you as you continue on your journey towards creating the dynamic classroom.

2 The Physical Set-up of the Classroom

The classroom environment that you create has a profound effect on the social, emotional, physical, and intellectual development of the learners you teach. To gain a positive attitude towards school and learning, your students must have visual stimulation, organization, space, and a feeling of warmth and security. Devoting time and energy to the planning and physical set-up of your classroom is well worthwhile. In fact, the learning environment can be and should be regarded as an important teaching or instructional strategy. How you set up the physical environment plays an important role in determining how your students will respond, learn, and relate to one another. An engaging environment is more likely to invite students to become involved and excited about learning. Just a few changes can bring about major results and can influence the sense of community in the classroom.

We suggest you think carefully about your room arrangement and how you can make it work for you.

One of the first things to do is to designate a meeting area where a variety of learning experiences will take place with the whole class. In this area, an essential part of your program will occur, including direct instruction, chanting, singing, presenting, sharing, and discussion. Bringing your students together to an area where they are in close proximity to you and to one another encourages open dialogue, group interaction, and a relaxed flow of ideas.

Next, it is important to consider how to set up student desks or tables. You will want to maximize the amount of space you have, while, at the same time, ensuring that students can work in cooperative groups. You may want to set up specific work areas, stations, or learning centres in the room where students will share, cooperate, and work together with a variety of materials and resources.

Setting up areas for materials that students will use, as well as for audio-visual and computer equipment, will help you use the physical characteristics of your room to best advantage. Placing a variety of storage facilities around the room or near the work areas provides students with easy access to resources and materials. It also encourages student independence and leadership.

A variety of display areas, with student work appearing on bulletin boards or walls, hanging from the ceiling, or resting on tables or shelves, enhances the appearance of your classroom and sparks interest in learning. An organized look to your classroom and clearly defined areas help students feel safe and secure. Motivation to achieve often increases as students see their work on display and feel pride and ownership.

Ensure that all your students are represented in the environment that you create in your classroom. The pictures, posters, signs, and so on should reflect the diversity in your classroom as well as in the school, district, and wider global community. Seeing reflections of the diverse backgrounds and cultures in the classroom through the student work encourages all students to feel valued and part of a community of learners.

Creating the Physical Set-up of the Classroom

◆ Establish a large-group meeting area (preferably carpeted) with a teacher's chair and chart stand or chalkboard within easy reach.

◆ Set up a work area (near a sink, if possible) for art, paint, and craft materials and activities. Prepare bins of craft and junk materials, such as paper (construction, tissue, wallpaper, shiny paper), felt, pipe-cleaners, tin foil, string, wool, and ribbon. Storing glue, tape, scissors, rulers, and staplers in labelled bins or on the counter permits easy access and cleanup.

◆ Set up work areas or learning centres close to the electrical outlets to facilitate the use of audiovisual equipment (tape recorders, CD players, overhead projectors) and computer technology. If possible, have a bank of computers in one area to facilitate specific teaching of computer skills. (Refer to Chapter 8, Technology and Learning.)

◆ Set up any other desired learning centres. (Refer to Chapter 6, A Learning Centre Approach.)

◆ Look at the furniture and storage equipment available to see if these are the appropriate size and height for your students.

◆ Set up the desks or tables to accommodate small groupings of students working together. Figure 2.1 shows some furniture arrangements you can try.

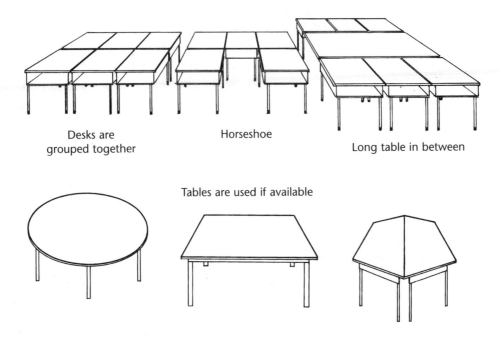

Desks are
grouped together

Horseshoe

Long table in between

Tables are used if available

Figure 2.1 *Possible furniture arrangements*

◆ Collect the equipment that will be housed in your room, such as computers, tape recorder, overhead projector and screen, and decide where these will be placed to their best advantage and use.

◆ Ensure that you have pencil sharpeners that work, trash cans, paper towels, and other essentials, such as chalk/whiteboard erasers, pencils, crayons, markers, rulers, paper, tape, and staplers.

◆ Set up shelves or other containers for storage and display of materials and resources. These may be placed near the work areas or around the periphery of the room for easy access by all students. Figure 2.2 illustrates some arrangements you can use.

Figure 2.2 *Ideas for storage*

Coloured tape to
organize surfaces

Cut-out plastic bottles

Variety of cans

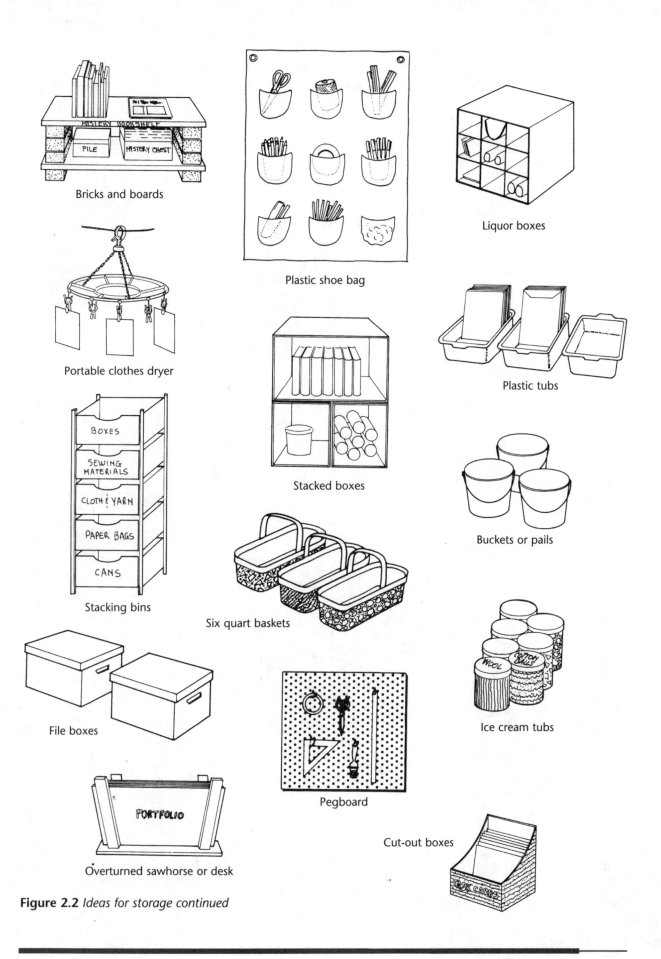

Bricks and boards

Plastic shoe bag

Liquor boxes

Portable clothes dryer

Stacked boxes

Plastic tubs

Stacking bins

BOXES

SEWING MATERIALS

CLOTH & YARN

PAPER BAGS

CANS

Six quart baskets

Buckets or pails

File boxes

Pegboard

Ice cream tubs

WOOL   COTTON BALLS

PORTFOLIO

Overturned sawhorse or desk

Cut-out boxes

TASK CARDS

Figure 2.2 *Ideas for storage continued*

♦ Determine areas for teacher and student displays. Be creative! Figure 2.3 shows some possibilities.

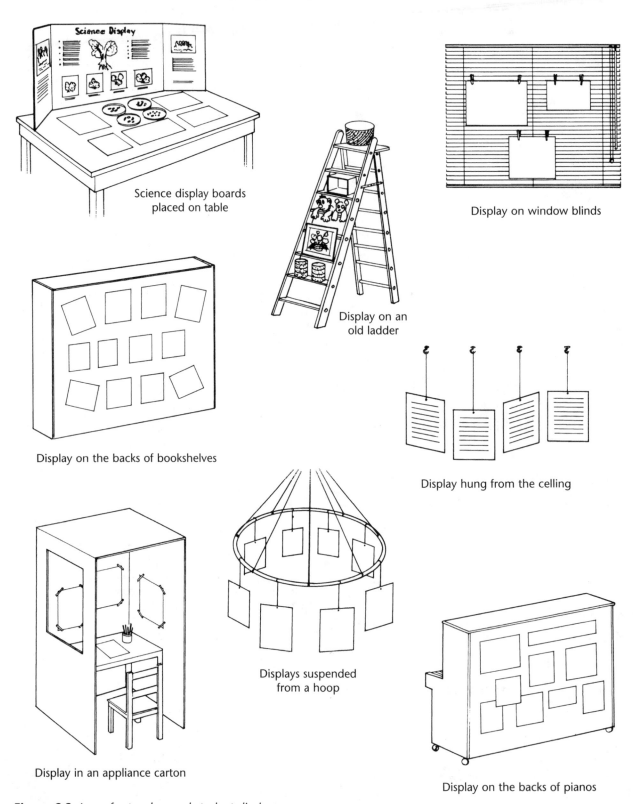

Science display boards placed on table

Display on an old ladder

Display on window blinds

Display on the backs of bookshelves

Display hung from the celling

Display in an appliance carton

Displays suspended from a hoop

Display on the backs of pianos

Figure 2.3 *Areas for teacher and student displays*

✦ Plan the different types of displays you will create on your bulletin boards. Remember to consider all the areas available for display, including the hall, your classroom door, or other convenient wall space.

✦ Depending on the effect you want to have, choose backing on your bulletin boards that is durable, colourful, or neutral. Some ideas for backing include fadeless paper, fabric, wallpaper, and paint.

✦ Think about the content presented in each display and ensure that you have a heading or title that captures the intended message. Here are a few examples:

Figure 2.4 *Effective display headings*

✦ One particular bulletin board, perhaps titled "Our Best Work," could present a variety of student work samples across various curriculum areas.

✦ Ensure that headings or titles are large enough to read, and that these and the displays are visually appealing and able to attract the attention of students and visitors.

✦ Headings or titles of displays do not need to be centred at the top of the bulletin board, but could be in the middle, at the bottom, or wherever. Be creative!

✦ Keep in mind that displays need not be one-dimensional, but rather, could feature student work or materials that are raised and off the backing, displayed with a ripple effect, off centre, or at different angles. Many possibilities exist. See Figure 2.5 for some ideas for bulletin board displays.

Figure 2.5 *Possibilities for displays and headings*

✦ Ensure that you have clearly defined areas, and that you can easily rearrange your learning environment to accommodate specific learning experiences as they arise. You may want to begin one way, and as the year progresses, change the room arrangement to suit the needs and interests of your students and program. Flexibility is the key! Figure 2.6 shows two examples of classroom set-ups.

Figure 2.6 *Two examples of classroom set-ups*

As you effectively construct the physical layout of your classroom environment, you will see how the overall set-up can and will invite your students to explore, interact, investigate, and learn. It is important that you continuously reflect on the use of space, organization, and accessibility of materials and resources in order to assess the overall effectiveness. Flexibility of structure, layout, and design is essential in creating a comfortable, secure, and dynamic classroom environment.

3 Timetabling

Finding time for everything and everyone is a continuing challenge in our daily lives and in the dynamic classroom. You will find that no one timetable can accommodate every teacher or student need, every style of teaching or learning, or every programming consideration. Learning takes time, and when preparing a timetable, you should remember to be flexible — flexible to adapt to your students' ever-changing needs, to unexpected changes in schedule, and to changes in planning and programming.

Class scheduling involves planning for blocks of time. *Horizontal* blocks of time, which might occur at the same time each day, are often necessary to meet school organizational requirements. You may find that time for physical education, French, or Spanish, which may be taught by someone other than yourself, usually needs to be scheduled first. In addition, scheduling for *preparation time* affects your timetable. It is ideal if your preparation time can be linked with that of a team partner so that you can engage in team planning during the school day.

Vertical blocks of time are essential in promoting longer and more sustained attention to tasks. These blocks of time accommodate more intensive, active investigations and provide opportunities for you to address specific areas of the curriculum. They also allow students to pursue their individual areas of interest or to plan collaboratively with you. When planning for these blocks of time, be sure to balance all curriculum areas, including language arts, mathematics, social studies, science and technology, and the arts. By taking an integrated approach to planning your units of study, you will be better able to accommodate the time needed for all subject areas.

When planning your day, you will want to include *input sessions* that allow time for large-group discussion, direct instruction, demonstration, and explanation. You will also want to provide *daily sharing times*. These times allow students to celebrate what they know, what they have learned, and what they have accomplished. Students' self-concept and confidence levels improve as they share and take pride in their efforts.

Exercising flexibility in timetabling is the key to effective scheduling. It allows you to tailor your plans to meet the particular needs and interests of your students on a daily basis.

Creating Timetabling Possibilities

✦ Schedule horizontal blocks of time for specific subject areas, such as French, physical education, and other subjects that might involve different teachers. Doing so will assist in the booking of the gym or other facilities, such as the music room or computer lab. Figure 3.1 illustrates horizontal blocks of time.

	Monday	Tuesday	Wednesday	Thursday	Friday
8:45					
9:15	Physical Ed.	Physical Ed.	Physical Ed.	Physical Ed.	Physical Ed.
9:45	French	French	French	French	French
10:30	Computer Lab				
11:30					
12:45			Music		Music

Figure 3.1 *Horizontal blocks of time*

✦ Try to arrange your preparation time so that it coincides with that scheduled for your team partner or for a same-grade teacher to facilitate planning and delivery of program.

✦ Once your horizontal blocks of time are scheduled, examine your timetable for larger vertical blocks of time. Figure 3.5 later in this chapter shows one example of a vertical block of time.

✦ To begin your year, choose one large block of time for language arts or two smaller blocks for reading and writing. Ensure that you allow sufficient time for read-aloud, shared reading, guided reading, independent reading, shared writing, modelled writing, and independent writing. Refer to Chapter 7, Literacy and Language Learning, for more information on these learning experiences.

- Choose a daily block of time for mathematics and ensure that you have opportunities for direct instruction, cooperative learning, and independent practice. Remember to address all the components of mathematics, including number and computation, measurement, geometry, data management, probability, and problem solving.

- Choose a large block of time for your integrated study, which may revolve around science and technology, health education, or social studies. These integrated studies may also address language, mathematics, and the arts.

- Ensure that your arts curriculum is integrated into your units of study. Chapter 5, Planning an Integrated Curriculum, offers some guidance. You should also allocate specific time throughout the week and year to a more direct focus on the arts.

- Allow time for flexible input sessions and for sharing when appropriate.

- At the beginning of the year, schedule time when you will introduce lessons to promote social skills and cooperation in small-group learning experiences. Chapter 4, Classroom Atmosphere, addresses these issues.

- Use one of the following timetables when implementing learning centres in your program. (See Chapter 6, A Learning Centre Approach.)

Example 1: *A Six-Day Cycle*

A rotation system is one way to begin a learning centre approach. If you set up six centres, students work in one of the six centres each day and then rotate to another centre the next day. The rotation cycle will be completed over six days. (See Figure 3.2.)

	Monday	**Tuesday**	**Wednesday**	**Thursday**	**Friday**	**Monday**	**Tuesday**
10:30 – 11:30	1st Rotation	2nd Rotation	3rd Rotation	4th Rotation	5th Rotation	6th Rotation	1st Rotation

Figure 3.2 *Six-day cycle rotation*

Example 2: *A Three-Day Cycle*

Once you and your students are comfortable with rotations, you may want students to visit two centres each day during one or two time blocks. It will take three days for the class to rotate through the six centres. (See Figure 3.3.)

	Monday	**Tuesday**	**Wednesday**	**Thursday**	**Friday**	**Monday**
10:30 – 11:30	1st Rotation	3rd Rotation	5th Rotation	1st Rotation	3rd Rotation	5th Rotation
1:15 – 2:15	2nd Rotation	4th Rotation	6th Rotation	2nd Rotation	4th Rotation	6th Rotation

Figure 3.3 *Three-day cycle rotation*

Example 3: *A Two-Day Cycle*

If your students rotate through three centres each day, it will take two days to complete the cycle. (See Figure 3.4.) With this type of schedule, your students spend the majority of their day working at learning centres. You need to be diligent in ensuring that you address major areas of the curriculum at these centres.

	Monday	**Tuesday**	**Wednesday**	**Thursday**	**Friday**
8:45	Writing	Writing	Writing	Writing	Writing
9:15	Physical Ed.	Physical Ed.	Physical Ed.	Physical Ed.	Physical Ed.
9:45	French	French	French	French	French
10:30 – 11:30	1st Rotation	4th Rotation	1st Rotation	4th Rotation	1st Rotation
12:45	*D.E.A.R.	*D.E.A.R.	*D.E.A.R.	*D.E.A.R.	*D.E.A.R.
1:15 – 2:15	2nd Rotation	5th Rotation	2nd Rotation	5th Rotation	2nd Rotation
2:30 – 3:30	3rd Rotation	6th Rotation	3rd Rotation	6th Rotation	3rd Rotation

*D.E.A.R. means **D**rop **E**verything **A**nd **R**ead.

Figure 3.4 *Two-day cycle rotation*

✦ If you monitor student movement among learning centres using a planning board or tracking sheet, the following timetables may prove useful. See Chapter 6, A Learning Centre Approach, for more information on how to implement planning boards and tracking sheets.

Example 1: *Focus on Learning Centres*

In this timetable (Figure 3.5), a separate block of time is designated for mathematics, where there would be several centres with mathematics as the focus. There would also be another block of time for integrated studies in language arts, social studies, science and technology, and the arts.

	Monday	Tuesday	Wednesday	Thursday	Friday
8:45	Writing	Writing	Writing	Writing	Writing
9:15	Physical Ed.	Physical Ed.	Physical Ed.	Physical Ed.	Physical Ed.
9:45	French	French	French	French	French
10:30 – 11:30	LEARNING CENTRE TIME (MATHEMATICS)				
12:45	*D.E.A.R.	*D.E.A.R.	*D.E.A.R.	*D.E.A.R.	*D.E.A.R.
1:15 – 3:30	LEARNING CENTRE TIME (INTEGRATED LANGUAGE ARTS/THE ARTS/SOCIAL STUDIES OR SCIENCE)				

Figure 3.5 *Focus on learning centres*

*D.E.A.R. means **D**rop **E**verything **A**nd **R**ead.

Example 2: *Focus on Integrated Studies*

This timetable (Figure 3.6) indicates that students are participating in active learning experiences for the greater part of the day. You must ensure that all curriculum areas are clearly addressed at the centres.

	Monday	Tuesday	Wednesday	Thursday	Friday
8:45	Writing	Writing	Writing	Writing	Writing
9:15	Physical Ed.	Physical Ed.	Physical Ed.	Physical Ed.	Physical Ed.
9:45	French	French	French	French	French
10:30 – 3:30	↕ LEARNING CENTRE TIME (INTEGRATED TASKS FOR ALL CURRICULUM AREAS) ↕				

Figure 3.6 *Focus on integrated studies*

◆ Create a weekly plan that meets your timetable needs and allows you to see the week at a glance. (See Figure 3.7.)

Time	Monday	Tuesday	Wednesday	Thursday	Friday
8:45 – 9:15	**Process Writing** Intro. Class Cooperative Big Book – Pioneer Life	**Process Writing** Cont. with Big Book	**Process Writing**	**Process Writing**	**Computer Lab**
9:15 – 10:15	**Language Arts** Whole Group Reading *Book Bins* ──▶ Guided Reading – Red Group	**Language Arts** Guided Reading – Blue Group & Green Group	**Language Arts** Guided Reading – Yellow Group & Red Group	**Language Arts** Guided Reading – Blue Group & Red Group	**Language Arts** Check Book Bin Work
10:15 – 10:30	RECESS	RECESS	RECESS	RECESS	RECESS
10:30 – 11:30	**Mathematics** Geometry – 3D shapes	**Mathematics** Number – 3-digit addition with regrouping	**Mathematics** Geometry	**Mathematics** Number	**Mathematics** Geometry
11:30 – 12:30	LUNCH	LUNCH	LUNCH	LUNCH	LUNCH
12:30 – 12:45	D.E.A.R.	D.E.A.R.	D.E.A.R.	D.E.A.R.	D.E.A.R.
12:55 – 1:30	**Phys. Ed.** Gymnastics	**Health** Nutrition	**Phys. Ed.** Gymnastics	**Music** Pioneer songs	**Phys. Ed.** Gymnastics
1:30 – 2:15	**Social Studies** Integrated Pioneer Unit	**Social Studies** Integrated Pioneer Unit	**Social Studies** Integrated Pioneer Unit	**Visual Arts** Integrated Pioneer Unit	**Language** Integrated Pioneer Unit
2:15 – 2:30	RECESS	RECESS	RECESS	RECESS	RECESS
2:30 – 3:30	**Social Studies** Integrated Pioneer Unit	**Social Studies** Integrated Pioneer Unit	**Science** Structures	**Visual Arts** Integrated Pioneer Unit	**Science** Structures

BLM T-1* **Figure 3.7** *Sample weekly timetable*

*Note: The CD-ROM symbol/BLM and number indicates that the figure is reproduced in the Blackline Masters on the interactive CD-ROM that accompanies this book. Teachers can manipulate the content of the masters to meet their particular needs.

- ✦ Review your weekly schedule and allocate the time you will need for specific learning experiences or direct instruction lessons in the different areas of the curriculum. Some lessons may require daily scheduling while others may occur only two or three times per week.

- ✦ Create a daily plan that meets your timetable needs. (See Figure 3.8.) You might want to use a plan that allows you to record specific time slots, learning expectations, tasks, assessment strategies, resources needed, and other considerations.

Time	Curriculum Area/Learning Experience	Grouping*	Learning Expectations	Description	Materials	Assessment
8:30 – 9:15	**Language Arts** – Process Writing	I	– use adjectives for describing	– in their writing folders, create one page of class coop big book on Pioneer Life	large paper, marker, pencils	Work sample – sentences include at least one adjective
9:15 – 10:15	**Language Arts** – Read-Aloud – Shared Reading – Guided Reading/Book Bins	W W W S	– understand main idea – use expression in oral reading – find main idea	– read *A Pioneer Life* – ask questions to elicit main idea regarding life then – read chorally passage from story – Blue, Green, Yellow: cont. with Book Bin work – Red: read *Pioneers Long Ago* – discuss new words, main ideas	Books: *A Pioneer Life* (6 copies) *Pioneers Long Ago* – Book Bins – Guided Reading record sheets	Observation – note who identifies main idea in large group – check bins on Friday – Running record
10:15 – 10:30	RECESS	RECESS	RECESS	RECESS	RECESS	RECESS
10:30 – 11:30	**Mathematics** – Number: addition	W S I	– able to add 3-digit numbers with regrouping	– use manipulatives to demonstrate regrouping process – exploration centres & small groups for reinforcement	Multilinks Centre tasks — see textbook, p.49 for centre tasks	Observation Work samples

*Grouping: W = Whole class; S = Small group; I = Individual

 **BLM T-2 Figure 3.8** *Sample daily plan*

◆ In reviewing your daily plan, decide how you will begin each day. Decide whether your students will meet as a large group as they enter, or become involved immediately in small-group or individual tasks.

NOTE: Traditionally, it has been the practice for primary students to meet in a large-group area as they enter the class. Instead, you might want to have them engage in individual tasks, such as reading or independent writing, doing a math problem, or working independently at learning centres. Doing this means that valuable time is not wasted waiting for you or for school announcements. You are also freed to respond to parents and concerns, take attendance, or collect notes. Time for large-group tasks, such as looking at the calendar and discussing the rest of the day's events, could be scheduled for later in the morning.

◆ Examine your daily timetable to plan for your students' transitions from one learning experience to another. Ensure that these transition times are smooth and well organized so that students always make productive use of their time. Chapter 4, Classroom Atmosphere, provides further information.

◆ If you are using homework planners, or agendas, schedule daily time for your students to record information in their planners. Decide when you will check that their planners are up-to-date and that homework is completed.

◆ Ensure that you allow time at the end of the day for students to tidy up and for you to distribute any notes going home. Bring closure to the day by having your students reflect on what they have accomplished and learned, and what they will do differently tomorrow.

In creating your timetable, remain flexible and open to changes. Expect to make adjustments to your timetable as you plan your program, establish routines, and encourage independence and confidence in your students. You may find that you will begin with one timetable but that you will change it as needs arise and as the year progresses.

4 Classroom Atmosphere

Creating a warm, caring, and non-threatening atmosphere in your classroom will not happen without careful thought and planning. Such a desirable atmosphere will help your students learn in exciting and meaningful ways. They will feel safe to take risks, express their views, and work well with others. With your help, they will become a community of learners where mutual respect and self-worth prevail.

In creating a positive and dynamic classroom atmosphere, you can readily apply Cambourne's seven conditions of learning. You can help your students believe in themselves and in the value of school and lifelong learning by *immersing* them in a wide variety of active/interactive learning experiences in a pleasant and safe environment. As you *demonstrate* respect and caring at all times, provide clear *expectations* for their learning and behaviour, and encourage *approximations* and risk taking, you are gradually building a positive classroom atmosphere. Your students will realize that people learn from and through their mistakes. They will become risk takers, decision makers, and problem solvers as they *practise* their cooperative skills and learn together. When they are given opportunities to help establish and monitor classroom rules and routines, they take ownership and begin to realize more and more that the *responsibility* for their actions and goal setting lies within themselves. Your job is to provide *feedback* and support, encouraging your students to move towards positive goals.

Managing the classroom is one of the most important aspects of the art of teaching. Good classroom management allows you to work with students in a positive and encouraging way. It allows you to use preventative measures to avoid unnecessary interruptions in the flow of your program to deal with the misbehaviours that will arise no matter how well you have planned your program. Internalizing and using a repertoire of effective classroom management strategies will allow you to get on with the business at hand: teaching your students in an exciting, motivating, and creative way.

You can actively encourage and demonstrate the importance of cooperation and collaboration by planning experiences in which students need to cooperate with others in order to learn. Students will find out that cooperation is a life skill and a necessary and fundamental requirement in today's society. Promoting cooperative, *heterogeneous* groupings in the classroom encourages students to participate in peer teaching. As students work together, they are given many opportunities to clarify their ideas. They develop better problem-solving and decision-making strategies. They gain respect for one another, are better able to appreciate another person's perspective, and become more accepting of other races, genders, cultures, and socioeconomic groups. They become more responsible, more independent, and more task-oriented, often gaining a more positive attitude towards school.

Although cooperative, heterogeneous groupings are usually best for meeting the needs of all your students, you will sometimes need to form *homogeneous* groupings. Such groupings can address specific academic, social, and emotional needs of individual students in your classroom. In the past, homogeneous groupings were seen as the only way to deal with individual differences. For example, teachers grouped the good readers together, the poor readers together, then all the rest. The existence of these static groups resulted in students being labelled, and some students carried these labels with them throughout their school years. Short-term, flexible, and purposeful homogeneous groupings are now the norm rather than the exception. Ideally, homogeneous groupings are temporary and are used as a forum for teaching at the point of need. When you observe that some students need a particular skill or concept, form a small, temporary group. Direct teaching in this small-group situation is an effective and meaningful use of your time.

If you create a classroom that promotes mutual respect, risk taking, peer teaching, decision making, problem solving, and cooperation, you are better able to serve as a facilitator of learning. As your students experience, experiment, and learn together, you are free to circulate, observe, analyze, assess, assist, and instruct individuals and small groups.

Creating an Effective Learning Atmosphere

✦ In creating a safe and cooperative atmosphere, use common sense and be alert: continuously survey your classroom; move around the room and among your students as they work and interact with others; keep your students in your line of sight, for example, do not stand with your back to your class at the board or in the gym; and project a sense of "with-it-ness," demonstrating that you are aware at all times of what is going on in your classroom.

✦ Always avoid sarcastic and negative comments, which can harm students' self-esteem.

✦ Remember to consistently stop and wait for all students' attention before you or someone else speaks. Never talk over your students' voices.

✦ Understand and use a repertoire of classroom management strategies to prevent minor misbehaviours from escalating. Those outlined below depend upon body language, facial expressions, and voice intonation (Bennett and Smilanich).

  1. *Proximity:* Move closer to students to indicate to them that you are there, watching and monitoring their behaviour.

  2. *The "look":* Communicate to students that what they are doing is inappropriate by looking directly at them for a few seconds and then smiling or nodding and carrying on.

  3. *The "pause":* Stop your lesson for a few seconds to wait until the minor misbehaviour ends.

  4. *A gesture:* Place your finger on your lips or put your hand up to indicate stop.

  5. *Use of a student's name:* Calmly say the student's name to acknowledge that you are aware of the behaviour and expect things to change. If you find yourself using the same name often, consider whether this strategy may be counterproductive. Some students seem to thrive on this attention for negative behaviour.

NOTE: Your body should resonate that you are in charge, but should also show that you are inclusive and welcoming. If one message becomes more pronounced than the other, you run the risk of seeming either too wishy-washy or too tough minded. Practising the five just-outlined strategies in front of a mirror would help you achieve that perfect balance in your body language.

✦ Think about why students misbehave. It is important to identify the underlying causes. Often, students are seeking attention because they lack positive interactions with adults and peers, or a feeling of self-worth. Children need recognition and attention, and if they do not receive them for positive actions, they will seek them in negative and unconventional ways.

✦ Ignore some minor misbehaviours so that the flow of your lesson is not unduly disrupted. If you stop every time to address misbehaviours, you may be reinforcing them as the students become encouraged by your attention.

✦ Ensure that your students know that you will follow through with appropriate consequences when necessary. Be consistent and predictable.

✦ Establish clear and consistent routines and procedures for your classroom. The following questionnaire, Figure 4.1, is a guide to help you establish these routines and procedures.

**Questionnaire for Establishing
Classroom Routines and Procedures**

What procedures do you have for student entry into the classroom?

What are your procedures for exit and entry for:

— fire drill?

— gym?

— library?

— lunchroom?

— other?

What are the student tasks upon entry:

— in the morning?

— after each recess?

— after lunch?

— after physical education?

What are your expectations for students:

— in large-group situations?

— in small-group situations?

— for individual tasks?

— for indoor recess?

— for the lunchroom program?

— for the gym?

— for the library/resource centre?

— for the computer lab?

— for learning centres?

— other?

**Questionnaire for Establishing
Classroom Routines and Procedures**

How do you call for students' attention when they are working individually or in small groups in the classroom? (Examples: STOP and LISTEN! Give me 5! Hands up!)

How do you recognize individual students when they want to contribute in a large-group situation? (Examples: have them raise their hands, pass a talking stick, call out responses.)

What do your students do when they finish their work?

What are your washroom use procedures?

What procedures do you have for storage of:

— students' personal belongings?

— students' completed work?

— students' work to be completed?

— students' materials and resources?

— teacher's resources?

— other?

How do you distribute materials to students during class time?

How do you distribute materials, work, and notices to go home?

How do you collect students' materials?

What cleanup procedures do you have for individuals, groups, and monitors?

What are your procedures for dismissal?

What are your procedures for collecting homework?

What other routines and expectations have you established to encourage appropriate behaviour and actions?

BLM T-3 Figure 4.1 *Questionnaire for establishing classroom routines and procedures*

◆ Continuously reflect on your program to ensure that you are meeting the needs and interests of all your students through careful planning and the implementing of exciting and dynamic lessons. Doing so should prevent misbehaviours due to students becoming frustrated or bored. (Refer to Chapter 5, Planning an Integrated Curriculum, and Chapter 6, A Learning Centre Approach.)

◆ Consider how long you are requiring your students to sit and listen for any one period of time. When students are required to sit and listen for a prolonged period of time, they tend to misbehave. A good barometer is to have them sit and listen for as many minutes as their age in years. For example, a six-year-old would be required to sit and listen for not much longer than six minutes.

◆ Plan for your students' transitions from one learning experience to another. Ensure that transitions are smooth and well organized by giving clear instructions and directions, having materials and resources ready for use, and thinking carefully about all routines to be followed. See Figure 4.2.

---

1. When students are required to line up or be dismissed, call them by groups, by the colours they are wearing, by the first letter of their name, by the month of their birthdays, etc.

2. When students are required to retrieve materials, either individually or for their group, stand near the materials to monitor any difficulties that may arise.

3. When you plan to have students work as partners or in groups, first explain *what* they have to do and then tell them *how* (as partners or in groups). Doing this will ensure that they pay full attention to the instructions.

4. Time your students as they move through a transitional period. Discuss the length of time they used and set goals to improve the time.

Figure 4.2 *Ideas for smooth transitions*

◆ With your students, brainstorm and develop rules and routines for your classroom, or a code of behaviour where appropriate consequences are clearly delineated. Some consequences are as follows:

- discussion/counselling
- recording of events and what was learned
- loss of privileges
- staying after school
- written communication with home to be signed and returned
- telephone contact with parent

- a conference with parent and student
- involvement with in-school resource staff or the principal
- payment for repair or replacement of damaged property
- community service
- informal suspension
- formal suspension
- alternative programming
- involvement with outside agencies

NOTE: *Always focus on providing logical consequences (vs. punishments), encouraging students to take responsibility for their actions and creating opportunities for growth, learning, and goal setting. Consequences should be directly related to the misbehaviour — a natural extension of the actions. Barbara Colorosa, in* Kids Are Worth It, *says it well: "Consequences need to be reasonable, simple, valuable, and practical."*

✦ Use your school's code of behaviour, if available, as a foundation for developing your own classroom code of behaviour.

✦ Involve your students in a variety of *team-building experiences* where the prime objectives are to promote teamwork, collaboration, cooperation, mutual respect, and a sense of community. Doing so will teach them valuable lessons in developing appropriate classroom behaviour and develop the skills necessary for effective cooperative group learning. The following learning experiences, several adapted from *Tribes: A New Way of Learning and Being Together* by Jeanne Gibbs, will assist you in building a community of learners. They can be used as stand-alone getting-to-know-you lessons, or as introductions to specific content-based lessons for a topic, theme, or unit of study.

Community Circle (Gibbs): Have your students sit in a large circle. Ask a question or give a sentence prompt, and have everyone in turn give a response. For example: "This morning I feel…" or "From this experience, I have learned…." It is important to establish norms before you begin: "You can pass if you wish, but you can't laugh at another's mistakes." At the end, ask questions about how well everyone listened, how everyone felt during the experience, and what was learned about the content or about themselves.

People Hunt (Gibbs): Give your students a list with specific criteria. Have them circulate to find people in the class who fulfill the criteria. They record the person's name in the space provided. This strategy helps the group meet, talk together, and learn about each other in a fun way. See Figure 4.3.

People Hunt

Student Name _____   Date _____

Find someone who:

1. _____Sally_____ has both a sister and a brother.
2. _____Sanje_____ was born outside Canada.
3. _____Sudeep_____ speaks another language besides English.
4. _____Michael_____ has more than two pets.
5. _____Kimberly_____ went on a trip recently.
6. _____Matthew_____ plays baseball or another sport.
7. _____Yung Hi_____ loves to eat pizza.
8. _____Brad_____ enjoys reading mysteries.

BLM S-4 Figure 4.3 *People hunt*

People Search Bingo (Bennett, Rolheiser, Stevahn): Provide each student with a blank card with 16 (or fewer) squares. Ask students to circulate and stop to talk with 16 different people in the room. Each time they stop, they *tell* the other person a *different* fact about themselves. This other person records the name and information in one of the blank spaces on his/her card. The game ends when one person completes a card and calls out "Bingo." Debrief this activity with the group by discussing what was learned about different students in the class. It is sometimes difficult for individuals to think of 16 different facts about themselves so you may want them to brainstorm before they begin. See Figure 4.4.

People Search Bingo

Robert has one brother.	Lisa went on a trip up north.	Joshua just read an exciting mystery novel.	Sylvia spent the summer at camp.
Matthew recently created a Web site.	Karen attended a skating competition.	Rena went to a basketball game.	Marnie went to a movie.

BLM S-5 Figure 4.4 *People search bingo*

Things in Common: Have students fold a piece of paper into four equal parts, and draw a circle in the centre. In groups of four, have them pass the paper so that each student can record information about themselves in one section until the paper contains information about all four students. Or, you might use a large piece of paper so that the students can all write in their section of the paper at the same time. Information might include number of brothers and sisters, place of birth, and hobbies. As they share information within their group, students record all the similarities they notice in the circle in the middle of the rectangle. This activity, also called a "placemat" activity, can be used when dealing with content information: each person is responsible for a different topic or role and records what they know about that topic or role in their section. They then record the similarities (or differences) in the centre circle. See Figure 4.5.

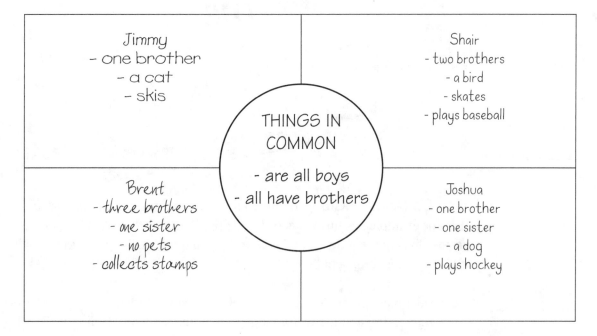

BLM S-6 **Figure 4.5** *Things in common*

Nametag Art: Make available arts and crafts materials, markers, scissors, and glue, and give each student a card with two holes punched at the top so string or ribbon can be hung to make it into a large nametag. Tell students to write their names in the middle of their cards. Decide on four facts you wish to know about your students and direct them to record the answers in each of the four corners of their nametags. Examples include their place of birth, a highlight in their life, something they do well, and the name of a favourite person, food, book, or movie. Invite the students to decorate their nametags using the craft materials. Afterwards, have them meet in small groups to discuss the words and illustrations they recorded on their nametags.

One variation is to involve the students in deciding what to record in each corner. You could include an added twist where three statements are true and one is false. The students could meet in small groups to discover which statement is not true.

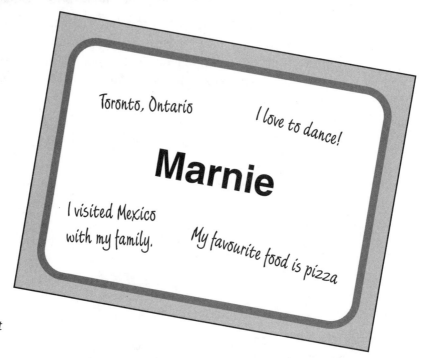

Figure 4.6 *Nametag art*

Lining Up (Andrini; Gibb): Invite your students to form a line in a specific order: for example, by birthdays or by the first letter of their favourite foods. Consider having them do this *without* talking and *with* talking. Lining up without talking adds to the challenge.

✦ Consider having your students participate in some learning experiences first *without* talking and then *with* talking (as in the strategy "Lining Up"). The following learning experiences concretely emphasize the importance of communicating with others while addressing the need for appropriate noise levels in different situations. They can also serve as a baseline to which you can refer later when discussing appropriate noise levels with your students.

Example 1: *Scrambled Sentences*

Have your students write one sentence about themselves on a strip of cardboard and then cut their sentences into individual word cards. They then form into groups of four to six and combine their word cards with the rest of their group's cards. Direct them to shuffle the cards and distribute them evenly to each person in the group. Their goal is to make a complete sentence using the word cards that they have been given. Emphasize *no talking* by displaying the words below on a chart or board.

Do not talk.
Do not take a word card from another person unless offered.
You can give word cards to others in your group.

Prompt your students to discuss how they felt about not being able to talk and how they helped in their group. Do the activity again, but this time *with talking*. Afterwards, invite your students to discuss the difference.

Example 2: *Newspaper Scramble*

Using individual pages from the newspaper, cut each page into 8 to 12 puzzle pieces depending on the age of your students. Put each set of puzzle pieces into individual envelopes. Give each group of students one envelope and have them distribute the puzzle pieces evenly among group members. The task is to put the page together again. Emphasize *no talking* by displaying the words below on a chart or board.

Do not talk.
Do not take puzzle pieces from others in your group unless offered.
You can give puzzle pieces to others in your group.

Afterwards, prompt your students to discuss how they felt about being unable to talk. What strategies did they use to accomplish the task? Direct the groups to change envelopes and try the activity again. This time, encourage them to talk. Have them discuss the differences.

Example 3: *Scrambled Poetry*

Find appropriate poems for your students. Record the lines from each poem onto individual strips of paper or cardboard. Mix up the strips for each poem and place them into individual envelopes. Record on the envelope the title, author, and source book of the poem. Have your students work together in small groups to put the scrambled poem back in the right order. Emphasize *no talking* by displaying the words below on a chart or board.

Do not talk.
Do not take a card from another person unless offered.
You can give a card to others in your group.

Prompt your students to discuss how they felt about being unable to talk. Direct the groups to change envelopes and try the activity again. This time, encourage them to talk. Have them discuss the differences. Students can also be encouraged to find other poems to add to the scrambled poetry collection. Instruct them to print each line of their poem neatly on strips of paper and then put them in an envelope. Ensure that they include the title, author, and source book of the poem on the front of the envelope. They should also include their own name so that anyone who is having trouble can ask them for help.

BLM S-7 Figure 4.7 *Cooperative group learning experiences*

✦ To begin a focus on cooperative learning, group your students heterogeneously, using the information you know about them. Ensure that each
group is composed of students with varying abilities who are able to help
and complement one another. Integrate into these groups any students with
special needs, such as those who are physically challenged or second language learners.

NOTE: *It is a good idea to begin by using partners or triads before you involve*
larger groups of students. The most effective number for a cooperative group
is four to six, but you should view this as a goal towards which you work.

✦ Ensure that each cooperative learning experience (Johnson, Johnson, and
Holubec; Bennett, Rolheiser, and Stevahn) incorporates the following
elements:

1. *Positive interdependence:* All members of a group work together
   towards successful completion of a task or achievement of a goal. All
   members can say, "I cannot succeed unless you succeed."

2. *Individual accountability:* Each member of a group is responsible for
   completing his or her portion of the task or goal. All need to demonstrate the learning. All members can say, "We cannot succeed unless I
   do my share, and I need to be able to demonstrate what we as a group
   have learned."

3. *Face-to-face interaction:* Group members need to interact and sit in
   close proximity to one another in order to work together successfully.

4. *Social skills:* Social skills should be taught and in place before cooperative learning experiences will be successful. Students need to learn the
   skills and techniques on how to work with others and in a group.
   Cooperative learning experiences often fail, not because the students are
   unable to work in groups, but because they have not been taught directly
   how to work in groups.

5. *Processing:* Evaluation of the group process allows students to reflect
   on what they did individually and as a group in order to set goals for
   future improvement.

** For comprehensive resources on cooperative learning and effective instruc-
tional strategies, see *Cooperative Learning: Where Heart Meets Mind,* by
Barrie Bennett, Carol Rolheiser, and Laurie Stevahn (Bookation Inc., Ajax,
Ontario, 1991 and *Beyond Monet: The Artful Science of Instructional*
Integration by Barrie Bennett and Carol Rolheiser, Bookation Inc., Ajax,
Ontario).

✦ Elicit from your students expectations for successful cooperative learning experiences and add these to the rules and routines you and your class generated earlier. Add some of your own ideas to the list. See some possibilities in Figure 4.8.

Expectations for Successful Cooperative Learning

- We respect the rights of others in the class and in our group.

- We never laugh at other people's mistakes.

- We are free to make mistakes, and we learn from and through our mistakes.

- We share resources, materials, and ideas.

- We always help a person in the group if he/she asks for help.

- We listen to what others have to say and ask questions if necessary.

- We praise the efforts and achievements of others.

- We take turns, do our share, and do our best.

- We avoid asking the teacher a question unless we have asked others in our group. ("Ask three before me.")

BLM S-8 **Figure 4.8** *Expectations for successful cooperative learning*

- Model, role-play, and discuss with your students appropriate social skills for working in cooperative groups. Some examples of such social skills include

  - listening actively,
  - taking turns,
  - sharing materials,
  - respecting the ideas and rights of others,
  - not making put-downs,
  - never laughing at others' mistakes,
  - making decisions,
  - solving problems,
  - praising others,
  - disagreeing agreeably,
  - resolving conflict, and
  - reaching consensus.

- Use a *T-chart* (Bennett, Rolheiser, and Stevahn) to explicitly teach your students the social skills necessary. The T-chart asks students to identify what a social skill sounds like and looks like and focuses the students' attention on concrete examples of appropriate behaviours. See Figure 4.9.

Student: _____		Date:_____
	T-Chart	
	Skill:_____	
See 👁		**Hear 👂**
What does it sound like?		What does it look like?
"That's a very good idea but I think we might consider…"		smiling
"I can definitely see your point."		head shaking up and down

BLM S-9 **Figure 4.9** *A T-chart*

- Use picture books, poetry, and short stories to stimulate discussion and common understandings about socially acceptable behaviours and human interaction. *Chrysanthemum*, by Kevin Henkes, and *In the Great Meadow*, by Skid Crease, are examples of excellent resources to use to stimulate such discussions. See Appendix 3: Favourite Children's Literature for other appropriate titles.

✦ Reinforce the social skills you have taught by encouraging your students to create related stories, scripts, poems, art, posters, or song lyrics and have them present their work to the class or school. For example, your students might present a role-play about praising others and receiving compliments, a student-written song about active listening, a play about good manners, or a puppet play or musical performance about respecting differences.

✦ Once your students are clear about the expectations of working in cooperative groups, and you have reinforced some necessary social skills, begin to incorporate cooperative learning structures into *all* areas of the curriculum. Some examples are outlined below.

1. *Jigsaw* (Aronson; Johnson, Johnson, and Holubec; Kagan): Assign students to heterogeneous home groups, with each group member having a number 1 to 4, and being given something to learn or do for the group. Students with the same number (e.g., all the 1s) join together to form an expert group to learn about types of Australian mammals, for example. Once all groups have completed their work, students rejoin their home groups. They then have the task of teaching their part to the other members of the home group so that everyone learns all the material. This structure works well in science or social studies–based programs where students are responsible for mastering content-related material.

2. *Think-Pair-Share* (Kagan; Bennett, Rolheiser, and Stevahn): Students first think individually about an issue, question, or topic, and then partner up with another student to share thoughts, ideas, and feelings. This structure is especially effective when used in large-group situations to ensure that all students are involved and thinking about the topic at hand. It allows rehearsal with a partner before a student participates in a large group, and maximizes student involvement as opposed to the traditional practice of asking a question where five students put up their hands. In this way, the entire class has the opportunity to articulate answers and stay on task.

3. *Roundtable* (Kagan; Bennett, Rolheiser, and Stevahn): This structure encourages cooperation as the group shares materials and systematically takes turns contributing. For example, each member of the group generates ideas about a common topic as the paper and pencil are passed from one to the next.

4. *Roundrobin* (Kagan; Bennett, Rolheiser, and Stevahn): This structure calls upon each team member to take a turn contributing to the discussion at hand. Group members may pass if they wish to do so.

5. *Corners* (Kagan): This structure encourages students to make a particular choice and then verbalize why. First, label the corners of the classroom with the words *Agree*, *Strongly Agree*, *Disagree*, and *Strongly Disagree*. Next, put a thought-provoking statement up on the overhead, chart, or board, and ask students to decide whether they strongly agree, agree, disagree, or strongly disagree. Direct them to move to the corner that best represents their position. Have them discuss with others in that corner why they made the decision to move there. If students are undecided, they can move to the middle of the classroom. Discuss with the whole group why particular decisions were made.

A variation of the corners structure is to display specific statements on the walls of the classroom and have students move to the statement that best represents their opinion, feelings, or position (Figure 4.10.) Once there, students should articulate why they have taken that position.

When I first learned to read, I felt like a clown at a circus.

When I first learned to read, I felt like a castaway on a deserted island.

When I first learned to read, I felt like a mountain climber.

When I first learned to read, I felt like an Olympic swimmer at the finish line.

Figure 4.10 *Example: Statements for corners*

Be careful that you choose statements that *will* create controversy and differences in opinion so that all students do not end up in the same corner. You might want to ask students to record on a slip of paper the corner they have chosen before they move so that they do not simply follow their friends.

6. *Graffiti* (Gibbs; Bennett, Rolheiser, and Stevahn): This co-operative learning structure helps students to generate ideas or thoughts around particular topics. Each group is given a piece of chart paper and asked to brainstorm words, phrases, or ideas on different topics or on different areas of the same topic. For example: "What words come to our minds when we think of pollution?" Each group will have a different question or topic. The chart paper is then rotated to another group whose members add on to the previous group's contributions. This activity continues until all groups have responded to all questions or topics.

7. *Mindmaps* (Bezan; Bennett, Rolheiser, and Stevahn): This cooperative learning structure involves students in creating visual images of thoughts, feelings, or ideas around a central topic, theme, or word. Each group is

given a piece of chart paper and directions to begin in the centre of the paper by recording the central image, word, or concept. They then begin to make connections for the purposes of brainstorming, summarizing information, and presenting key ideas or images. The visual images that they create should demonstrate the relationships between and among all the concepts and ideas recorded. Students use linking graphics such as arrows, bubbles, and chains to show the connections. Using a variety of different colours enhances and emphasizes the points and facilitates the organization of the information shown on the chart paper. Figure 4.11 shows a mindmap.

Figure 4.11 *Mindmap (illustrates feelings and thoughts that students might have when they are new to a country or school)*

✦ After any cooperative group learning experience, have the students assess their individual contributions to the group as well as their success in the total group process. Figures 4.12 and 4.13 provide examples of group and self-assessment forms respectively.

WORKING TOGETHER

Did we share? ☺ ☺ ☹

Did we take turns? ☺ ☺ ☹

Did we say something nice to each other? ☺ ☺ ☹

Did we help each other? ☺ ☺ ☹

BLM S-10 Figure 4.12 *Group assessment form*

Evaluating Your Group Work

Group Member's Names: _Nadia_
Edison
Steven

My Name: _Jennifer_   Date: _Mar. 9_

☑ 1. I listened to others while they were speaking.

☑ 2. I offered my own ideas and information.

☑ 3. I asked others for their ideas.

☑ 4. I shared the materials and supplies.

☐ 5. I asked my group for help when I needed it.

☑ 6. I helped someone in my group.

☑ 7. I took my turn and encouraged others to take their turns.

☐ 8. I praised someone in the group.

BLM S-11 Figure 4.13 *Self-assessment form*

✦ Continue to build close relationships with your students. Engage them in conversation, showing that you are interested in what they have to say. Know when to listen and when to step in. Become sensitive to their needs and interests, and ask carefully thought-out questions.

✦ Promote appropriate classroom behaviour by providing genuine praise, encouragement, and positive reinforcement whenever possible. Catch someone doing something good.

NOTE: Be specific when you provide praise. Rather than making a general comment, such as "You were great today," point out specific areas that are noteworthy such as "You participated extremely well in your group. I noticed that you shared and took turns." As well, continue to use specific praise for academic achievements, such as "Your use of colour for the background in your painting is effective."

✦ Use more direct intervention if the strategies above do not produce the necessary change in behaviour. The following are examples of direct intervention:
  • Provide a choice to the student (e.g., "You can choose to sit quietly on the carpet or you can return to your seat until you are ready to attend to the lesson.")
  • Have a discussion or conference with the student in a location where other students cannot overhear. Avoid centring out the student in front of others, which can possibly spark a power struggle. Be specific by naming the misbehaviour and outlining the logical consequences.
  • Follow through with logical consequences and ensure that your students know these in advance.
  • Develop a verbal or written contract, as outlined in Chapter 6, A Learning Centre Approach.

✦ Teach your students strategies to monitor and control their own behaviour. These include breathing deeply and counting to ten, using the steps to problem solving such as STOP, THINK, PLAN, and DO, reflecting on their behaviour by writing in a journal, or drawing a picture to express their feelings.

✦ Involve parents and your administrator when necessary.

✦ In extreme cases, have students monitor their own behaviour throughout the day or week via a behaviour checklist. This checklist can be used with individual students, a small group, or a whole class. For example, as shown in Figure 4.14, students could monitor positive behaviours daily, reflecting upon their actions and continuing to set goals for improvement.

Name: _Steve_   Week of _Oct. 3_

DID YOU HAVE A GOOD DAY?

BEHAVIOURS	Mon.	Tues.	Wed.	Thurs.	Fri.
Did you stop, listen, and follow directions well?	✓	✓	✓	✓	✓
Did you listen carefully while others were speaking?	✓	✓	✓	✓	✓
Did you work quietly?	✓	✓	✓	✓	✓
During work periods, did you stay at your centre, desk, or table?	No	✓	No	✓	No
Did you complete the work assigned for the day?	Math Incomplete	✓	Science Incomplete	✓	Reading Incomplete
Did you cooperate with others?	✓	✓	✓	✓	✓

Comments: _Steven has shown some improvement in self-control this week. He continues to need reminders to stay at his table to complete his work. Please discuss with him. He has his reading response to complete for homework._

Teacher's Signature: _S. Smith_   Parent's Signature: _____

BLM S-12 **Figure 4.14** *Behaviour checklist*

✦ Consult educational and resource personnel when necessary in order to obtain further information, suggestions, strategies, and program modification for specific students.

- Former teachers can provide necessary background information and strategies that have proved successful in previous years.
- Special education teachers can be asked to share their expertise.
- The school nurse can provide important data, including a medical history or information regarding the home situation. The nurse can also make home visits to gather pertinent information that may have an effect on a student's progress in school.
- Psychologists can be requested to administer formal assessments to determine psychological, social, and/or emotional strengths and difficulties.
- Administrators and other available resource personnel can offer suggestions, strategies, and support.
- Outside agencies can be contacted.

** An excellent resource is *Classroom Management: A Thinking and Caring Approach*, by Barrie Bennett and Peter Smilanich (Bookation Inc., Ajax, Ontario). It contains classroom-tested strategies for managing student behaviour and will help you with establishing and maintaining an effective classroom atmosphere.

✦ Continuously monitor your students' behaviour inside and outside of the classroom to ensure that *bullying* is not a concern. Watch out for students displaying these characteristics: withdrawal, avoidance, frequent absences, or aggressive reactions. They may be victims of a bully. Often, some students who display the characteristics of a bully are victims themselves and are reacting to a bullying situation. In these cases, intervene directly, involving parents and administrators in discussion with the students and in follow-up actions.

✦ To avoid bullying situations, involve your students in proactive discussion and in activities such as using literature to engage in discussions about bullying, role-playing using assertive language, writing letters to the editor or to an advice columnist, creating posters about bullying, and writing stories and scripts to do with bullying.

✦ Keep records on bullying incidents in order to look for patterns and have concrete data when talking to parents and administrators. Invite the students involved to write their own versions of what happened and attach these to the bullying incident report. Very young children might illustrate the incident. Figure 4.15 shows a bullying incident report.

Bullying Incident Report

Date of Incident: _Dec 8, 2000_   Time of Incident: _2:35 pm_

Names of Students Involved: _John Smith, Sudeep Sang, Alison Banks, Dana Crandall_

Description of Bullying Incident: _Name calling_

Reported by: _Mrs. Taylor_

Statements: _See attached_

Witnesses: _Mrs. Taylor_

Intervention: _discussion with the principal_

Parent Contact: _parents were called_

Signatures: _S. Schwartz_

 **BLM T-13** Figure 4.15 *Bullying incident report*

✦ Inform your students' parents about how they can help their children deal with bullying. See Figure 4.16.

Dear Parents,

According to recent research, bullying is an aggressive type of repeated behaviour that should be actively discouraged by parents and teachers alike. Without question, bullying inflicts a great deal of pain on its victims.

Here are some tips to help you empower your children when they come face to face with a bully:

• Ask your children how their peers treat them. Children often hide the fact that they are being bullied. Watch, listen, and ask questions.

• Increase social opportunities for your children. Encourage them to invite other children and groups of children over to your house or on outings. Encourage sleep-overs. The more socially accepted a child is, the less opportunity there is for bullying to occur.

• See that children in groups have things to do. Bullying flourishes when children are together but have nothing to do.

• Enroll your children in classes or groups that develop strengths in activities that are valued by peers. Even children who do not love sports may like bowling, karate, or chess. The more confident your children feel, the less likely they will be bullied.

• Monitor the TV programs your children watch. Much programming on television reinforces the idea that aggression is the only way to deal with conflicts.

• Do not expect children to work out the problem of bullying on their own. Bullying is not an insignificant disagreement between children; it is aggressive repeated behaviour. *Always* intervene. Adults have a crucial role to play in the socialization of children. Consistency is important. Let all children know that bullying is never condoned.

• Talk to other parents. Where there is one victimized child, there are likely to be others.

• See that your children have a grounding in assertive behaviour. Ask them what they can do or say when faced with a bullying situation. The first real line of defence against a bully is self-confidence.

• Teach your children that fighting and aggressive behaviour are not appropriate. Help them to develop viable self-defence strategies, such as protecting their faces and heads from contact, calling for help, and running away. Counter-aggression to any form of bullying actually increases the likelihood of continued victimization. It usually aggravates the situation, sometimes causing the victim to be blamed.

I hope you find these tips helpful if you suspect that your child is being bullied.

Let the principal or me know immediately when problems occur. We can help and support you and your children in dealing with bullying.

Sincerely,

B. Golden

B. Golden

BLM P-14 **Figure 4.16** *Sample letter to parents re: bullying*

It is important to continually assess your own actions and program to determine whether you are using the necessary strategies to ensure an effective classroom atmosphere. Figure 4.17 provides a checklist that you can use to measure your success.

Checklist for Creating an Effective Classroom Atmosphere

Check for:

❑ clear and consistent routines

❑ appropriate classroom management strategies to prevent and respond to misbehaviour

❑ effective lesson plans to teach the necessary social skills

❑ appropriate learning experiences that suit the ages and stages of students

❑ cooperative learning structures integrated into all aspects of the curriculum

❑ involvement of others including parents, other professionals, and administrators, when necessary.

Figure 4.17 *Checklist for creating an effective classroom atmosphere*

If you have provided for all of the above considerations, you will be well on your way to establishing and maintaining an atmosphere that promotes a safe, secure environment where mutual respect and self-worth prevail.

# Planning an Integrated Curriculum

P*lanning is a process of thinking and preparing.* When planning a party, event, or trip, your advance thinking and prior preparations contribute to the overall success. This process is similar to what you do in your classroom as you prepare the road map to guide your students on their learning journeys. Your responsibility, as a teacher, is to be intentional in the directions in which you lead your students.

Assessment and evaluation are inherent parts of the planning process. You practise them when you find out and build on what your students know and can do, value, and learn and when you track student progress, monitor achievement, and modify your program to meet the needs and interests of your students. *Assessment and evaluation drive your program.* Since we live in times of accountability and open communication, it is expected that you will report student progress, build upon their strengths and successes, and help them deal with needs and areas of weakness. These expectations require that you have recorded evidence about how you work with your students and what outcomes ensue. They can also serve as an impetus to self-assessment and reflection.

Planning is a shared and articulated activity which calls for problem solving and collaboration. Co-planners include your students, colleagues, other professionals, and your parents and community. Valuing your students as co-planners in the planning process helps them gain a sense of ownership of their learning and of curriculum content. As you work with your colleagues and other professionals, you gain a broader perspective and range of ideas. Parents feel validated and develop a sense of confidence when they, too, are included in the planning process — they gain understandings about the responsibilities they share as partners in the process of educating their children. Thoughtful planning, when clearly and consistently communicated, becomes the important bridge that allows all participants to believe that our educational process is both effective and accountable.

Systematic planning helps to ensure that district and school expectations are met for each grade, division, and course of study. It provides meaningful direction for students, clarifies program and learning expectations, and maximizes use of time, resources, and materials.

Be aware that the planning you do becomes even more important when you are absent for a prolonged period of time or even for one day. When an occasional teacher takes over your classroom program and routine, it is critical that plans are in place to ensure consistency for your students. Also, when an administrator or parent asks about your program, detailed plans serve as a valuable record of your teaching and learning journey each day and throughout the year.

When you view planning as an important component of your role as a teacher, then *what* and *how* you plan take on greater significance. When you look at what you plan, *integration* should become one of your guiding principles. Integration allows you to help your students see relationships and patterns as they make the connections between and among various curriculum areas. Integration exemplifies the real world as students link their many background experiences and understandings to the various themes, topics, or issues in the curriculum. An integrated curriculum also assists you in addressing the multitude of expectations across the curriculum.

Although each curriculum area contains specific knowledge, skills, and attitudes/values that students need to learn, the *process* of learning that occurs in all curriculum areas is seen to be similar. In all curriculum areas, children take part in *active learning experiences,* such as communicating, interacting, reflecting, observing, exploring, following directions, predicting, problem-solving, and decision-making. Active learning experiences extend curriculum areas and encourage integration and personal connections.

An important component of how to plan an integrated curriculum is *balance* — a balance among the various curriculum expectations and content areas, among learning expectations (knowledge, skills, attitudes/values), among large-group, small-group, and individual learning opportunities, and among the variety of instructional strategies available. Balance helps enable students to learn and grow in any real-life situation.

When you begin to plan, you need to consider the various types of plans necessary for an effective program. *Long-range* plans help you to envision your year at a glance and the sequential path you will take. *Short-term* plans are the more detailed outlines of the themes, topics, issues, or units of study within your yearly long-range plans. *Weekly* and *daily* plans map out and confirm timetabling possibilities. *Lesson* plans provide the framework for the delivery of the important lessons in your themes, topics, issues, or units, and outline the specific learning expectations as well as the assessment and evaluation strategies. *Mini-lessons* are brief instructional moments for teaching knowledge, skills, and attitudes/values to large groups, small groups, or individuals.

The process of planning is an essential part of creating an integrated curriculum, and teachers can and will approach it in unique ways. There are many entry points into the planning process. You need to make decisions on how you will plan, and as you become more proficient with the process, you will develop your own style. Your planning process will become a journey of discovery for both you and your students.

Long-range Planning

In developing your long-range plans, you will need to envision your year at a glance and decide on the sequential path you would like to follow.

As you begin to organize your long-range plans, consider a number of important elements. You will want to ensure a balance among the main curriculum areas of language arts, mathematics, social studies, science and technology, physical and health education, and the arts, along with their corresponding content strands. By achieving a balance among these curriculum areas and within the strands, you ensure that the knowledge, skills, and attitudes/values in each area will receive the appropriate instructional emphasis throughout the year.

Along with balance, you will want to consider *when* you will address each of the major themes, topics, issues, or units stemming from each curriculum area. By looking at your year in terms of blocks of time, such as terms or semesters, you will be better able to determine when each unit will be addressed and which units can integrate well together. Be sure to look for the links among various curriculum areas in order to facilitate the planning for integration. As you decide where these links exist, consider the best time of year to implement certain topics. For example, it would be most fitting to plan an integrated unit on plant growth during warm weather when you and your students could explore the outdoor growth environment in your neighbourhood or city.

School- or *district-wide* planning will have an impact on your own classroom long-range plans. Often, districts develop far-reaching goals for individual schools and classrooms based on data collected or standardized testing results. As they target specific areas for improvement, the implications for individual classroom teachers can be extensive. You will need to investigate what school- or district-wide plans exist and how they will affect your own planning.

As your long-range plans begin to take shape, you will want to carefully consider the availability of resources and materials, including teacher resources, student materials, equipment, and possible human resources. The more you plan ahead, the more successful you will find the path chosen.

Creating a Long-range Plan

◆ Examine and become familiar with the major curriculum areas, content, and student learning expectations you will need to address for your grade level(s).

◆ When planning your year, keep in mind not only the learning expectations for your grade level(s), but also school plans; division or team plans; assessment and evaluation practices that might have an impact at a specific time of year, such as standardized testing initiated by the province/state, district, or school; the needs and interests of the students and the community; teacher resources, student materials, and equipment available; and the interests, talents, and availability of other teachers and resource staff, volunteers, and administrators.

◆ Be flexible when thinking of human resources. You may know specific volunteers or resource staff who are available only at certain times of the year. In these cases, you will need to plan around their schedules if you want them to be involved with your class. The same is true of specific physical resources and equipment such as videos, computer labs, keyboards, or print material where access may be limited to specific time periods.

◆ Consider the school year as divided into distinct blocks of time, such as three terms or two semesters. Decide what you hope to accomplish in each major curriculum area in each block of time.

◆ Choose one curriculum area with which to begin your planning. Decide which specific topics you need to address at your particular grade level and *when* you will address each topic depending on the blocks of time available and the estimated length of time required for completion of each unit.

NOTE: Social studies is a good curriculum area with which to begin. For your first unit of a new school year, you may wish to do an integrated unit titled "Getting to Know You" or "Looking at Our Roots" which will provide you with valuable information about your class and community. In this opening unit, students are encouraged to research their family histories, backgrounds, and cultures. You will find this a good way to value the experiences of each student as well as establish baseline literacy skills from which to evaluate growth in knowledge, skills, and attitudes/values.

◆ Choose another curriculum area, decide on the specific topics to address for your grade level, and plan *when* you will address each of them.

◆ As you choose subsequent curriculum areas and specific topics, keep in mind opportunities for links between and among various topics. For example, a science unit on structures would integrate easily with a social studies unit on the community. The curriculum areas need not be addressed in any specific order as long as all curriculum areas are addressed throughout the year.

◆ If you are teaching a combined grade, make decisions about how you will meet the expectations for two different grade levels. You may decide to teach two separate units to each group of students, or combine the learning expectations from the two different grade levels to create one new integrated unit.

◆ Keep in mind how you will group your students, ensuring a balance of groupings (large group, small group, individuals).

◆ Consider the time, space, and instructional strategies that you might use. These will be planned and recorded in more detail in your integrated unit plans. (Refer to the section on short-term planning in this chapter.)

◆ Be flexible and open to change and possible obstacles to planning and implementation.

◆ Record your long-range plans on a planning sheet which can be enlarged for easy use. The intent is that you would be able to see the whole year at a glance. See Figure 5.1. Use this planning sheet to check for balance among curriculum areas over the course of the year. Continue to keep in mind the many possibilities for integration that may not be clearly indicated on the pages. Figures 5.2 and 5.3 are other examples of long-range planning sheets.

Long-Range Planning Sheet

Curriculum and Content Areas		Fall	Winter	Spring
Mathematics	• Number	*· adding, subtracting, counting, estimation, place value*		
	• Measurement	*· linear – measure "me"*		
	• Geometry	*– desk, class*		
		– our wt. Kg.		
	• Pattern & Algebra	*· mass graphing*		
	• Data Management & Probability	*· solid shape structures, pattern blocks, geoboards*		
Language	• Listening	*· reading friendship books, "me" poems, student published.*		
	• Speaking	*· writing personal narratives, stories, journals, responses*		
	• Reading			
	• Writing	*· storytelling*		
	• Viewing	*· focus on authors, format, publishing*		
	• Representing			
The Arts	• Drama	*· role playing "Round Trip" mime mirror group*		
		· group dynamics		
	• Dance	*· songs: "You are My Friend" "Climb Every Mt." rhythm instruments lummi sticks (chants)*		
	• Music	*· name art, silhouettes paper plate people, line design, puppetry modelling colour*		
	• Visual Arts			
Science	• Life Systems	*· structures expt.-towers, bridges, using different materials: straw, plastic, pins, wood sticks, plastic stirs*		
	• Matter			
	• Energy			
	• Structures			
	• Earth and Space			
Social Studies	• History	*· me, family, neighbourhood, community, mapping skills, interviewing skills, community helpers*		
	• Geography			

BLM T-15 Figure 5.1: *Long-range planning sheet*

Year-at-a-Glance Planning Sheet

Curriculum Area(s)	Topics/Themes/ Issues/Units	Timeline	Integration Possibilities	Consider • Teacher Resources • Student Materials • Out-of-the Classroom Excursions • Human Resources • Other?
Social Studies	Pioneers	6 weeks	Mathematics – cost of living Science – growing plants Drama – role playing	A Pioneer Story by Barbara Greenwood

BLM T-16 **Figure 5.2** *Year-at-a-glance planning sheet*

Year-at-a-Glance Monthly Planning Sheet

Curriculum Area(s): _Social Studies/Science_
(Themes, Topics, Issues, Units and Resources/Materials)

September *Looking at Our Roots*	October *Structures* *Community*
November *Pioneers* *Growth*	December
January	February
March	April

BLM T-17 **Figure 5.3** *Year-at-a-glance monthly planning sheet*

Short-term Planning of a Topic, Theme, Issue, or Unit

When engaged in short-term planning, or the planning of a *topic, theme, issue, or unit of study,* input from your students is invaluable. One way to launch your unit is to ask your students what they already know about the topic or theme, what they need or want to know (their questions), and how they think their needs and interests can be met. This strategy, KWL, or Know, Want to Know, Learn (Ogle), is an effective baseline activity to begin any unit or new learning experience. You are, in essence, using a diagnostic assessment strategy to help guide your program based on your students' knowledge, experiences, and questions in this area. When you revisit this baseline at a later point in the unit, you will have a concrete record of growth over time to add to your assessment data. As well, you are negotiating the curriculum with your students as they gain a voice and input into the program.

Throughout the year, you should encourage your students to assess, evaluate, shape, reshape, and restructure their own learning opportunities. The curriculum, themes, issues, and interactive learning experiences become more relevant because they are built on the backgrounds, needs, interests, and everyday life experiences of your students. Students from a variety of diverse cultures and backgrounds will feel comfortable and part of the class. Students with low self-esteem will grow in confidence and competence as their views are heard and valued. As they develop a positive attitude towards school, all students will move towards meeting the goal of becoming lifelong learners.

As you plan your themes or units of study, take into consideration the learning styles and multiple intelligences of the students in your class. You, as the teacher, need to recognize that all students have strengths and it is incumbent upon you to maximize those areas while helping students to build their confidence in areas where they are less proficient. By identifying the intelligences in which students excel, you will be better able to plan learning experiences that incorporate those strengths and use those strengths to learn in areas needing growth. "If we provide students the opportunity to develop the full range of their intellectual capacities and teach them how to use their multiple ways of knowing in the learning task, they will learn the things we are trying to teach them more thoroughly than if we only permit them to learn in the more traditional verbal/linguistic and logical/mathematical ways," (Lazear).

Using a multitude of methods and instructional strategies to expand and enrich your integrated unit provides many benefits. You will become better able to see the needs and interests of your students, the subject areas and learning expectations that are to be addressed, and the variety of integrated learning experiences possible. You will also become better able to maintain the balance necessary, and you will become a partner and guide in the teaching and learning process, learning along with your students.

Creating a Short-term Plan

+ Select the curriculum area(s) you will be addressing.

+ Identify the specific topic, theme, issue, or unit of study.

+ Determine the timelines required: the approximate number of weeks the unit will last (review the section on long-range planning), and the time during the day when you plan to address this unit (see Chapter 3, Timetabling).

+ Think about what you, the teacher, already know about this topic, theme, issue, or unit, what related experiences you have had, and what questions you have.

+ Collect, briefly examine, and organize the available teacher resources, guidelines, commercial resources, and student materials related to this topic and strive to see the "big picture."

+ Brainstorm with teaching partners, if available, words and phrases associated with this topic, theme, issue, or unit. You might want to record your ideas on Post-it notes or cards so that you can more easily sort and classify later. Brainstorming will encourage you to expand your thinking beyond specific learning expectations (which are often content-based and may not by themselves engage students in the active and interactive process of learning). It will also encourage you to activate *your* prior knowledge; foster interest and ownership in the theme, topic, issue, or unit of study; and actively engage you in thinking creatively about what you will plan for your students. See Figure 5.4 for an example of a brainstormed list of words on a particular topic.

Pioneers		
dress	education	settlements
- clothing	- teacher's role, salary	- water
- energy	- code of conduct,	- shelter
- gender differences	discipline, strap	hardships
- equality	- reading, writing,	- disease
homes	arithmetic	- war
- heating	- rote learning	- weather
- oil lamps	- slates	economics
- lanterns	food	- money
- furniture	- churning butter	- barter system
- utensils	- grinding flour	- fur trade, trading
- inventions	- making bread	- Hornbooks
- construction	- grains, fruits,	- Little House on
- building bees	vegetables	the Prairie
occupations	- animals (meat)	- Bonanza
- blacksmith	transportation	
- merchant	- covered wagon	
- carpenter	- horse	
- miner	- buggy	
- fisher	- boat	
- miller	- ship	
- farmer	- canoe	

Figure 5.4 *Brainstormed list*

✦ Brainstorm with your students for a similar list before you begin your lessons. You will gain important baseline information about what your students already know about the theme, topic, issue, or unit of study, and involving students in the planning process will increase their sense of ownership and interest.

✦ Using your brainstormed list (Figure 5.4) and the active "doing" words that appear in Figure 5.5 below, create a web of possible learning experiences associated with your theme, topic, issue, or unit of study. Figure 5.6 shows a web of learning experiences that uses the active "doing" words.

Bloom's Taxonomy

Knowledge

listing

labelling

identifying

naming

recording

locating

matching

observing

Comprehension

describing

summarizing

explaining

illustrating

paraphrasing

discussing

capturing the main idea

Application

applying

constructing

simulating

interviewing

modelling

demonstrating

charting

graphing

gridding

exploring

investigating

Analysis

analyzing

comparing

contrasting

surveying

analyzing data

sorting

classifying

making connections

Synthesis

creating

designing

composing

modifying

inventing

predicting

producing

researching

imagining

wondering

Evaluation

problem-solving

judging, rating, ranking

assessing

evaluating

defending

deciding

justifying

debating

criticizing

questioning

Figure 5.5 *Levels of intellectual behaviour*

> **NOTE:** *Figure 5.5 presents Bloom's Taxonomy (Bloom and Drathwohl), a well-known taxonomy, or classification of levels, of intellectual behaviour important in learning. Bloom identified six levels within the cognitive domain, ranging from basic knowledge to evaluation. His taxonomy is used by many teachers as a tool to encourage learners to move to higher, more divergent levels of thinking and learning. It is also useful as a check for balance in the thinking and learning experiences teachers provide for their students.*

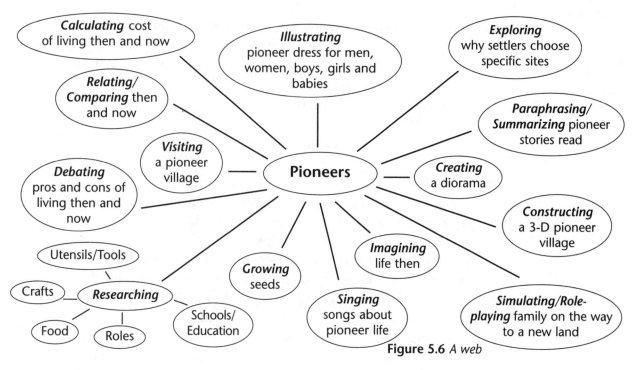

Figure 5.6 *A web*

of learning experiences

◆ Think about the integration possibilities you see. Colour-code the learning experiences on your web into different curriculum areas. For example, circle all the mathematics learning experiences in blue, all the science learning experiences in red, etc. You will be able to easily identify the natural integration possibilities without forcing integration. You can then plan accordingly, turning to the appropriate curriculum documents to determine learning expectations. See Figure 5.7.

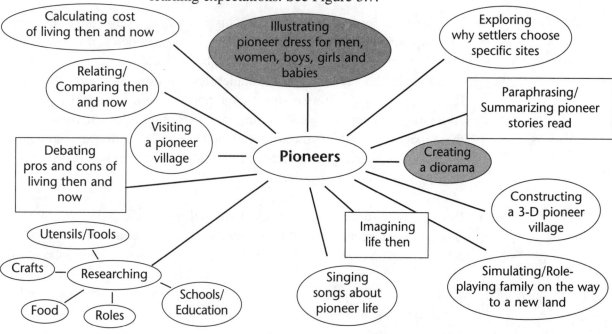

Figure 5.7 *A colour-coded web*

◆ Examine the curriculum documents you will need for this theme, topic, issue, or unit and select the student learning expectations to be addressed in the one or more curriculum areas you have identified. Think about what you want your students to know, be able to do, and feel or value at the end of this theme, topic, or unit of study.

◆ Look at all possible documents for integration opportunities.

◆ Think about and record the types of diagnostic, formative, and summative assessment strategies you will use. See Chapter 11, Assessing, Evaluating, and Reporting, for information on key strategies.

◆ Decide on the diagnostic assessment tools you will use to find out what the students already know, what experiences they have had, and what they want to know or what questions they have in relation to the expectations you have chosen to address in this unit of study. Some diagnostic assessment tools you might use are KWL (what I know, what I want to know, what I learned); observation; interviews and conferences; inventories, questionnaires, and surveys; and a test or quiz. Refer to Chapter 11, Assessing, Evaluating, and Reporting, for information about them.

NOTE: The diagnostic assessment will serve as your baseline and will help to guide your program. An extremely important part of the planning process, it can also serve as part of your introduction to the overall unit. Referring to the baseline at a later date will allow you to see what your students have learned over time.

◆ Decide on the formative assessment tools you will use throughout the unit. This assessment involves ongoing tracking of your students' progress over time. Formative assessment tools you might use include ongoing observation, anecdotal notetaking, work samples, tests or quizzes, checklists, conferences, peer- and self-assessments, and portfolio assessments. Chapter 11, Assessing, Evaluating, and Reporting, provides more information about these tools which allow you to check whether your students are learning what you are teaching. That needed information will help you make decisions as to next steps to take.

◆ Decide on the summative assessment you will use at the end of your unit. Some summative assessment tools you might use are unit tests, portfolio assessments, self-assessments/final reflections, peer assessments, speeches, oral and written reports, and project displays and presentations, including audiotapes, videotapes, drama, songs, visual presentations, and multimedia computer presentations. Chapter 11, Assessing, Evaluating, and Reporting, provides information about these tools.

◆ Decide on the overall criteria you will use to determine the success of your students' learning during this unit of study. You could create a rubric to clearly identify the criteria by which the students will be evaluated in relation to the expectations that you have chosen to address. See Chapter 11, Assessing, Evaluating, and Reporting, for information on how to create a rubric.

◆ Begin to explicitly plan the learning experiences in which your students will take part. Review your brainstormed list of words, active learning experiences web, and integration possibilities, and make connections to the expectations you have decided to address.

◆ Review the teacher resources, guidelines, commercial resources, and student materials related to this topic and decide what you will use.

◆ Find out what possible human resources are available and try to arrange for these people to visit with your students, or to communicate with them via other means, such as e-mail, telephone, or letter.

◆ Collect or order any media resources (e.g., stories, poetry or songs on audiotapes, CDs, videos) and computer software that would be relevant to the topic, making sure that they are appropriate to your students' maturity level and interests.

◆ Decide how you will introduce your theme, topic, or unit of study. For example, if your class is going to study pioneer life, you might decide to dress as a pioneer, read a story about pioneer life, show a film or video about pioneers, do some role playing, conduct a lesson using rote learning and relate it to pioneer life, or bring in an artifact and have students guess what it is and what its purpose was.

NOTE: *Any of the above introductions could provide you with diagnostic assessment data about your students. Keep in mind that other diagnostic assessments that you have planned, such as KWL, could also serve as a viable introduction to your unit.*

◆ Decide which learning expectations will need teacher-directed lessons. (Refer to "Lesson Planning" and "Creating a Lesson Plan" later on in this chapter.)

◆ Prepare a flexible plan, recording the learning expectations to be addressed and the learning experiences that will be used to teach those expectations. Sequence the learning expectations and experiences in the order that you plan to present them. Remember to take into account the past experiences, needs, interests, learning styles, and expectations of your particular group of students. Some students may take one day to accomplish a certain task; others may take a week. Also, once you are into the unit, you may find that the order of learning experiences must be changed. Flexibility and a focus on meeting the needs and interests of your students are key to effective programming. Figure 5.8 provides an example of a flexible plan.

Learning Expectations	*Learning Experiences*
Students will	*Students will*
1. articulate the many roles of people in a pioneer community	role-play the various roles in a pioneer community
2. describe the buildings in a community	create dioramas that illustrate the various pioneer buildings
3. identify how life has changed since pioneer times	prepare a report that explains aspects of community life that might be different between then and now

Figure 5.8 *A flexible plan*

◆ If you choose to use learning centres for students to explore, reinforce, refine, or practise some of the learning expectations to be addressed in the unit, decide how you will set up your centres, how students will use and move through them, and how you will track and assess students' work. Use a planning sheet to document the centres and what will be accomplished at each centre. Refer to Chapter 6, A Learning Centre Approach, for guidance.

◆ Ensure that you use a range of instructional strategies in your lessons that involve direct instruction, independent activity, and small-group cooperative learning.

◆ Plan for a variety and balance of groupings, including whole class, small group, heterogeneous, homogeneous, ability, and interest. Ensure that your groupings are flexible to meet the needs and interests of your students.

◆ Consider the learning environment or space in your classroom. You may need to organize or rearrange the furniture, the meeting spaces, the display areas, the storage areas, your learning centres, and your audiovisual or technological requirements. Chapter 2, The Physical Set-up of the Classroom, provides helpful guidance.

◆ If you have decided to take your students on an out-of-classroom excursion to address some of the learning expectations in your unit, ensure that you have made all the necessary arrangements and preparations. (See Chapter 9, Out-of-Classroom Excursions.)

◆ Check that you are planning and modifying your program for students with special needs. Ask yourself these questions:
  • Have I provided support for those who are struggling?
  • Have I provided support, such as visuals, simplified use of language, and peer buddies, for second language learners?
  • Have I provided enrichment for those who need a challenge?
  • Have I addressed different learning styles?
  • Have I addressed the multiple intelligences of my diverse group?

◆ Decide on the homework you will assign to accompany this unit and the learning expectations it will address.

NOTE: *See Chapter 10, Homework: A Window into the Classroom, for information on how homework experiences allow parents to see what you are doing and what you value in your program and to become involved with your program in a positive way.*

◆ Decide how you will share your plans with parents and communicate student progress. You might use a class newsletter, an after-school meeting, an informal invitation to your classroom, phone calls home, certificates of achievement, or formal reports. See Chapter 12, Partnerships with Parents, for more information.

◆ Decide how you will celebrate and share the learning with your students and with others. Possible activities include an authors' festival, a literacy or arts celebration of learning, a mathematics evening, a computer evening, a science fair, a musical concert, an open house, invitations to the classroom, a scavenger hunt through the classroom or school, a photo display, a slide show (photographs showing students in action), a video, and newsletters.

◆ You may want to use a unit planning template to guide your short-term planning. A template appears as Figure 5.9.

Main Curriculum Area:	Topic/Issue/Unit:	Timeline:	Physical Environment:
Other Curriculum Areas:			

Learning Expectations:

Assessment

Diagnostic	Formative	Summative
☐ Observation	☐ Observation	☐ Portfolios
☐ Anecdotal Notes	☐ Anecdotal Notes	☐ Unit Test
☐ Interview	☐ Work Samples	☐ Self-assessment
☐ Conferences	☐ Test/Quiz	☐ Peer-assessment
☐ Inventories/ Surveys	☐ Checklist	☐ Final Reflection
	☐ Conference	☐ Speeches
☐ Test/Quiz	☐ Peer-assessment	☐ Projects
☐ Questionnaires	☐ Self-assessment	☐ Presentations
☐ KWL		☐ Reports, Oral/Written

Grouping* W | S | I	Learning Experiences:	Materials/Resources	Modifications
	Introductory Lesson		
	Culminating Lesson		
	Out-of-Classroom Excursions		

Homework/Parent Communication/Celebrating the Learning

BLM T-18 Figure 5.9 *Unit planning sheet template* *Groupings: W = Whole class; S = Small group; I = Independent

BLM T-19 BLM T-19, which appears only on the CD-ROM accompanying this book, provides a four-page workbook for planning a short-term unit.

Lesson Planning

Lesson plans guide your instruction as you approach the task of meeting the needs and interests of your students on a daily basis. In creating a lesson plan, you are considering the planning and preparation that you must do before the lesson and the way that you will deliver the lesson.

If your lesson is part of a unit of study, it is important to think about how it fits into the overall flow of the unit and what your students have already learned before it. If it is an introductory lesson to your unit or a final summary lesson, it could be considered part of your diagnostic or summative assessment for the unit. However, lessons are not always linked to your units of study and can stand alone in order to teach specific knowledge, skills, or attitudes/values.

In planning your lessons, you need to think about what you want your students to learn (learning expectations), how you will know they have learned it (assessment), and how you will adapt or change the lesson if necessary (modifications). Also, consider the materials and resources you will require for the lesson, as well as the groupings you will use, and the timing required. In recording your lesson plan, you may want to include a section for personal notes, reminders, homework, and other considerations such as space modifications.

In the actual delivery of the lesson, you will need to think about how you will engage the students in learning. Designing an effective lesson delivery is like designing a dynamic presentation to any audience. Both should include a motivating introduction or beginning, objectives that are openly shared with participants to outline purpose and direction, content where the key concepts are outlined, modelled, practised, and internalized, and a conclusion that inspires thoughtful reflection. These key elements are not meant to be a rigid step-by-step formula or recipe to be applied to each and every lesson. Instead, you are encouraged to carefully and deliberately consider the elements when planning your lessons and make decisions on which elements to use and on which order to use them. Teaching then becomes a conscious decision-making process. The strength of this delivery model lies in the myriad of combinations that are created by the teacher for each lesson (Wolfe; Hunter and Russell).

Recording specific plans for major lessons is an important exercise for teachers new to the fundamental structure of lesson design and delivery. As you internalize the structures inherent in effective lesson design, it becomes less essential to record the specific details of each of your lessons. The basic components of your lessons can be included in a point-form daily plan.

Teachers create more detailed lesson plans for their short-term integrated units of study. For example, once you have the "big picture," or a sense of where you are going and the expectations you will be addressing in a theme, topic, issue, or unit of study, you are ready to outline the important lessons in the unit. These detailed lesson plans become an integral part of the short-term planning process.

Although it is important to be accountable, lesson plans should not be carved in stone. You should be able to modify your plans to meet your students' needs and interests. In fact, the art of teaching lies in the ability to adapt, change, and revise lessons and plans as required.

Creating a Lesson Plan

- ✦ Think about the background information that your students bring to the lesson.
- ✦ Choose the learning expectations (the knowledge, skills, attitudes/values) that your specific lesson will address.

NOTE: You may also want to record specific learning expectations that are not content-based, but rather address certain social skills that your students may need to learn. These are different than the academic learning expectations for your unit. (See Chapter 4, Classroom Atmosphere.)

✦ Decide on the specific formative and summative assessment strategies you will use in order to determine how well your students achieve the identified expectations for this particular lesson. It is assumed that the diagnostic assessment completed at the beginning of your unit is guiding your lessons. (See Chapter 11, Assessing, Evaluating, and Reporting.)

✦ Decide on the materials and resources you will need to teach this lesson: literature, textbooks, audiovisual equipment, teacher resources, technology, student materials, and manipulatives.

✦ Decide on the delivery of your lesson by considering the elements of lesson design (Hunter and Russell):
   • introduction, hook, or mental set;
   • purpose and learning expectations shared in student language;
   • body of the lesson including these aspects: providing input and sharing information, modelling and demonstrating, practising the learning (guided and/or independent practice), and checking for understanding; and
   • conclusion, closure, or wrap-up to the lesson.

A detailed description of lesson design components appears as Figure 5.10.

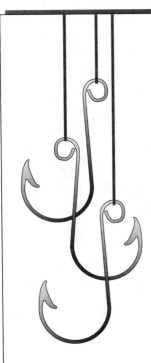

Introduction, hook, or mental set

The mental set is perhaps the most important part of your lesson as it sets the stage for engaging the learner. It should motivate and inspire your students to participate and become immediately involved. It allows you to link the past experiences of your students (through questioning or activities) to the learning objectives and expectations of the lesson. Depending on the type of learning experience used, this introduction to your lesson can range in time from thirty seconds to a full day. Here are some examples of effective mental sets:

• a powerful read-aloud
• a lively song, poem, or chant
• a thought-provoking question
• a photo, picture, movie, or video
• an interesting quote
• a full-day out-of-the-classroom excursion
• an unusual prop or artifact

Purpose and learning expectations shared (in student language)

For each lesson, you will need to decide how you will share the purpose and learning expectations using vocabulary and language that are appropriate to your students' specific age and maturity level. When you inform your students about the purpose of the lesson, you are answering the questions "What's in it for me?" and "Why are we doing this?" Sharing the purpose and expectations builds ownership and motivation and is key to making the lesson meaningful and relevant. You may want to consider varying *when* you share the purpose of the lesson. Depending on your purpose and learning expectations, you might want to wait until the end of the lesson or share it during the lesson.

Body of the lesson

Providing input: You do not have to deliver input in a didactic, teacher-directed way. Instead, you could read aloud to students, ask students to read material independently, or have your students sing a song, watch a video, listen to a tape, look at pictures, participate in drama, or go on a field trip, for example. Students also acquire information and input from each other, as in a cooperative learning lesson such as a jigsaw. (Refer to Chapter 4, Classroom Atmosphere.) During the body of the lesson, it is advisable that as many of the multiple intelligences as possible be tapped, in order to involve all learners in an auditory, visual, tactile, and kinesthetic way. Knowledge of learning styles and multiple intelligences benefits teachers as they strive to involve all students in an active way.

Modelling and demonstrating: Doing this for your students provides them with clear examples of what the learning looks like and sounds like. It increases memory by giving students visual and concrete cues, it helps to provide variety to your lessons, and it generates interest.

Practising the learning (guided practice and/or independent practice): In this part of the lesson, students are given time to experiment, experience, and apply their understandings. Practice is extremely important and allows students to consolidate the key learnings and to gain confidence and competence. To be effective, it should relate to the learning expectations and the appropriate level of thinking of your students. Practice activities often occur after the input and modelling, when the students are ready to apply what they have learned to a real and meaningful situation. Practice illustrates the transfer of learning to new situations.

- *Guided practice* is when the students follow instructions and practise with support and guidance from the teacher.

- *Independent practice* is when students work on a task by themselves or in a group with minimal teacher support.

Check for understanding: When you check for understanding, you help to increase students' success. You can see where you should intervene before students become frustrated and uncertain during a lesson. When you stop to ensure understanding throughout the lesson, you are better able to adapt and modify to meet the needs and interests of your students. With experience, you will become better able to *read* your students to see the learning and understanding that occur — this is the *"art"* of teaching. Ways to check for understanding include asking a few key questions, doing a think-pair-share in partners or a think-pair-square with four students, or making a statement and encouraging a thumbs-up or thumbs-down response to indicate that they agree or disagree with the statement.

Conclusion, closure, or wrap-up to your lesson

Every effective lesson should have a conclusion that calls for thoughtful reflection by the students. Encourage the students to tie together the key learnings: to summarize, synthesize, or consolidate them in some way. Teachers tend to leave out closure when they underestimate the time it takes to complete parts of the lesson. Careful consideration of timing will allow you greater opportunities for closure. Ways to close a lesson include sharing in a small or large group, taking a gallery walk where students circulate to look at work accomplished, and calling for an oral or written response before students can exit. This is sometimes called a "ticket-out-the-door" strategy, where students are required to articulate an oral response or hand in a written response as they exit.

Multiple Intelligence Reference.

Figure 5.10 *The components of lesson design.*

BLM T-55 to T-59 *BLM T-55 to T-59 provide samples of completed lesson plans.*

✦ In order to achieve the goal of meeting the needs and interests of all your students, examine your lesson and decide how you will target the multiple intelligences of your students. When planning a lesson, Thomas Armstrong suggests you ask yourself the following questions:

How can I use the spoken or written word?   *(linguistic)*

How can I bring in numbers, calculations, logic, classifications, or critical thinking?   *(logical-mathematical)*

How can I use visual aids, visualization, color, art, metaphor, or visual organizers?   *(spatial)*

How can I bring in music or environmental sounds, or set key points in a rhythm or melody?   *(musical)*

How can I involve the whole body or hands-on experiences? *(bodily-kinesthetic)*

How can I engage students in peer or cross-age sharing, cooperative learning, or large group simulation?   *(interpersonal)*

How can I evoke personal feelings or memories, or give students choices?   *(intrapersonal)*

NOTE: *It is not necessary that you plan to include tasks that tap into every intelligence in every single lesson, but you should balance the use of the intelligences across a number of lessons. Armstrong writes: "You won't always find ways of including every intelligence in your curriculum plans. But if this model helps you reach into one or two intelligences that you might not otherwise have tapped, then it has served its purpose very well indeed!" It is important to note that an eighth intelligence has recently been identified. Described as the naturalistic intelligence, it involves using nature and the outdoors in learning (Armstrong).*

✦ Determine whether you need to put in place modifications for specific students. Consider

- decreasing a student's workload
- setting up a peer-tutoring situation
- increasing time allocated for task completion
- scribing for the student
- providing different modes of response, such as orally or in pictures
- providing direct teacher assistance
- providing further use of visual aids or manipulatives
- having a conference with a student
- using a timer to help with time management
- using different forms of technology

◆ Include in your lesson planning any personal notes or reminders you might need to have on hand for this lesson.

◆ If you decide that what needs to be taught requires only a brief lesson, teach a mini-lesson, either planned in advance or taught at the point of need. A mini-lesson can occur at the beginning of an activity, during a lesson to ensure understanding, during a conference with a student or group of students, or even when students are lining up for recess. Modelling, demonstrating, and think-aloud strategies can be seen as types of mini-lessons, where you make the learning explicit by sharing what is happening in your mind.

NOTE: Read-aloud experiences provide numerous opportunities to use mini-lessons to teach specific skills. For example, reading a simple pattern book to young children allows you to point out punctuation, capital letters, rhyming words, plurals, initial consonants, blends, and compound words. Reading a novel provides many opportunities to point out literary elements such as characterization, climax, and epilogue. See Chapter 7, Literacy and Language Learning, for more ideas.

◆ Modify or create your own template of a lesson plan. A template should include all the components of a lesson plan yet each lesson does not necessarily have to include every component of lesson design in a step-by-step fashion. Figures 5.11 and 5.12 and BLM T-22, which appears only on the CD-ROM accompanying this book, may prove helpful.

PLANNING THE LESSON

Date: _____   Title of the Lesson: _____

Curriculum Area: _____   Unit of Study: _____

Background Information: *Where does this lesson fit into your overall unit planning – introductory, middle, culminating?*

Learning Expectations: *What skills, knowledge, attitudes/values do you expect your students to learn?*

Academic: Social:

Assessment Strategies: *How will you assess the learning expectations?*

❑ Observation   ❑ Learning Log/Journal   ❑ Presentation/Performance
❑ Anecdotal Notes   ❑ Self-assessment   ❑ Audio/Video Technological
❑ Work Samples   ❑ Peer-assessment   Presentation
❑ Interview/Conference   ❑ Rubric   ❑ Project
❑ Checklist   ❑ Oral Reports
❑ Other

Indicators: *How will you know that they have achieved the expectation? What will it look like?*

Modifications: *How will you change the lesson to meet the needs of individual students?*

❑ Increase: *time, space, amount*   ❑ Scribe   ❑ Use manipulatives
❑ Decrease   ❑ Oral explanation   ❑ Include visuals
❑ Change   ❑ Peer Tutor/Partner ❑ Extend
❑ Other

Materials/Resources: *What will you need to prepare in advance?*

Teacher Resources	Human Resources	Student Materials

Personal Notes/Reminders/Homework/Other Considerations:

BLM T-20 Figure 5.11
Lesson plan template #1

DELIVERING THE LESSON

Timing	Grouping* W S I	Lesson Design:	Materials/Resources
		Mental Set:	
		Sharing the Purpose/Objectives:	
		Body: *(Input, Modelling, Check for Understanding: Guided Practice, Independent Practice)*	
		Closure:	

*Groupings: W = Whole class; S = Small group; I = Independent

LESSON PLAN

Date: _____   Title of the Lesson: _____

Curriculum Area: _____   Unit of Study: _____

Background Information:	Grouping:

Learning Expectations:	Assessment:

Lesson:

- ❏ Mental Set
- ❏ Sharing the Purpose/Objectives
- ❏ Input
- ❏ Modelling
- ❏ Check for Understanding
- ❏ Guided Practice
- ❏ Independent Practice
- ❏ Closure

Bloom's Taxonomy:
- ❏ Knowledge
- ❏ Understanding
- ❏ Application
- ❏ Analysis
- ❏ Synthesis
- ❏ Evaluation

Multiple Intelligences:
- ❏ Linguistic
- ❏ Logical/Mathematical
- ❏ Spatial
- ❏ Musical
- ❏ Bodily-Kinesthetic
- ❏ Interpersonal
- ❏ Intrapersonal
- ❏ Naturalistic

Modifications:

Personal Notes/Reminders/Homework/Other Considerations:

 **BLM T-21** Figure 5.12 *Lesson plan template #2*

 BLM See BLM T-22 on accompanying CD-ROM for lesson plan template #3.

✦ You may wish to use Figure 5.13 as a checklist on the planning process.

Checklist on the Planning Process

The following are some questions to guide your thinking:

Have you collected and examined
- ❏ Ministry documents and curriculum learning expectations?
- ❏ board guidelines and resources?
- ❏ school plans?
- ❏ available published and commercial teachers' guides or resources?
- ❏ available student materials?
- ❏ media and computer technology resources and links?
- ❏ available human resources?
- ❏ sites for possible out-of-classroom excursions?

Have you determined the learning expectations you will focus on and address in terms of whether they are
- ❏ knowledge based?
- ❏ skill based?
- ❏ value based?
- ❏ social skills based?
- ❏ a combination of the above?

In assessing student progress and program effectiveness, have you used
- ❏ specific criteria for the expectations you have chosen to address?
- ❏ a variety of diagnostic, formative, and summative assessment strategies?
- ❏ a student tracking or record-keeping system?

Have you planned
- ❏ tentative timelines?
- ❏ the appropriate learning experiences?
- ❏ lessons using lesson design components?
- ❏ direct instruction?
- ❏ cooperative learning small-group activities?
- ❏ independent student activities?
- ❏ integration with other curriculum areas?
- ❏ the groupings you will use?
- ❏ the arrangement of classroom space?
- ❏ modifications for specific individual needs?
- ❏ homework experiences?
- ❏ communication with parents?
- ❏ celebrations of student learning?

BLM T-23 **Figure 5.13** *Checklist on the planning process*

Weekly and Daily Plans

As your long-range, short-term, and lesson plans begin to take shape, you will want to focus on the *weekly and daily planning process* to ensure smooth implementation of the programs that you have envisioned. *Weekly* plans which allow you to see your week at a glance show specific lessons, tasks, and learning experiences taking place over the course of the week. They help you see the direction you are heading. *Daily* plans allow you to focus in on each lesson and on the routines that accompany your teaching day. Weekly and daily plans can include a record of the specific routines that you will be reinforcing to help in the smooth running of your program.

Weekly and daily plans often outline the lessons, learning experiences, and tasks in which your students will be involved, along with the corresponding expectations, materials needed, and assessment required. For experienced teachers, these can take the place of detailed lesson plans on a day-to-day basis, while essential and detailed lesson plans are incorporated into the integrated unit planned for that period of time.

Weekly and daily plans put your thoughts and ideas into immediate practice. They have much to do with timetabling procedures as you begin to decide when certain learning experiences, unit tasks, lessons, and so on will occur within your weekly and daily schedule. These plans will depend on the timing of other school requirements, such as physical education, French, and the arts, if other teachers work with your students in such curriculum areas.

In essence, weekly and daily planning cannot be separated from timetabling. In Chapter 3, Timetabling, you will find procedures and specific examples of different timetabling possibilities on a weekly basis. We invite you to review these possibilities and decide what works best for your class.

Effective planning, whether long term, short term/unit, or lesson planning, helps you to prepare a viable road map to guide your year. The planning procedures outlined in this chapter represent *one* way to plan your program. In no way should they be construed as set plans to be followed in a lockstep fashion. Planning effective programs requires that you take into account a multitude of factors, including your students' past experiences, needs, interests, and learning styles, your own unique way of organizing and recording your thinking, and the requirements of your school, board, and district. The more you experiment with the planning process, the more expertise you will develop as you chart a course to guide yourself and your students' learning.

6 A Learning Centre Approach

Learning centres provide opportunities for students to work together in small groups, interacting, sharing, and cooperating with one another as they reinforce, practise, apply, and refine previous learnings. Students participate in tasks that help them to internalize and consolidate what they learn, often with minimal teacher intervention or support. At learning centres, students also experiment, explore, question, discuss, and reflect, thus participating in discovery learning, the process of *learning how to learn*. The tasks and learning experiences at learning centres are usually closely tied to curriculum goals and should be clear, comprehensible, and relevant to your students' cognitive, physical, social, and emotional stages of development.

In taking a learning centre approach, you make decisions in your planning to include one or more learning centres in your program. A learning centre approach does not necessarily mean that specific areas in the classroom must be designated as learning centres. Some centres may be permanent, some may be portable or easily moved, and some may be temporary, used for a specific purpose for a short period of time. A learning centre is as varied as the imagination.

At learning centres, students will often be presented with a choice of learning experiences at various levels of difficulty. They will begin to take greater responsibility for their own learning, becoming better decision makers and problem solvers. Your students will gain a greater willingness to take risks in these small-group situations. As they gain confidence in their own abilities, they will become more self-motivated and independent and will begin to evaluate themselves more critically.

In a learning centre approach, peer teaching is facilitated and students gain valuable leadership skills and confidence. Little pressure to compete with others develops because this approach to learning emphasizes cooperation, collaboration, and sharing of materials, resources, and ideas.

Collecting and preparing learning materials is easy with a learning centre approach. Resources and materials are shared to a great extent, and only a few students need the same materials at any one time. It is not necessary to have class sets of texts or other materials at learning centres. Instead, funds can go towards acquiring class libraries of literature and a variety of manipulatives, including magnifying glasses, thermometers, measuring instruments, and manipulative mathematics materials. The materials and resources for centre tasks should be accessible and readily available.

A learning centre approach also facilitates integration and assessment. Since a number of curriculum areas are interconnected, integration can occur naturally through learning centres. Assessment can become a manageable and meaningful task when students are actively involved in learning centre work. As you circulate, observation and anecdotal notetaking are facilitated. Peer- and self-assessments after students complete centre tasks will promote reflection and goal setting, both for work habits and academic quality of work.

As your learning centres become an increasingly integral part of your overall program and your students develop as independent workers, you will become accustomed to a variety of learning experiences occurring at the same time in different areas of the classroom. You will circulate, encourage, instruct, model and demonstrate, provide guidance, and ultimately promote independence. As well as learning along with your students, you will serve as a facilitator of learning, a full partner in the teaching/learning process.

Creating Effective Learning Centres

✦ Examine your classroom environment, and decide which *permanent* learning centres you will create and *where* these will be located. Permanent learning centres may remain all year long. Possibilities include a listening centre, a reading corner, an art area (preferably near a sink), a computer centre (near electrical outlets), a design and technology centre, and a mathematics centre (housing mathematics texts and manipulatives).

NOTE: *Keep in mind that a centre need not be a physical space. If space is limited, all materials necessary for a centre can be stored in labelled bins, buckets, folders, or other containers that can be taken by the students to any area in the room or school or to a designated work space. The school's resource library can also be used as a designated area for small-group or centre work.*

✦ Decide which centres will involve generic learning experiences. Such experiences are not directly related to a theme or unit being studied. For example, a generic computer centre may focus on tasks such as keyboarding, word processing, skill teaching, and graphic design. It is beneficial to keep generic tasks available for students to work on as they complete assigned tasks from a given unit of study.

♦ If you will be using learning centres as part of an integrated unit, examine the small-group and individual learning experiences you have planned and decide which ones would be well addressed at either a permanent or new learning centre. For example, during the study of weather, student tasks at your computer centre may include creating a database that will record the information gathered about the weather in a particular area and creating a spreadsheet to analyze data collected during a field trip to a weather station. Chapter 5, Planning an Integrated Curriculum, may also prove helpful.

♦ The following types of centres can be created for either generic or unit-related use: a mathematics centre (see Figure 6.1), a writing centre, an arts centre, a puppetry centre, a drama/dress-up centre, a nature centre, a science centre (see Figure 6.2), an invention centre, a take-apart centre, a magnets centre, a design and technology centre, a music centre, a sound centre, a mapping centre, a water centre, a sand centre (see Figure 6.3), and a blocks or structures centre (see Figure 6.4).

Figure 6.1 *A mathematics centre*

Figure 6.2 *A science centre*

Figure 6.3 *A sand centre*

Figure 6.4 *A blocks or structures centre*

✦ For each learning centre you plan, decide on and record the name and tasks, the learning expectations you will be addressing, the materials you will need, the assessment practices you will use, and the method of tracking student work. See Figure 6.5 for a sample planning template.

Learning Centre Name and Tasks	Learning Expectations	Assessment	Materials Needed	Tracking
Reading Centre - read/respond (see generic task cards) - record books read - read aloud and tape-record reading	- read a variety of fiction and non-fiction materials for different purposes - express clear responses to written materials	- tape recording of student reading aloud - self-evaluation - teacher comments on reading logs	- novels - picture books - student-authored books - poetry - anthologies - reading logs - reading folders - task cards - tape recorder - blank cassettes	- reading log to record books read and responses completed

BLM T-24 Figure 6.5 *Sample planning template for learning centres*

◆ Examine the tasks at each centre carefully to ensure that they represent meaningful and relevant learning experiences. Students should have opportunities to do the following:

- reinforce, practise, apply, refine, and consolidate their skills and knowledge;
- interact, communicate, reflect, investigate, discover, and explore;
- choose from tasks at varying levels of ability;
- work with open-ended tasks (no right answers);
- make choices, solve problems, make decisions, and take risks;
- participate in cooperative learning experiences;
- receive ongoing feedback and assessment; and
- participate in peer- and self-assessment.

NOTE: *Since learning centres are meant to target independent or small-group experiences, it is critical to ensure that students possess the basic skills and knowledge necessary for completion of tasks. For example, if a task at a reading centre requires students to identify the main character, they must have an understanding of main character from previous learning experiences.*

◆ Ensure that for each centre you have signs and labels, clear instructions, concrete manipulatives, materials easily accessible to students, and storage and display areas for materials, resources, and student work.

◆ Collect, sort, and prepare the materials and resources needed for each centre. Figures 6.6 and 6.7 may help you with organization.

THINGS TO DO FOR THE *Structures* CENTRE

Materials to Collect		Things to Prepare
Equipment	**Manipulative Materials**	
☑ paper	☑ straws	☑ signs
☑ pencils	☑ pipe cleaners	☑ task cards
☑ crayons	☑ pins	☑ student worksheets
☑ scissors	☑ Plasticene	☑ games
☑ glue	☑ junk (boxes, tubes)	☑ student folders/ scrapbook
☑ filmstrip projector	☑ wooden stir sticks	❏
❏	☑ plastic stir sticks	❏
❏	❏	
Student Resources		**Other**
☑ Books on Structures		
☑ Filmstrip "Structures in Toronto"		
☑ Picture File "City Structures"		

BLM T-25 Figure 6.6 *Checklist for planning a centre*

Name of Centre	Learning Experiences	Materials Needed
Structures	– Build a bridge structure using the materials	tubes, rolled newspaper, tape, scrapbook, sketch pencils, photos of structures
	– Sketch different structures	

BLM T-26 Figure 6.7 *Teacher's chart for planning a centre*

♦ Once you are comfortable with using learning centres in your classroom, involve the students in the collection and preparation of materials.

♦ Involve the students in decisions about where to store and display their work. (See Chapter 2, The Physical Set-up of the Classroom.)

♦ Examine your timetable and decide *when* you will have students working at the centres. (See Chapter 3, Timetabling.)

♦ Decide on the maximum number of students allowed at each centre at any one time. The ideal number of students at a centre is four to six.

♦ With your students, take the time to establish rules, routines, and expectations for the centres. Promote the following practices:

  • Work cooperatively with others.

  • Complete work within an acceptable period of time.

  • Use materials appropriately and clean up each work area.

  • Move on to another task (or centre) when work is completed.

  • Keep tracking sheets up-to-date.

NOTE: *Students beginning to work in centres need to learn routines, expectations, and responsibilities. They need to strengthen their self-direction and independence, and develop positive attitudes towards learning and working at centres. When learning centres are first introduced, it is important to provide learning experiences that require a minimum of teacher direction and support in order to establish the basic rules, routines, and expectations. Take the time that is needed to ensure that routines are firmly in place.*

♦ Allow for input sessions prior to learning centre time. In these sessions, centre tasks are introduced, specific skills are taught, or large-group theme-related learning experiences occur. When introducing new learning experiences at various centres, stagger the instructional input over a few days. By doing so, your input sessions will not become overly long and unwieldy.

♦ Allow time for sharing after each learning centre time. During sharing, student work is highlighted, questions and issues are aired, and learning is articulated. Students could also engage in assessing their behaviour and quality of work.

♦ Decide on how you will *begin* to use learning centres. The following options provide you with three possibilities for implementing learning centres in your program.

Managing Learning Centres in Your Classroom

◆ Decide how best to move your students to and through centres. There is no one way to organize and manage a learning centre approach. Below are some options.

Option 1: Use learning centres when assigned tasks are completed.

This approach introduces the concept of learning centres to both teachers and students, but with it, learning centres may be perceived as an add-on, not as an integral part of your program. As well, when students use centres only after their work is completed, the centres remain unused for large portions of the day.

Option 2: Use a sign-up system or schedule.

This approach indicates specific times when students will use the learning centre or indicates the order of use by students. See Figure 6.8.

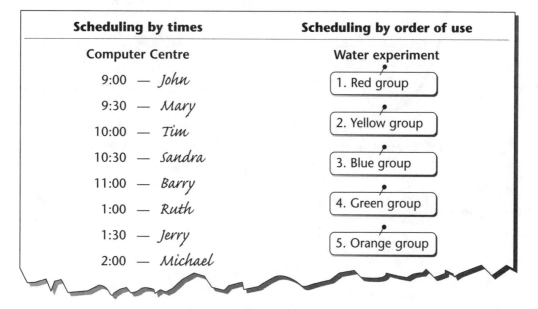

Figure 6.8 *Sign-up system or schedule*

Option 3:   Use a rotation system whereby students move systematically through centres in set groups.

This system allows teachers greater control over *when* and *where* students will work. A group rotation method ensures participation by all students in all centres over a specified period of time. It also allows the teacher and the students to become accustomed to many things occurring simultaneously in the room.

TYPES OF ROTATION SYSTEMS

a. Write group names on cards and post on a chart or board using tape, pins, or magnets. (Magnets may be taped to the back of the cards for easy movement on a magnetic board.) Prepare centre name cards and attach them to the board or chart. As the groups rotate through the centres, move all the name cards forward so that the chart reflects the rotation cycle. (See Figure 6.9.)

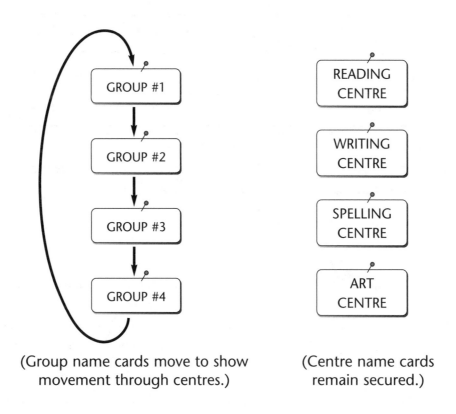

(Group name cards move to show
movement through centres.)

(Centre name cards
remain secured.)

Figure 6.9 *Group rotation chart*

b. The rotation wheel contains group names on the inner circle and centre names on the outer circle. These centre names can be written on cards and attached to the wheel by paper clips or clothespins to facilitate frequent and easy changes. The two circles are attached in the centre by a paper fastener. For each rotation, the inside circle is turned once so that students can see in which centre they are to participate next. (See Figure 6.10.)

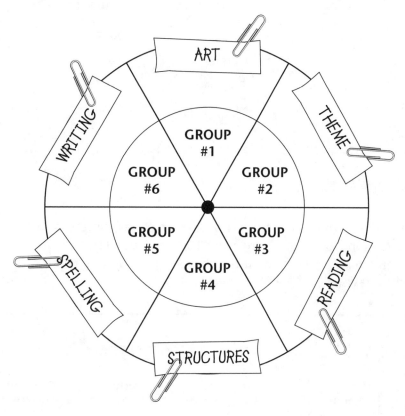

Figure 6.10 *Rotation wheel*

Option 4: Introduce a planning board sign-up.

Use a planning board to present a menu of learning centre opportunities from which students will choose. Students choose to work at specific centres on an individual basis and form self-selected groups. Each student decides the order of learning experiences and the necessary time to complete tasks.

> **NOTE:** *To avoid the possible chaos of 30 students approaching the planning board at the same time and having to wait to choose, you might want to assign a short, directed task to be completed prior to choosing a centre at the planning board. Since students will finish the assigned task at different times, they will approach the planning board a few at a time.*

TYPES OF PLANNING BOARD SIGN-UPS

a. Write the names of the centres on a board or chart. Students either sign up beneath a centre name or move their magnetized nametags under the appropriate column. (See Figure 6.11.)

Reading	Writing	Math	Puppetry	Structures
Marnie	Sonya	Kim	Aaron	Mark
Saul	Edison	Matthew	Kaari	Naseeb
Karen		Hyussein		
Nadia		Rena		
Mike				

Figure 6.11 *Planning board: centre sign-up*

b. Write the centre names (and/or show pictures) on the pockets. Student name cards (and/or photos) are placed in the pockets of the centres chosen. (See Figure 6.12.) Each student may have more than one name card to indicate the day's tasks.

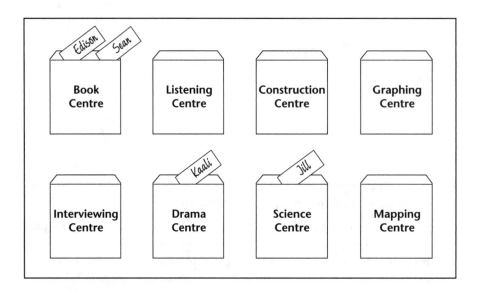

Figure 6.12 *Planning board: names on cards*

---

c. Write the centre names on the cards. Students place the cards for the centres chosen into their own name pockets. The number of centre cards available indicates the number of students allowed there at a time. (See Figure 6.13.)

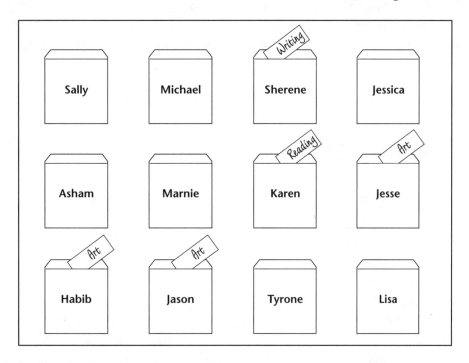

Figure 6.13 *Planning board: names on pockets*

d. Write the centre names on cards. The number of pockets beside each centre card indicates the number of students permitted at that centre at one time. Students place their name cards in the pockets for the centre chosen. (See Figure 6.14.)

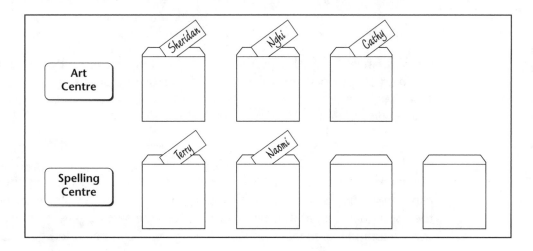

Figure 6.14 *Planning board indicating number of students at a time*

e. Write a number on the pocket to indicate how many students are allowed at the centre at any one time. Students move their name cards to the appropriate pockets, but also sign on the sheets below the centre pockets. They put checks beside their names when the work is completed. (See Figure 6.15.) This type of planning board promotes peer teaching because students who have questions can ask for help from those students who have already completed the task.

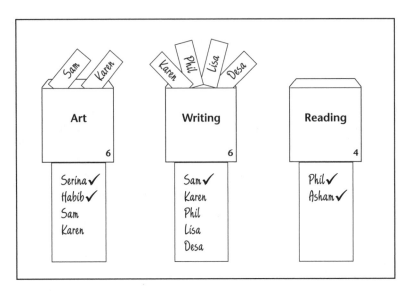

Figure 6.15 *Planning board indicating number of students and sign-up*

Option 5: Use tracking sheets.

These provide a method of monitoring student movement through centres. Students choose a learning task from the tracking sheet and mark the appropriate place when completed. These sheets are kept in desks or personal bins, stored in folders or envelopes, or glued into scrapbooks or notebooks.

Tracking sheets may also be used in conjunction with group rotations or with planning boards because they serve as records of student work accomplished. They can include sections for student self-assessments as well as sections for teacher and parent comments.

---

a. The tracking sheet in Figure 6.16 can be used in two ways. Very young students can simply choose one task at a time and put a check, sticker, or date stamp in the appropriate box as they begin or complete the task. For slightly older students, some learning experiences on the tracking sheet can be coded, for example, by star or colour. Students are instructed to alternate between coded and non-coded tasks. The coded tasks might represent experiences in which you want all your students to participate. These could be either skill-building or exploratory.

Name: Aaron					
The week of ___Jan. 9___ to ___Jan. 13___					

Activities	Monday	Tuesday	Wednesday	Thursday	Friday
Painting 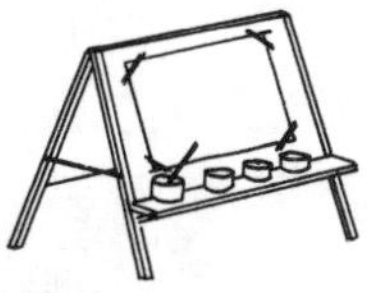			✓		
Cut and Paste 		✓			
Water Table 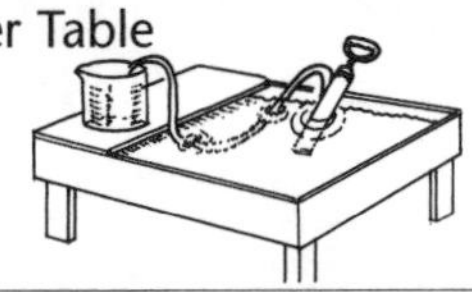			✓		
Home Centre 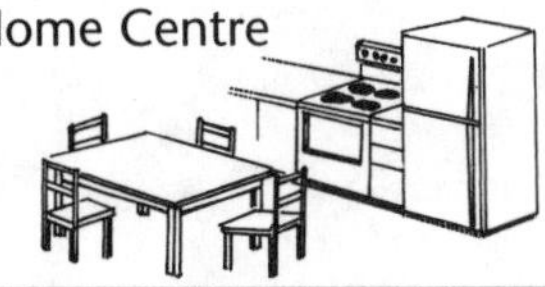	✓	✓			
Listening Centre 				✓	
Book Centre 	✓			✓	

BLM S-27 Figure 6.16 *Tracking sheet for primary students*

b. On the tracking sheet in Figure 6.17, students choose their learning experiences and record the name of the centre, the date started, and the date completed.

Centres	Date Started	Date Completed
1. Math	Feb. 9	Feb. 9
2. Structures	Feb. 10	Feb. 11

BLM S-28 Figure 6.17 *Tracking sheet: date started and completed*

c. On tracking sheets similar to that shown in Figure 6.18, young students begin to assess their own work and behaviour. They colour in descriptive faces to illustrate how well they think they worked at each centre.

MY TRACKING SHEET				Name: Matthew
Listening Centre	☺	😐	☹	Date Mar. 9
Reading Centre	☺	😐	☹	Mar. 6
Writing Centre	☺	😐	☹	Mar. 10
Math Centre	☺	😐	☹	
Art Centre	☺	😐	☹	Mar. 5
Odds 'n' Ends	☺	😐	☹	

BLM S-29 **Figure 6.18** *Tracking sheet: self-assessment using descriptive faces*

d. Students use the style of tracking sheet shown in Figure 6.19 to comment on how well they did at each learning centre.

MY TRACKING SHEET			Name: Daisleon
Centres	**Date Started**	**Date Completed**	**Comments (Self-assessment)**
1. Music	Mar. 2	Mar. 4	I think my words are coming out much more clearly now.
2. Spelling	Mar. 5		
3.			

BLM S-30 **Figure 6.19** *Tracking sheet and comments*

e. In Figure 6.20, students use a rating scale of 1, 2, 3, or 4 to indicate their accomplishments. Teachers and students can decide whether to rate behaviour, work habits, or quality of work.

Centres	Date Started	Date Completed	Rate Yourself: 4: Wow! 3: Good! 2: Just okay. 1: Could be better!
Structures	Dec. 8	Dec. 9	4

BLM S-31 Figure 6.20 *Tracking sheet and rating scale*

f. The tracking sheet in Figure 6.21 illustrates a distinction between teacher-directed learning experiences and student-chosen ones. It clearly indicates which learning experiences *must* be accomplished and which ones students may choose to do over the course of one or more days.

MY TRACKING SHEET	Learning Experiences	Monday	Tuesday	Wednesday	Thursday	Friday
THINGS I MUST DO	Reading	✓	✓	✓		
	Math	✓	✓	✓		
THINGS I WANT TO DO	Spelling	✓	✓	✓		
	Writing	✓	✓	✓		
	Printing	✓	✓	✓		
	Art					
	Drama		✓			
	Listening	✓				
	Games & Puzzles		✓			

Name: Roy
Date: April 19

BLM S-32 Figure 6.21 *Tracking sheet: Musts and wants — primary*

g. The tracking sheet in Figure 6.22 also illustrates musts and wants and applies to a weekly period of time.

MY TRACKING SHEET	Name: _Tyrone_
MUSTS	Week of _June 15_

✔	Choose 10 words, 2 activities
✔	Math: 1 arithmetic, 1 measurement, 1 geometry, 1 problem solving
✔	Read and make a book jacket
	Finish your interview/news articles
	Make a want ad or display ad
✔	Create a comic strip

WANTS	
	Planting activities
	Puppet play
	Magnetic board
✔	Computer-keyboarding

BLM S-33 Figure 6.22 *Tracking sheet: Musts and wants — junior*

h. The format in the tracking sheet in Figure 6.23 permits tracking of tasks over a lengthy period of time. Students must be involved in the top seven tasks, and then can choose from the next five.

Name: _Debra_   Starting Date: _Dec. 8_

MY CHECKLIST OF LEARNING TASKS

Learning Tasks	Date	My Comment	Teacher's Comments
1. Community Walk	Dec. 8	This was fun.	You set a fine example on our trip – Good Work. MC
2. Alphajobs booklet	Dec. 10	This was hard.	You tried hard to complete this task. MC
3. Interview			
4. Comparative graph	Dec. 11	I learned that graphs give me a lot of information.	Your graphs were detailed and accurate. Bravo!! MC
5. "Roll" model			
6. Earning and spending			
7. When I grow up			

BLM S-34 **Figure 6.23** *Tracking sheet: Checklist of learning tasks*

i. Students can use charts, such as in Figure 6.24, to have a written record of the tasks to be completed.

Centre	Tasks	Date Completed	Comments
Theme	Which animals live on land, in water, or in air?	Mar. 6	I found that most animals live on land.
	Which animals are vertebrates and which are invertebrates?		
	What do they eat? Choose a card and do research.	Mar. 7	I now know that monkeys are omnivores.
	Complete the food chain and webs.		
Talking	Sort the buttons/animal pictures/models.	Mar. 4	This was fun.
	Tell about your favourite animal.		
Reading	Read an animal fable.	Mar. 12	I didn't like the ending, because it didn't make sense.
	Read and tape an animal poem.		
	Find more animal poems.		

ANIMAL STUDIES TRACKING SHEET   Name: Sarah

BLM S-35 Figure 6.24 *Tracking sheet: Tasks described*

j. The format shown in Figure 6.25 allows students to record the date, the name of the centre, and other pertinent information each time that they begin work at a centre. Teachers can easily see how much time a student spends at a particular task. Some students may take many days to complete work at a centre. Others may pass through many centres in one day.

MY TRACKING SHEET

Name: _Lyle_

Today's Date	Name of Centre	Description of Each Learning Experience I Worked on or Completed	Comments
Mon. Mar. 6	Diorama Centre	I did Cinderella and the Prince dancing at the ball.	I'm proud of my box.
Mon. Mar. 6	Spelling	I finished my crossword puzzle.	It was fun.
Tues. Mar. 7	Mapping	I started my imaginary map of Hansel and Gretel's trip.	I had trouble starting.
Wed. Mar. 8	Mapping	I'm working on my map.	😐
Thurs. Mar. 9	Mapping	I finished the map.	I worked hard on it.

BLM S-36 **Figure 6.25** *Tracking sheet: Time spent at centres*

k. A log or journal such as in Figure 6.26 allows students to plan and organize their day's accomplishments. They write what they plan to do and later reflect upon what they have accomplished. Teachers can also comment and assess daily.

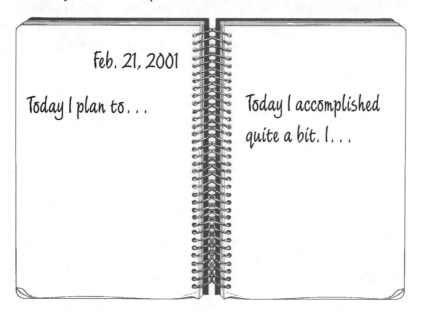

Figure 6.26 *Student Log*

Assessing the Learning at Centres

✦ In order to assess learning at the centres, refer back to the assessment strategies you outlined in the chart (see Figure 6.5) as you planned your centres. The assessment strategies you have chosen should address the learning expectations you have selected for each centre. (See Chapter 11, Assessing, Evaluating, and Reporting.)

✦ Observe individuals and small groups of students as they work at learning centres. Record pertinent information as anecdotal notes. Assessing students at centres can be quite manageable since you are focusing on a small number of students at any one time.

✦ Use tracking sheets that include an assessment component to encourage self-, peer-, and teacher-assessment.

✦ Create checklists or rubrics that indicate the criteria for achievement at each learning centre, and share these criteria with students before they begin working at learning centre tasks. Doing so is essential in providing clear expectations for success. Developing the criteria in collaboration with students builds ownership and commitment.

NOTE: You might want to include criteria on your checklists or rubrics that outline necessary social skills, as well, to encourage appropriate behaviour and work habits.

✦ Closely observe, assess, and assist those students who consistently do not complete tasks within an acceptable time frame. A contract can be set up between you and such a student. Involving parents in this process can prove beneficial. Figures 6.27, 6.28, and 6.29 provide examples of student contracts.

My Contract

I, _Stephen_____, agree to finish

_____my research project_____

_____my French story_____

_____

_____

_____

by _Mon Jan 15_____
                         (due date)

_____Stephen_____   _____M. Jones_____
   Student's Signature   Teacher's Signature

Comments: _____

_____

_____

    _____   _____
   Student's Initials   Teacher's Initials

BLM S-37 Figure 6.27 *Student contract #1*

My Contract

What I *must* do today . . .   _Math_____

_____Spelling_____

_____Finish the pictures for my book_

_____

What I *might* do today . . .   _cut and paste_____

_____

_____

_____

_____Sandi_____   _____B. Golden_____
   Student's Signature   Teacher's Signature

BLM S-38 Figure 6.28 *Student contract #2*

Contract

Date: _Dec. 8_

I, _Michael_, agree to _finish my Pioneer research project by Dec. 15._

If I do what I have agreed to, I will _be a hall monitor at recess for one month._

If I do not do what I have agreed to, I will _stay until 4 pm. each day until I finish._

This contract is in effect for _2 weeks._

Michael
Student's Signature

B. Golden
Teacher's Signature

Kate Samson
Parent's Signature

S. Schwartz
Principal's Signature

 **BLM S-39** **Figure 6.29** *Student contract #3*

Final Thoughts

Learning centres can prove to be a valuable addition to your classroom program. As you begin to implement a learning centre approach, you will find your students becoming more independent and self-motivated, as they make choices and work together cooperatively. It is important to continuously evaluate and reflect on the learning centres you have created to ensure that they provide opportunities for students to reinforce, apply, practise, refine, and consolidate their learning, to make choices, to solve problems, to make decisions, and to take risks. Successful implementation of learning centres will engage your students actively and help them to discover and grow as they *learn how to learn*.

7 Literacy and Language Learning

Literacy is the cornerstone of all learning and success in school. Before children begin their formal education, they have already learned a tremendous amount about language. The foundations for their future learning, not simply in the language area but in all aspects of the curriculum, are laid during their early years. As children learn to speak, they watch, listen, interact with language, and begin to make meaning from the sights and sounds around them. As they begin to read, write, draw, and represent their understandings, they use language in all aspects of their lives. Everything they do revolves around their confidence and ability to read and write, listen and speak, view and represent.

Literacy cannot be viewed as merely a subject to be learned in school, as it impacts on all aspects of learning, both in the classroom and in the world beyond. As the learners in your classroom acquire and learn to apply literacy skills, they move towards becoming proficient, independent users of language.

As a teacher, you are responsible for ensuring that you honour and value the language experiences, backgrounds, cultures, and diversity of your students. You need to provide rich contexts and environments for learning to occur. In your language program, you need to integrate reading, listening, and viewing, as well as writing, speaking, and representing, in a supportive and dynamic environment, one that fosters independent and critical thinking. During reading, viewing, and listening experiences, students are immersed in information and make sense of it in light of their prior knowledge, experience, and understanding. They then demonstrate their new learnings in a variety of ways. This demonstration of their meaning making is evidenced when they write, speak, and represent aspects of their learning. In this environment, where many opportunities for literacy experiences exist, all the components of language are seen to be interconnected.

Children begin to see themselves as readers as they look closely at books and notice the print in their environment. They attach meaning and build relationships between print and the spoken word. They are read to often, learn to listen carefully, and develop a positive attitude towards reading and books. As they develop and grow, they read often and with fluency, in a wide variety of genres, always for meaning, information, and enjoyment. They speak about their reading, listen to others read and speak, and write about what they read in order to share their understandings. They represent their learnings using a variety of mediums, read what they write, and share what they represent.

Children begin to see themselves as writers as they write and represent with clarity, imagination, and in an organized manner. They want to write because they have a purpose and an audience for their writing. They speak to clarify ideas for their writing, they listen to others read and speak, and they read and view the world around them to get ideas for their writing. They respond to questions about their writing, and represent their ideas through the use of line, form, design, media, and technology. Once children see themselves as authors, researchers, and artists, writing becomes a motivational tool for development in all other areas of the curriculum.

With an equal emphasis placed on listening and speaking, children learn to present their thoughts, ideas, and feelings with confidence. They talk about their writing before, during, and after they compose. They listen to good reading models often and talk about their reading and writing experiences. They have frequent opportunities to communicate with peers and adults in meaningful situations. This emphasis on "talk" provides opportunities for students to develop critical thinking skills. They are better able to organize their thoughts and convey information in both formal and informal situations.

As students take in meaning through reading, listening, and viewing, and produce new meaning through writing, speaking, and representing, the components of language are seen to be interwoven, one into the other, in a cyclical pattern, with meaning as the ultimate goal. An effective literacy program has a profound influence on all aspects of the curriculum, and as you develop your philosophy and implement your program, you will see your students become more and more motivated in every way.

Creating a Language-rich Environment

✦ Ensure that your classroom is rich in print and provides many opportunities to stimulate language development. (For examples of excellent print and language-stimulating resources, see Appendix 3: Favourite Children's Literature.)

✦ Collect and have available a wide variety of print material. Choices include

- fiction books
- novel sets

- non-fiction books
- poetry

- picture books
- big books
- wordless books
- predictable books
- pattern books
- anthologies
- levelled text sets
- books with accompanying tapes or CDs
- read-along books on CD-ROM and other software to encourage reading and writing
- author studies (multiple titles by the same author)
- character studies (multiple titles about the same character)
- student-authored books

- recipe books
- textbooks
- encyclopedias
- dictionaries
- thesauri
- magazines
- newspapers
- telephone directories
- television guides
- crossword puzzle books
- joke and riddle books
- catalogues
- atlases
- maps
- travel brochures

✦ Collect and have available a wide variety of materials, resources, and equipment that stimulate literacy learning experiences and cross-curricular connections. These include the following:

- posters
- charts
- songs
- labels
- lists
- task cards
- message boards
- felt boards
- magnetic boards
- mailboxes
- writing materials

- a student author display (student of the week)
- a library corner
- puppets, materials to make puppets
- puppet stage
- costumes and props for dramatic play
- blocks and building manipulatives
- sand and water activities
- audiovisual equipment
- computers

◆ When choosing resources for your classroom, ensure that they are suitable for your students' level of maturity and appropriate to your program needs. Resources should also be durable and cost efficient, as well as representative of people of varying abilities, lifestyles, ages, races, religions, and cultures.

◆ Ensure that the visual images and resources in your classroom environment represent the diversity of your own student population as well as that of the broader, global community. Students need to see many groups represented in order to honour and value those not necessarily in their immediate sphere of life.

◆ When choosing your resources, check to see that these are free from stereo-typical language or images.

NOTE: Some resources, including literary classics, can contain negatively biased stereotypical material. If you feel that the material may still have some relevancy and usefulness to your program, it is essential that you address the bias and stereotyping by involving your students in relevant discussions and debates. Be sensitive to the feelings of individual students in your classroom.

◆ Ensure that your reading corner is well stocked, and that books and resources are on display and accessible in many areas of the classroom. You may need to borrow books from the school or neighbourhood library in order to have many books in your classroom.

◆ Make available a wide variety of non-fiction reading materials at varying levels of difficulty to correspond to topics, themes, issues, or curriculum units of study for your grade and interest level.

◆ Provide a wide variety of writing materials, such as paper in a range of colours, sizes, and shapes, blank and lined, ready-made into booklets; writing tools, such as pencils, pens, markers, and chalk; sources of writing ideas, including class-generated topics listed on posters or charts, a table displaying artifacts to stimulate discussion, and theme books and materials; and publishing materials, such as cardboard, paper with adhesive backing, wallpaper, staplers, string, wool, dental floss, and needles (to sew books together).

◆ Provide your students with both reading and writing folders, either commercially produced or student-made, to serve as working files as they engage in the reading and writing process.

◆ Create an area in your classroom where authors and illustrators are highlighted and celebrated. Featuring a professional author or illustrator and celebrating an Author/Illustrator of the Month helps to develop a sense of authorship. This focus introduces students to different styles of authorship and illustration, and provides them with models for their own personal writing.

✦ Devote a section of your class to student-authored books. When your students write and publish their own books, they see firsthand the link between reading and writing. Students bring a new understanding to their own reading and to subsequent writing tasks, because they have inside knowledge about and experience with the development of storylines, characterization, and setting. In working with non-fiction material, they learn about procedural writing, point of view, research, and report writing. Students become motivated when reading and rereading their own and their peers' writing. See Figure 7.1.

Figure 7.1 *A "Hot off the Press" display of student-authored books*

✦ Use environmental print in your classroom. The signs, labels, posters, billboards, ads, and so on in students' environment can represent young children's first opportunity to bring meaning to print. These opportunities help to make necessary links to students' prior experiences.

NOTE: *For children just beginning to read and write, you might want to set up an area in your classroom that features pictures of traffic signs, fast food restaurant signs, and exit/entrance signs, or bring in samples of cereal boxes, store bags, magazine ads, and more. Students will recognize these signs and symbols from their experiences outside the classroom and begin* *to associate the reading process with print conveying meaning. This helps them to see themselves as readers.*

✦ Label all your bins, buckets, storage containers, and centres.

✦ Create signs for your walls, doors, and bulletin boards that convey messages for students to read, such as a *We Can Read* bulletin board, a welcome sign, or students' names on your classroom door. For young children, ensure that signs and resources are at their eye level.

✦ Create a **word wall**, a large, visual representation of words that students learn and use in their everyday life, both in the classroom and beyond. The words on a word wall are usually arranged under each letter of the alphabet or under other phonetic representations of the alphabet, and new words are added as students acquire new vocabulary. Students can refer to the word wall during reading and writing. (See Figure 7.2.)

Figure 7.2 *Word wall*

✦ Create and post, on an ongoing basis, lists of words that correspond to the themes or units being studied. Word families, such as "all" words — *fall, ball, mall,* etc. — are also good choices for word lists.

✦ Post rules and routines established for and with your students. Chapter 4, Classroom Atmosphere, provides guidance in this area.

✦ Use a chart for a morning message which allows students to read for a purpose as they begin their day. As they approach the chart individually, or more likely, in partners or groups, they help each other to bring meaning to the print. Often, the morning message shows the outline of events/tasks for the day, thus providing students with a sense of organization and a clear direction for the day's tasks. (See Figure 7.3.)

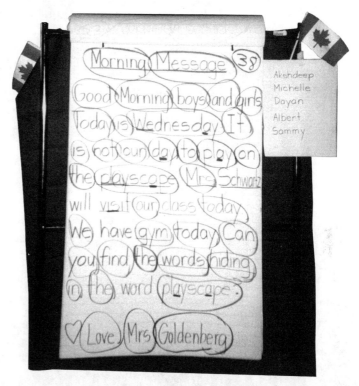

Figure 7.3 *Morning message chart*

✦ Work with students' names, and put them on display in a variety of ways. Names are usually the first words that students recognize, read, and write, so they are important.

✦ As you introduce poems, chants, or songs, record them on chart paper for display around the room. These should be left up for a prolonged period of time so that students can continuously refer to them for words, phrases, and ideas. You might also want to give students a smaller, individual copy of each poem, chant, or song for inclusion in their own reading booklets.

✦ Display a variety of commercial posters for students to read, ones that highlight poetry, favourite children's books and authors, memorable sayings, and thoughts of the day. Often, publishers, distributors, or bookstores will give away free posters that highlight children's books or events.

Creating Opportunities for Quality Listening and Speaking Experiences

✦ Provide frequent opportunities for oral language development by allowing students to express, clarify, and rehearse their thoughts and ideas verbally, in partners, in small groups, and to the whole class. They can gain practice speaking and listening in the following settings and circumstances:

- large- and small-group discussions
- problem-solving activities
- sand and water activities
- a dress-up/drama centre
- a nature centre
- felt or magnetic board activites

- storytelling opportunities
- activities with blocks, puzzles, games, and toys
- a puppet centre
- a construction centre
- recording of oral language samples on audiocassette tapes

✦ Provide specific opportunities to reinforce good listening skills. For example, have students listen with headphones to taped material, listen to adults read aloud frequently, respond to whole-class or small-group presentations, do echo clapping activities, and follow oral directions.

Figure 7.4 *Students present a puppet show using handmade puppets.*

Figure 7.5 *Students dress up for a skit.*

NOTE: *Involving students in storytelling, drama, and the arts is an excellent way to encourage and develop their listening and speaking skills as well as foster creativity, imagination, positive attitudes, and self-confidence. Drama spans role-play, tableaux (freeze frames), puppetry, and scriptwriting and should be a valued part of every program.*

** An excellent resource for drama is Larry Swartz's *Dramathemes* (Pembroke Publishers) which provides suggestions and clear outlines on how to use children's literature to invite students and teachers into the world of drama.

Creating Opportunities for Focused Viewing Experiences

✦ Provide opportunities for focused and directed viewing experiences, and allow time for sharing. As students begin to observe with a new focus and understanding, they become more critical and perceptive in the way they view the world around them. They begin to view things from a variety of perspectives. Focused viewing possibilities include

- examining illustrations, format, or organization in books;
- looking at pictures, posters, photos, and slides;
- viewing filmstrips, films, videos, and television programs and commercials;
- interacting with computer programs;
- attending plays and other presentations;
- using cameras or binoculars during out-of-classroom excursions; and
- using magnifying glasses, microscopes, or telescopes during science experiments.

Figure 7.6 provides an illustration of a focused viewing experience.

Figure 7.6 *A student uses a magnifying lens to observe the life in a terrarium.*

Creating Opportunities for Creative Representing Experiences

✦ Encourage your students to represent their learnings using a wide variety of media and technology. Doing so provides students with integrated learning experiences and better allows those students who are less linguistically inclined to express their thoughts, ideas, and feelings. Options include

- paintings
- papier mâché work
- videos
- scripts
- computer graphics
- slide shows

- drawings
- filmstrip creations
- photographs
- poetry
- dioramas
- Web pages

Figure 7.7 *Students using computers.*

Ed Bock/Firstlight.ca

Creating Opportunities for Meaningful Reading Experiences

✦ Continue to keep in mind your knowledge and understanding about the reading process.

- When students read, they apply a variety of strategies to construct meaning. As they incorporate all cueing systems into their repertoire of learning strategies, they begin to understand that print conveys a message. As they use the **semantic** cueing system, they bring all their prior knowledge and experience about print into play; as they use the **syntactic** cueing system, they begin to understand how the grammar of language works; and as they use the **grapho-phonemic** cueing system, they are able to see the connection between sounds and symbols. When readers are attuned to all three cueing systems and use them efficiently, they bring meaning and understanding to what they have read.

- Along with the three cueing systems, readers use a variety of other strategies to unlock meaning. These reading strategies include using illustrations, graphs, charts, and other visual cues, reading ahead, rereading, guessing, and skipping the word.

- Readers also incorporate an understanding of how text is laid out or organized to predict how to go about reading the print. For example, menus, recipes, dictionaries, and textbooks all have specific formats that help the reader make decisions about how to read and comprehend that particular type of text. Proficient readers bring all of these strategies together and use them to sample the text, predict what it might be about, and confirm their predictions as they strive to make meaning.

✦ Plan for a wide variety of meaningful reading experiences. Include the following on a regular basis in your program.

- **READ-ALOUD**

Daily read-aloud immerses students in a wide variety of quality literature, as well as providing them with models of good reading behaviours (intonation of voice, expression, fluency, enjoyment). It encourages discussion and extends thinking while opening students to new worlds and customs. It provides opportunities for students to develop author-illustrator awareness and encourages them to become more critical readers and writers. All teachers, not just those in the primary grades, should value read-aloud as a vital part of their literacy programs. This meaningful reading experience should occur at least three times each day, in different contexts and situations. Beyond a regular read-aloud story time, you can read aloud in all areas of the curriculum. Read-aloud opportunities exist as you read from textbooks, reference books, or other non-fiction material, articles, newsletters, and memos. A good idea is to read poetry or riddles as students line up to go outside for recess or for lunch. Any time you share the reading process with students, you are providing them with an excellent opportunity to see reading as a valued, relevant, and meaningful pursuit.

Plan your read-aloud experiences to complement your program. As you do so, consider carefully what you do *before, during,* and *after* you read aloud. Before you read aloud, you are activating prior knowledge, setting the context, setting purposes for reading, generating interest and motivation, and finding out what students already know. Figure 7.8 provides some direction.

Before the read-aloud:

Retell	Relate	Reflect
- Talk about/discuss/describe the cover, title, pictures, author, illustrator - Give information about the story/text	- Talk about what this makes you think of…what it reminds you of - Make connections to own experiences *(self)*, other books, characters, or plot *(text)*, or issues *(world)*	- Predict what this story/text is about - Ask questions

During the read-aloud, stop at intervals to:

Retell	Relate	Reflect
- Discuss key points - Notice details - Visualize	- Continue to make connections to *self, text, world*	- Continue to predict, infer, determine importance - Ask questions

After the read-aloud:

Retell	Relate	Reflect
- Describe the parts you liked or disliked - Point out/notice details, significant parts - Identify/name/list key concepts and main ideas - Retell ideas or events in sequence - Summarize	- Make connections to *self, text, world* - Compare - Contrast	- Draw conclusions - Make judgements about the text - State opinions - Synthesize/share insights and new learnings - Predict, infer, determine importance - Ask and answer questions/wonder

 **BLM T-40** Figure 7.8 *Before, during, and after read-aloud or guided reading*

** A good resource to use to complement the Retelling, Relating, Reflecting framework (Schwartz and Bone) is *Strategies That Work: Comprehension to Enhance Understandings* by Stephanie Daniels and Anne Goudis (Stenhouse Publishing/Pembroke Publishers in Canada).

• **D.E.A.R.***

D.E.A.R. time (Drop Everything and Read) is an extremely important part of every student's day as it provides in-school reading practice and develops the habit of reading for pleasure. This time for self-selected reading can also be called S.Q.U.I.R.T. (Sustained, Quiet, Uninterrupted Reading Time), or U.S.S.R. (Uninterrupted, Sustained, Silent Reading). Often, very young children will role-play reading behaviours as they look at the pictures and talk out the story — and the period is far from quiet. Beginning readers vocalize their reading, but as they become more confident and proficient, they will read silently. Giving students time to read for pleasure helps establish and nurture a love of reading.

The amount of time allotted for D.E.A.R. should correspond to the age and stage of your students. Younger students might spend only five to ten minutes each day reading for pleasure in the classroom, while older, more proficient readers could read self-selected material each day or every other day for as long as 30 or 40 minutes. With older students, it is still necessary to increase time in increments as you establish the routines necessary for D.E.A.R. time. Take your cues from your students as to how long they can sustain independent reading.

You may want to consider scheduling D.E.A.R. as soon as students enter the classroom, either in the morning, after lunch, or after a recess break. In these situations, you might have students put their books out on their desks or tables before they go out for recess/lunch or leave for the day. In this way, they will be able to start reading right after they enter the classroom. A good management idea is to ask that your students exchange books within their seating group only, to avoid having them take time to look for another book to read during D.E.A.R. You might also have them choose more than one book. When students are actively engaged in a task as soon as they enter the classroom, it frees you to deal with individual student needs or concerns that might arise, to talk to parents who might come to the door, to collect notes and permission slips, or to take attendance.

*This term was introduced by Andrea Butler and Jan Turbull in *Towards a Reading-Writing Classroom* (Australia; Primary English Teaching Association), p. 49.

• SHARED READING

In shared reading, students participate in choral reading and whole-class or small-group oral reading of big books, stories, poems, songs, chants, and chart stories. As students read together, they are not singled out, but begin to feel more confident in the group. In a risk-free environment, their voices are carried along by the stronger voices in the group, and they begin to recognize familiar and oft-repeated words. Students recognize patterns in language as they hear, read, and internalize the patterns in predictable books. These reading experiences can lead to meaningful writing, speaking, and representing extensions. Students become more aware of the rhythm and cadence of language as they sing, read, and chant together.

• PAIRED READING

Reading together in pairs allows students to read and discuss in a risk-free environment. The more fluent readers will often take on leadership roles while the beginning and developing readers gain valuable exposure to higher levels of reading material. Paired reading is an ideal way to promote the reading of novels or chapter books. It is also an excellent opportunity for buddy reading programs. Partnerships are formed with other teachers in the school (or in neighbouring schools) as older students are encouraged to read to, with, and for younger students (refer to "Paired Reading Guide" in Chapter 12, Partnerships with Parents).

• GUIDED READING

Guided reading provides support for the reader as the teacher guides students through the reading. As children progress in their reading ability, it is essential to help them through the process of understanding and gaining meaning from text. In this small-group learning experience, students are grouped together by instructional reading level to read the same levelled text. The groupings, based on assessment data collected on an ongoing basis, should always be flexible and temporary with students moving in and out of them according to their particular needs and interests.

Guided reading is a time to talk about a text, predict what might be in that text, and guide students through the initial encounter. You might ask students what they think the story is about after examining the title, cover, and illustrations throughout. You might also talk through the story as students look at the illustrations. A discussion about unfamiliar words that they might encounter would also be beneficial so as to activate as much prior knowledge as possible. The more readers know about the text before they read, the more successful they will be in the actual reading.

For beginning readers, you might first rehearse the reading by having the group choral-read the story together before they read it to themselves. Older, more proficient readers should also take part in guided reading as they predict, set purposes for their reading, read silently, discuss specific elements, and reflect on the meaning of the text. You might also want to focus more on non-fiction texts as a basis for their instruction. Guiding students through unfamiliar, expository text before asking them to read it independently will ultimately allow them to better understand what they are reading and to be better able to gather the needed information that non-fiction offers.

NOTE: Avoid round-robin reading where students read a portion of a text orally, one at a time, without rehearsal, in a group situation. This method is not conducive to creating a positive attitude towards reading. Students can experience anxiety and frustration when they are reading orally in a group without having had time to rehearse beforehand. Read-aloud without prior rehearsal should be used only in a one-on-one situation with the teacher for the purpose of assessing reading progress.

• ORAL READING

Oral reading is an effective learning experience when students have time to rehearse and polish their delivery. It enables students to develop the good expression, intonation, and phrasing necessary to present text aloud effectively. Read-aloud, shared reading, and paired reading provide students with the necessary practice to prepare for the oral reading experience. Readers' Theatre is clearly an example of a purposeful oral reading learning experience. Other examples might be choral reading or singing, poetry reading, sharing a favourite part of a book, newspaper, or magazine article, sharing jokes or riddles, presenting commercials or radio shows, sharing their own writing, presenting a speech or project, taping stories, recording and reading minutes of class meetings, and beginning an announcer's club where students make class and school announcements over the public address system.

** A good resource to refer to is *Good-bye Round Robin: 25 Effective Oral Reading Strategies* by Michael F. Opitz and Timothy V. Rasinsky (Heinemann/Irwin Publishing).

• READERS' THEATRE

Readers' Theatre allows students to become intimately familiar with the structure and pattern of language in a passage or story. As students take on the roles of narrator and readers, they dramatize the text through words and improve their oral reading fluency through the repeated practice that Readers' Theatre provides. This learning experience can also be an ideal opportunity to demonstrate clearly the interconnected relationship between the processes of writing, speaking, and representing, and reading, listening, and viewing. As students begin to write adaptations to stories used in a Readers' Theatre experience, audiences can read, listen to, and view what they have created.

• NOVEL STUDIES

The use of novels or chapter books is most appropriate for readers who are gaining some fluency in reading. Having students come together to read and respond to a novel helps to foster a love of reading, provides opportunities for sharing and responding in many ways, and introduces a variety of authors, types of novels, and genres of literature. It also allows the reader to interact with a text for a more sustained, intense period of time. There are a number of ways to program for novel studies in a classroom. Two possibilities are highlighted below.

Whole-class novel study: The whole-class approach is used to introduce, model, and reinforce the strategies that students will need to use later, when reading novels individually. It is usually tied to a theme or unit of study being addressed. It provides a model for students and an opportunity to introduce and discuss parts of a novel, such as character, setting, plot, sequence, and climax. In this approach, the teacher usually selects the novel, introduces it in a unique and attention-catching way, and models discussion and follow-up learning experiences. The use of a reading response journal as a follow-up learning experience is a particularly effective strategy, as are creative responses in visual arts, drama, and music. On the other hand, the ten-questions-to-answer-per-chapter approach has been found to stifle enthusiasm for reading.

Small-group novel studies: With a small-group approach, the teacher is able to tailor the choice of the novel to the students' interests and needs. Each group may be reading the same novel or members of the small group could be reading novels about a similar theme or topic. The groups can be homogeneous in ability so that the teacher can involve the students in guided reading, where specific skills can be taught, or the groups can be heterogeneous, where students might engage in paired reading and help each other through the text. The discussion and follow-up learning experiences are key to small-group novel studies. Small-group novel studies are often organized as literature circles which are outlined below.

• LITERATURE CIRCLES

Providing students with the opportunity and time to discuss their thoughts, feelings, and ideas about a text promotes skill and comprehension in reading and enjoyment of the reading process. In literature circles, small groups of students take on specific roles and come together on a regular basis to discuss, make connections, question, and wonder. Usually, these heterogeneous groups are no larger than six to eight students who are either reading the same text, different texts that share a similar theme, or a variety of completely different texts. Whatever they are reading, be sure to provide the groups with guidelines for discussion so that they can derive the maximum benefit from their meetings. Also, the assignment of specific roles encourages individual accountability as students share within their groups.

In launching literature circles in your classroom, it is important to introduce your students to the expectations and structure, and have them clearly understand each role through discussion, modelling, and role-play. You may want to begin with one group at a time. As each group becomes comfortable with and confident in the structure of these booktalks, you can let all groups meet at the same time while you circulate between and among them, acting as a facilitator and guide to the process. With this approach, it is important to structure your groups carefully to ensure that group members are able to work cooperatively and to help each other if needed. Figure 7.9 shows roles that students can assume during literature circles. Figure 7.10 provides a sample procedure for literature circles. A good idea is to plan a culminating task where students create a group mindmap, poster, dramatization, or presentation as a summary of their learning.

Literature Circles

Procedure:

1. Read and understand the specifics of each role identified below.
2. Choose a different role for each time you meet with your group.
3. Read the assigned reading material in advance, and come prepared to serve in your role for each session.

Session 1: Reading Material: _King of the Castle by Kathy Stinson, Chapters 1-3_

Date: _____ Time: _1:00 p.m._

_____ Kim _____   E. Illustrator: _Germaine_
_____ Meda _____   F. Facilitator: _Mike_
_____ Laureen _____ G. Recorder: _Silvan_
her: _Farhan_

erial: _Chapters 4-7_

Time: _1:00 p.m._

_____ Meda _____   E. Illustrator: _Mike_
_____ ureen _____   F. Facilitator: _Silvan_
C. Questioner: _Farhan_   G. Recorder: _Kim_
D. Vocabulary Enricher: _Germaine_

Session 3: Reading Material: _Chapters 8-12_

Date: _Jan. 24_ Time: _1:00 p.m._

Roles:
A. Summarizer: _Laureen_   E. Illustrator: _Silvan_
B. Connector: _Farhan_   F. Facilitator: _Kim_
C. Questioner: _Germaine_   G. Recorder: _Meda_
D. Vocabulary Enricher: _Mike_

Roles for Literature Circles

A. Summarizer: ❑ summarizes the reading for the group (a brief retell of the most important parts and issues).

B. Connector: ❑ relates or finds connections between the ideas in the text and their own lives, other texts, or the real world

C. Questioner: ❑ raises puzzling questions from the text for the group to consider

D. Vocabulary Enricher: ❑ finds new and interesting words from the text and draws the group's attention to them and their meaning

E. Illustrator: ❑ illustrates something of interest in the text to share with the group

F. Facilitator: ❑ makes sure the group stays on task, that everyone participates, and that the group keeps to a time line

G. Recorder: ❑ takes notes of the most important points during the literature circle discussion

BLM S-41 Figure 7.9

Roles for literature circles

BLM S-42 Figure 7.10 *Sample procedure for literature circles*

Sources: Adapted from *Literature Circles* by Harvey Daniels (Pembroke Publishers) and *Guiding the Reading Process* by David Booth (Pembroke Publishers), p. 54.

• READING RESPONSE

For any reading program to be meaningful, it is important to provide students with an opportunity to respond to what they have read in a variety of ways. Students need to be able to share their ideas, reactions, and opinions, both in written and graphic formats. They need to respond by expressing their thoughts in writing, answering relevant questions, making inferences, drawing images, and creating representations of any or all aspects of the text they are reading. Whatever the format the response may take, ensure that students understand the nature of the response and what is expected of them. Present models of exemplary responses to them.

Below are some different formats for reading response.

Using a reading response journal: Students respond in writing, sharing their thoughts, feelings, opinions, and questions about the plot, characters, setting, issues, information, etc. The use of prompts often helps to provide a structure and support for students as they build confidence and competence in their abilities to respond. The following prompts can prove helpful, especially if they are modelled at every opportunity throughout the program.

I noticed that... I especially liked... *(retell)*

This makes me think of... This reminds me of...
This makes me feel... *(relate)*

I wonder why... Now I realize... *(reflect)*

(Schwartz and Bone)

See **BLM S-43** for a sample reading response book.

Using graphic organizers: These visual models help to organize and represent learnings to facilitate recording of ideas and thinking. The following are examples of graphic organizers commonly used:

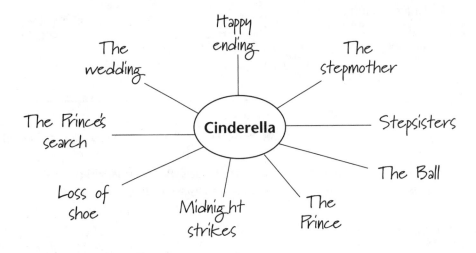

Figure 7.11a *Graphic organizer on a fairy tale theme* — Web

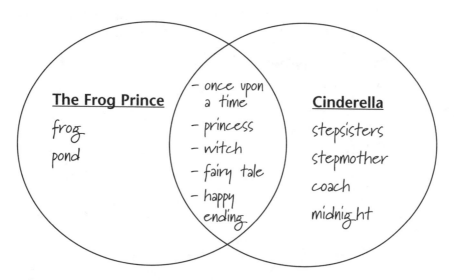

Figure 7.11b *Graphic organizer on a fairy tale theme* — Venn Diagram

In the Venn diagram:

The Frog Prince
frog
pond

(overlap)
– once upon a time
– princess
– witch
– fairy tale
– happy ending

Cinderella
stepsisters
stepmother
coach
midnight

Figure 7.11c *Graphic organizer on a fairy tale theme* — Story Map

Story Summary Sheet

Title: The True Story of the Three Little Pigs

Author: Jon Scieszka

Characters: Alexander T. Wolfe
3 Pigs
Reporter
Lawyer

Setting: jail house

Plot: A.T. Wolfe tells his story

Problem:

Solution:

BLM S-44 **Figure 7.11d** *Graphic organizer on a fairy tale theme* — Story Summary Sheet

Using follow-up questions: Questioning strategies that focus on a variety of levels of thinking, such as comprehension, analysis, synthesis, and evaluation, help to push students to be critical problem-solvers and decision-makers and to use language to articulate their ideas. It is important to avoid assigning a list of simple recall questions where students are required only to regurgitate facts and figures found in the text. Students need to not only read the words and phrases but read between the lines and beyond the lines, as they infer, analyze, predict, and more.

Using a book report format: Book reports can be in oral or written format and usually require that students summarize, present specific parts, and make recommendations about books read. Book reports should be varied to increase motivation (e.g., presented in a booklet format, as a commercial or advertisement, or on a poster) and should be displayed or shared with others. Figure 7.12 shows a book report format that can be used throughout the time students are reading a book; it incorporates tasks to be completed *before*, *during*, and *after* the reading.

Inside

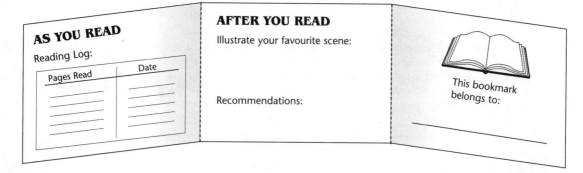

BEFORE YOU READ

Title:

Author:

Other books by the same author:

Story predictions:

AS YOU READ

New vocabulary:

Questions raised:

AFTER YOU READ

Story summary:

Outside

AS YOU READ

Reading Log:

Pages Read	Date

AFTER YOU READ

Illustrate your favourite scene:

Recommendations:

This bookmark belongs to:

_____

BLM S-45 Figure **7.12** *A three-fold bookmark as a book report*

Using art, music, and drama: Students respond to reading material by representing their thoughts, feelings, and ideas through drawing or painting, creating a song, rap, or chant, role-playing, and dramatizing. Figure 7.13 shows possible small-group reading response tasks that are arts-based and specifically geared as follow-up to a novel.

SHADOW PUPPETS

Materials Needed:
- overhead projector and screen
- black construction paper
- variety of paper and materials (glue, scissors, tape)
- acetate
- paper fasteners
- pipe cleaners, straws

Visual Arts Concepts:
- shape and silhouette
- animation

Task:
Turn a segment of the novel into a moving picture by working with shadow puppets on an overhead projector. Characters and settings can be created from cut black construction paper or bristol board. Limbs or other parts can be attached with paper fasteners. Details can be drawn on clear acetate and attached with tape. Pipe cleaners or straws can be used to move the figures on the overhead screen. Try adding other translucent or opaque materials for texture and variety. Rehearse your presentation; add dialogue or a narrative if you wish.

DIORAMA

Materials Needed:
- a shoe box
- scissors, glue, tape
- Plasticine

Visual Arts Concepts:
- three-dimensional art form
- geometric and organic shapes/forms

Task:
Create a scene in a box to illustrate your part of the story. Be prepared to retell what is happening in your scene.

PAPER SCULPTURE

Materials Needed:
- construction paper and variety of other paper
- glue, scissors, tape

Visual Arts Concepts:
- three-dimensional art form
- geometric and organic shapes

Task:
Recreate the main characters as three-dimensional figures using cut and torn paper.
Start with basic geometric forms using construction paper; these can be attached with tabs or glue flaps or masking tape. Add details by scoring, folding, curling, piercing, crumpling, creasing, layering, and weaving the paper. Try adding colour with construction paper or markers. Make certain that these 3-D creations can stand on their own! You might need to make a stand or base.

SOUNDSCAPE

Materials Needed:
- found or class-made instruments
- audiotape and tape recorder

Music Concepts:
- vocal control
- variety, projection, articulation
- pitch, rhythm, timbre

Task:
Think about the different sounds and noises that occur throughout the novel. How does the author help us to hear them? In movies, the soundtrack is the part that you hear — music, noises, voices, singing, and various other sounds that accompany the images. As a group, create sounds and music for your portion of the novel. Use instruments, the keyboard, your own voices, and anything else that you can find to make sounds that will allow others to "hear" a portion of the novel. Tape-record your soundscape so others can hear it.

DRAMATIZE IN COSTUME

Materials Needed:
- a box containing a variety of costumes
- construction paper and cut-and-paste materials

Drama Concepts:
- role-playing
- concentration or focus
- improvisation

Task:
Make the characters and incidents in this section of the novel come alive through playmaking. Use the costumes and props to visually communicate a sense of character or personality. (You may want to make a few simple props out of paper.) Not everyone has to be a living thing, though; some group members can assume the roles of inanimate objects. Try to make your acting as convincing as possible through your imaginative use of movement, voices, gestures, facial expressions, and positioning. Rehearse your scene; add narration for effect.

Source: Acknowledgments to Bob Phillips, at the Ontario Institute for Studies in Education/University of Toronto, for some of the above ideas

BLM S-46 Figure 7.13 *Arts-based reading response tasks for a novel*

Using task cards: Students respond by using task cards which are specific to a text or generic in nature. These tasks are geared to the instructional reading and maturity levels of the students. Figures 7.14 and 7.15 show sample task cards.

---

1. Create a chart in your reading notebook that looks like the following one:

What I already know	What questions I have	What I learned

2. Before you read the book that you have selected, fill in the first column with any facts that you know about _____.

3. Fill in the second column with any questions you have about _____.

4. After you have read the book, record any new information you have learned about _____.

BLM S-47 **Figure 7.14** *Sample task card re: non-fiction*

---

1. Choose a partner with whom to share your buddy journal.

2. Read two chapters of your novel.

3. After you have read two chapters, write an entry in your buddy journal. As you write, describe key ideas, make connections, ask questions, and share insights.

4. Exchange your journal with your partner. (If your partner is in the middle of reading his/her book, continue to read your book until he/she is finished and can exchange journals with you.)

5. Respond to your partner's entry by making encouraging statements, making connections, and asking questions.

6. Return your partner's journal and begin to read the next two chapters.

7. Repeat numbers 1 to 6 until you have completed reading the novel.

BLM S-48 **Figure 7.15** *Sample task card re: a novel study*

Using a Tic Tac Toe board: Make a Tic Tac Toe board to organize *generic* reading response tasks as follow-up to a text. Figure 7.16 provides a sample Tic Tac Toe board, which should be created on a large, laminated piece of poster board. Use tape to attach the cards to the board so that you can change the reading tasks whenever you feel it is necessary. When changing the tasks, make sure that they represent a balance of writing, speaking, and representing experiences. Also, the students should have record sheets to record books read and tasks completed. They write the title of the book and the date completed on their record sheet in the corresponding box that represents the task that they have chosen to complete. The object is to create a tic tac toe with the tasks chosen. A tic tac toe can be diagonal, straight across, or down. When students have created a tic tac toe, they hand in their record sheet and begin a new one. Figure 7.17 provides a sample record sheet.

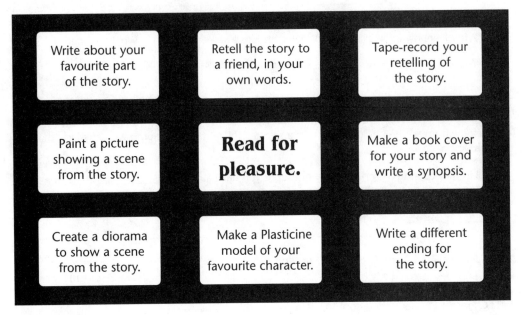

Write about your favourite part of the story.	Retell the story to a friend, in your own words.	Tape-record your retelling of the story.
Paint a picture showing a scene from the story.	**Read for pleasure.**	Make a book cover for your story and write a synopsis.
Create a diorama to show a scene from the story.	Make a Plasticine model of your favourite character.	Write a different ending for the story.

BLM S-49 **Figure 7.16** *Tic Tac Toe task cards*

TIC TAC TOE RECORD SHEET

Name: Loreen Lee

Date Started: Jan 19
Date Finished: Jan 22

Title: Chrysanthemum Date: Jan 20	Title: ___ Date: ___	Title: ___ Date: ___
Title: ___ Date: ___	**"FREE"** **READ FOR PLEASURE** **"FREE"**	Title: ___ Date: ___
Title: ___ Date: ___	Title: ___ Date: ___	Title: Whoever You Are Date: Jan 22

BLM S-50 **Figure 7.17** *Tic Tac Toe student record sheet*

• READING IN THE CONTENT AREAS

Reading opportunities throughout the curriculum are vital components of a balanced literacy program. Students need to know that not only do they *learn to read* for pleasure, but they also *read to learn*. They read to obtain facts, knowledge and skills and to learn about people, places, and things. It is important to show students that specific skills and strategies apply when reading non-fiction texts.

Just as you teach them to reread, skip, sound out, and look for smaller words in fiction, when you teach them to read expository texts such as textbooks or reference books, you must bring their attention to the clues to meaning found in that type of text. These include looking at the pictures, graphics, diagrams, captions, headings, and subheadings, noting highlighted, bolded, or italicized words, checking key word lists often found at the front or back of the book, reviewing any sidebar information, and studying the table of contents, index, and glossary.

By taking jot notes as they read, students are able to refer back to items that might help them make sense of the text. They can read a passage and recite back to themselves what they have just read. They often need to slow down their reading to focus more on the meaning to gain a fuller appreciation and understanding of the content. All of these strategies are important to ensure that reading non-fiction is a satisfactory and enlightening pursuit for all readers.

Creating Opportunities for Meaningful Writing Experiences

✦ Continue to keep in mind your knowledge and understanding about the writing process. As you involve students in process writing, they work through the same phases of writing as professional authors — pre-writing, drafting, revising, editing, and publishing for an audience.

Pre-writing: Students search for, contemplate, and choose topics to write about during the pre-writing phase. They experience, discuss, brainstorm, question, rehearse, and clarify their ideas. They talk out, plan, organize, and make connections. They articulate their purpose for writing, reveal a sense of voice, select appropriate vocabulary, and orally revise and apply conventions. They might engage in a variety of storytelling and role-playing experiences. Teachers often provide the impetus for writing as they involve students in a variety of learning experiences across the curriculum. Be sure to allow some choice of topic in order to give students ownership over their topics and writing forms.

Drafting: This is the "write-it-down-as-fast-as-you-can" phase, the phase in which thoughts and ideas are recorded onto paper (or keyboarded into the computer). Here, the emphasis is clearly on the content and meaning of the writing.

Revising: During this phase, students are encouraged to *"revisit"* or take another look at the content of their writing. They change, rearrange, add to, omit, and improve the ideas in their drafts.

Editing: When students, in collaboration with the teacher, decide to present and share their writing with an audience, they recognize the need to edit: to proofread and to polish the mechanics of their writing. It is at this phase that they concern themselves with spelling, grammar, and punctuation.

Publishing and sharing: Students present their chosen pieces of writing to an audience in a variety of ways and formats.

NOTE: Not every piece of writing will go through all phases of the writing process. Beginning writers might participate only in the pre-writing, drafting, and sharing phases. Also, some writing, such as personal writing and reflection, is not meant to be shared. You need to be aware of each writer's developmental stages, and to help him/her understand the purpose or intention of the writing.

✦ Provide for a wide variety of meaningful writing experiences. Be sure to include the following on a regular basis in your program.

• **JOURNAL WRITING**

Journals, diaries, or logs provide students with opportunities to express their thoughts, feelings, ideas, insights, and reflections in written format. Journal writing usually remains speech-like or in draft format as it is not intended to be shared with a wider audience. It is important to monitor what students are writing in journals as it can provide insights into their feelings of self-esteem and sometimes reveal difficulties that need to be addressed. Since journal writing can be a very personal experience for students, be sure to respect a student's request for privacy, should that occur. The student could fold back the page and mark "Confidential" on the outside to indicate to you that he/she would prefer a particular entry not be read.

Several different kinds of journals exist:

Reading response journals: Students record their reactions to literature in response to a reading experience such as read-aloud, literature circles, novel studies, or independent reading. (See the section on reading response earlier in this chapter.)

Buddy journals: In buddy journals, students practise written conversations with their peers within a framework of firmly established routines for the exchange of journals. This strategy can be used to respond to literature and to follow up on a class event, experience, discussion, or debate. The use of e-mail facilitates online buddy journals, where students improve their computer technology skills at the same time as they are communicating their ideas and improving their writing skills.

Communication via e-mail eliminates the routines of exchanging journals and facilitates writing at different times during the day. E-mailing also assists teachers in the monitoring of buddy journals. Students can learn to c.c. or copy their messages to the teacher who then acts as the reader on the side, commenting on the entry only when the need arises.

Dialogue journals: In this type of journal, students also practise written conversations but in this instance, they can do so with their teacher, parents, or other adults, such as an author or illustrator. Adults have a unique opportunity to model grammatically correct and effective writing as they respond to the students' entries. This way of demonstrating to your students correct grammar, spelling, and punctuation is much more meaningful than the use of worksheets. Responses and questions asked need to be genuine and to reveal the teacher/parent as an interested participant in the process.

Learning logs: In learning logs students record what they are planning to do and what they have learned, or how they have solved a problem and what strategies they have used to do it. This practice can be used in all areas of the curriculum including mathematics and science where communication is a vital component of the learning process. It allows students to think critically, analyze problems, and communicate or articulate their understandings.

- ## MODELLED WRITING

As students begin to experiment with or refine their writing skills, it is essential that they see good writing models. Teachers model and demonstrate how ideas are generated, organized, and recorded, and show how these ideas can be formatted, revised, edited, and prepared for an audience. Modelled writing should be both planned and spontaneous. Teachers share models of different formats, structures, and methods as they engage students in direct teaching experiences, and in their own response to students' writing. It is also important that students see teachers writing for their own purposes and needs in order to understand the relevancy of learning conventional writing skills and strategies.

- ## SHARED WRITING

In this learning experience, either a student or the teacher can act as scribe as participants collaborate to record ideas, thoughts, events, reactions, and/or opinions, usually during whole-class or small-group mini-lessons. Often, the teacher will be the sole scribe, but will always take the cues from the students as they negotiate the message to be recorded.

• LANGUAGE EXPERIENCE

This learning experience resembles shared writing and modelled writing as you capture students' thoughts and ideas on a chart, board, or overhead. The language recorded stems from the students as you scribe their own words to encourage reading and an understanding of phonemic awareness, grammar, and spelling. This is a good opportunity for teachers to find out what students already know about a subject, and can be used as a diagnostic assessment at the beginning of a unit of study. A good idea is to record each student's name beside their contribution on the chart. (See Figure 7.18.)

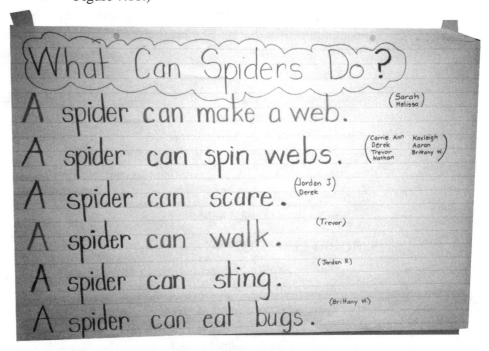

Figure 7.18 *This language experience chart identifies the students who contributed to it.*

• INDEPENDENT WRITING

During independent writing time, students use the skills and strategies learned during modelled and shared writing to create their own pieces. Independent writing can grow out of both student-selected and teacher-generated topics. It is vital that students be allowed to choose their own topics for writing; it is just as important that teachers involve students in more focused writing, where the topics are negotiated with the students and are relevant and meaningful to their interests, needs, and abilities, as well as to the curriculum. As students become more knowledgeable in and comfortable with the writing process, independent writing will take on even greater significance in their writing progress as they experiment with different ideas, formats, and purposes for their writing. During this time students begin to feel like authors, often making decisions about which pieces of writing to share or take to publication.

• LEARNING PHONICS, GRAMMAR, AND SPELLING

Children need to learn about sound/symbol relationships or phonics in order to write, and need to use this knowledge and understanding in order to read. The use of phonics as a beginning writing strategy is essential for young writers, who experiment with letters, sounds, and words. However, always remember that phonics, grammar, and spelling need to be put into the context of real writing opportunities, not handled as external, independent worksheet exercises that do not allow for the transfer of skills learned. The most effective way that students will learn about sound/symbol representation, or develop phonemic awareness, is to approximate spellings during mini-lesson, modelled, shared, and independent writing experiences. As teachers model and share writing, they talk about sounds, letters, and combinations of letters and sounds, how different words are spelled, and why they are spelled that way; they also talk about how language patterns are organized and used. The rules of conventional spelling and grammar need to be modelled, and those rules need to be practised as students attempt to write down their own thoughts and ideas.

• WRITING IN THE CONTENT AREAS

Just as *reading* in the content areas is vital to a balanced literacy program, so too is *writing* in the content areas. Here, students begin to understand that they write to show what they have learned. Most often, writing in the content areas means writing expository or non-fiction material, so students should be taught how to record information collected, how to organize that information, and how to present it for an audience. Teaching students how to take jot notes will provide them with the skills necessary to collect data as they research topics of need or interest. Demonstrating the use of graphic organizers will assist them when they attempt to sort and classify the information they have collected. Providing them with models of how to *publish* their information will help them see a purpose for the different formats available.

Organizing a Balanced Literacy Program

With so many components to consider, implementing a balanced literacy program often poses a challenge. Consider the following ideas which are intended to help make your planning and implementation more manageable.

✦ Set aside one large block of time for language arts or two smaller blocks of time for meaningful experiences in reading, writing, listening, speaking, viewing, and representing.

✦ Ensure that you read aloud several times throughout the day.

- In your focus on reading during your language arts block, include time for reading response, shared reading, guided reading, and independent reading.

- In your focus on writing during your language arts block, include time for journal writing, shared writing, modelled writing, and independent writing.

- Ensure that you are integrating meaningful literacy experiences into other content areas of the curriculum throughout the day, week, term, and year. Figure 7.19 provides a visual representation of a balanced literacy program.

A BALANCED LITERACY PROGRAM

The Reading Process
- cueing systems
- reading strategies

The Writing Process
- pre-writing, drafting, revising, editing, publishing
- phonics, spelling, grammar

Reading, Listening, Viewing

Writing, Speaking, Representing

Read-aloud

Reading response
Shared reading
Guided reading
Independent reading
Reading in the content areas

Journal writing
Shared writing
Modelled writing
Independent writing
Writing in the content areas

Figure 7.19 *A balanced literacy program*

A Focus on Reading

There is no *one* way to organize a reading program. The following ideas represent ways to begin.

- As part of your language arts block, schedule time for reading daily. Remember that very young, emerging readers should not be expected to read at the same time; instead, reading opportunities should be provided throughout the day. When Kindergarten and early Grade 1 students are just

beginning to understand that print conveys a message,
guided reading groups while the rest of the class is in
not dependent on an ability to read text. As more of t
readers, you can schedule a specific time for reading

BLM S-43

✦ Encourage your students to use reading folders to ho
response work. (A reading response book appears a⸱
The book, however, does not appear as a figure in this chapter.

✦ Introduce your students to a reading record sheet or log. See Figures 7.20
and 7.21 for samples.

Name: _Rena_	MY READING LOG			
Date	**What I'm reading**	**Pages read today**	**What it's about**	**Rating** 1: Wow! 2: Good 3: Okay 4: Could be better
Jan. 15	Elbert's Bad Word	25	It's about a boy who says a bad word that comes out of his mouth and looks like a spider.	1

BLM S-51 **Figure 7.20** *Sample reading record sheet #1*

Name: _Marnie_	MY READING RECORD				Term: _2_
Title	**Author**	**Date started**	**Date completed**	**Number of pages**	**Comments**
The Bee Tree	Patricia Polacco	Jan 8	Jan 11	29	I loved the way the grandfather described reading as honey and sweet.
The Girl Who Hated Books	Manjusha Pawagi	Jan. 12	Jan 14	23	This book makes me think of the book and movie Jumanji when the animals came to life.

BLM S-52 **Figure 7.21** *Sample reading record sheet #2*

+ Provide a reading notebook for each student, so that students will have a manageable way to organize any reading follow-up tasks.

+ Determine your students' reading levels and abilities through the use of diagnostic assessment. (See Chapter 11, Assessing, Evaluating, and Reporting.)

+ Prepare follow-up tasks depending on the curriculum expectations and the needs and interests of your students.

+ For your language arts block, plan a variety of meaningful reading experiences and consider integration possibilities and management strategies so that students are working independently while you work with small groups or individuals.

+ To facilitate planning, organization, and management, consider implementing a *Reading Bin Time* where students read and respond to a variety of materials geared specifically to their levels of reading ability. The premise of Reading Bins is to allow your students to work independently and on an ongoing, continuous basis so that you, the teacher, gain maximum flexibility to meet the specific needs of small groups and individuals. The key to making this method of organization successful is to ensure that the routines are firmly established before you begin to meet with small groups or individuals.

Preparing for Reading Bins

1. Use the information about your students' reading abilities that you have gathered through the use of diagnostic assessment strategies, and divide your students into three to five instructional reading groups.

NOTE: *When students are grouped into instructional levels, it is essential that these groupings be flexible and tied to their progress in reading ability. Students should move in and out of different reading groups and bins as their reading abilities and interests change and grow. Remember that all homogeneous groupings should be flexible and temporary — never static. You don't want students to become labelled or have difficulty changing perceptions about that label.*

2. Colour-code three to five plastic bins or tubs to represent the three to five reading levels.

3. Gather reading materials that correspond to the instructional reading levels you have determined through your assessment to place in each bin. There are many ways to choose materials for the bins. You might decide to place different materials in each bin, making sure that your

students understand that each group will deal with all the different types of texts at some time during the year. Doing this guards against students feeling that only some readers will be using picture books, poetry, novels, or non-fiction, or whatever. It is important that all groups have experience with many genres throughout the year. One group might be reading a novel set while another reads from a bin of picture books. You then would require only enough copies of a novel set for one group at a time.

If you use picture books or non-fiction texts in a bin, it is advisable to have at least 25 to 30 different titles to ensure that there is enough reading material for students at that level. Alternately, you might decide to have all groups working with the same type of text at the same time, possibly using a theme or unit of study as the basis for selecting the material. This facilitates the integration of other content areas into your reading program. For example, each group might have a science-fiction novel set in their bin that corresponds to a science unit on space. The important thing to keep in mind is that the novel set, or any of the material in each bin, would correspond to the instructional level of that group.

** Good references for you to refer to when deciding on levels of texts are *Guided Reading, Matching Books to Readers*, and *Guiding Readers and Writers, Gr. 3-6,* by Irene C. Fountas and Gay Su Pinnell.

4. Place each student's reading folder, reading record log sheet, and reading notebook in the appropriate bin for easy access and storage. (Not all groups need to use the same reading log or tracking sheet; reading log sheets can be tailored to the needs of each group of students.)

5. For each group, prepare follow-up tasks that are generic in nature or that correspond directly to the texts with which the students will be working during Reading Bin Time. Ensure that tasks, which could be presented on cards, are meaningful and purposeful learning experiences that will address the expectations required for your grade level.

6. Check to make sure that your bins are ready for use. Ask yourself if you have put the materials identified in Figure 7.22 in each bin.

READING BIN CHECKLIST

Student materials:

- ❏ Reading folder
- ❏ Reading workbook
- ❏ Reading record log/sheets

Instructions for students:

- ❏ Task cards (generic or specific to the text), or
- ❏ Reading response journal, or
- ❏ Multiple copies of task sheets in labelled envelopes or
- ❏ Tic Tac Toe record sheets

Reading texts (to be varied as appropriate):

- ❏ Picture books (25–30) or
- ❏ Non-fiction books (25–30) or
- ❏ Anthologies or
- ❏ Novel set(s)

BLM T-53 **Figure 7.22** *Reading bin checklist*

Using Reading Bins

1. Organize your timetable to include at least 30 minutes, three to five times a week, for work in the Reading Bins. In addition, ensure that you have allocated time for D.E.A.R., read-aloud, shared reading, etc. A possible timetable pertaining to Reading Bins is outlined below in Figure 7.23.

Timetable	Date: _____
8:45	D.E.A.R. (students stop for any announcements)
9:00	Whole group lesson (read-aloud, direct instruction, shared reading, language experience)
9:15	Reading Bin Time and Guided Reading with one group at a time (once routines are firmly established)

Figure 7.23 *Possible timetable for Reading Bins*

2. Introduce the Reading Bins to one group at a time so that the students know what is expected of each group.

3. Ensure that students are seated *heterogeneously* as they work at their Reading Bin tasks so that they can cooperate with and help one another in the different reading and follow-up tasks when necessary.

NOTE: *It is very important that students sit with peers at varying levels of reading ability so that students don't perceive that all the "good" readers are together and all the "poor" readers are together. When you want to work with one particular group of readers for guided reading or to check Reading Bin work, merely call them up from all the work groups situated around the room and have them convene at a meeting area with you. Once the time with you is over, they can return to their original, heterogeneous work groups.*

4. Ensure that your routines are firmly in place before you begin to work with small groups or individuals. Achieving this could take a few days or a few weeks.

5. Begin to work with small groups or individuals on other meaningful reading experiences such as guided reading, shared reading, literature circles, or novel studies. When you do so, use materials that are appropriate to their reading levels but *different* from the materials in their Reading Bins. Remember that Reading Bins are intended for independent, ongoing, and continuous learning experiences and are meant to allow you the time and opportunity to work with small groups or individuals.

6. Meet with each group as needed to discuss, track, or assess the work being completed during Reading Bin Time. Your goal is to check with each Reading Bin group at least once per week. You might set specific times for each group to meet with you. These times could be written on the chalkboard to promote independent time management.

✦ Continue to examine your timetable to ensure that you have carefully planned a balance of reading opportunities throughout the days and weeks. Doing so will encourage your students to remain committed, enthusiastic, and motivated throughout the year.

A Focus on Writing

There is no *one* way to organize a writing program. The following ideas represent some ways to begin.

✦ As part of your language arts block, schedule time for writing daily. Do not expect very young writers to write at the same time. Writing opportunities should be provided throughout the day. By placing a message pad near a toy phone in the house centre or by leaving stationery near a mailbox, you are providing invitations to even the youngest student to write. These invitations help young writers to see the purposes and opportunities for writing throughout their day.

✦ With your students, discuss writing as a process, and tell them that they will be working through the same phases of writing as professional authors.

✦ Encourage your students to use their writing folders to house their writing. An effectively organized folder has two or three pockets, which may contain and organize draft writing, edited and polished pieces, topic ideas and lists, ongoing records, titles of books, and lists of most commonly used words.

✦ Have your students use a writing record sheet such as the one shown in Figure 7.24.

WRITING RECORD SHEET

Name: _Sandy_

Date started	Theme/Title of writing	First draft	Revised	Edited	Published: Tell how	Teacher's comments
Jan 12	My trip to California	✓	✓	✓	Pop-up Book	I especially enjoyed the visuals you used.
Jan 23	Medieval life					

BLM S-54 **Figure 7.24** *Sample writing record sheet*

- ✦ Become a writer yourself and serve as a model for your students.

  - Make lists with your students.
  - Write messages or letters to your students and parents. (Use school or personalized stationery, or use Post-it notes for brief comments and questions about students' work.)
  - Write poems, stories, and riddles, and share your work with your students.

- ✦ Become a storyteller for your students and model storytelling skills. Encourage your students to become effective storytellers. Thinking like a storyteller should assist them in the pre-writing phase.

** A good resource to use is *Telling Stories Your Way: Storytelling and Reading Aloud in the Classroom* by Bob Barton (Pembroke Publishers).

- ✦ Allow students to choose their own topics for writing often. You can foster this by providing stimulating artifacts, pictures, photos, films, filmstrips, books, CDs, magazines and newspapers; storytelling experiences; opportunities for role-playing; opportunities for picture making and creative art; and meaningful experiences, such as class events, field trips, group activities, and performances.

- ✦ Involve students in lessons that demonstrate the different phases of the writing process: pre-writing, drafting, revising, editing, and publishing/sharing.

Pre-writing: Lessons might span brainstorming, using artifacts beginning with a picture, creating word association webs, using story maps, role-playing, dramatizing, and working with puppets.

Drafting: Develop expectations for draft writing with your students. Here are some pointers to pass on:

- Write down your thoughts and ideas as quickly as you can.
- Cross out any words, phrases, sentences, or paragraphs that need changing; do not use an eraser during the drafting phase, as this might slow down the flow of your ideas.
- Write on every other line to allow space for your revisions.
- Use only one side of the paper so you can revise, cut and paste, and reorganize your writing.
- Use looseleaf paper so you can revise large sections of your writing.
- Use a writer's notebook for your ideas and writing attempts.
- Save drafts to computer disks using "save as" to ensure that all drafts are maintained.

Revising: Keep in mind the following while students are revising their work.

- Model good questioning techniques at every opportunity.

- Reinforce the use of *who*, *what*, *when*, *where*, *why*, and *how* questions.

- Demonstrate the cut-and-paste feature when using the computer for word processing.

- Brainstorm and use word webs to generate alternatives for overused words such as *said*, *asked*, and *walk*.

- Advise students to use the thesaurus to find alternate words to use.

Editing: Lessons address the use of the dictionary and the use of the spelling/grammar check on the computer. Quotation marks, appropriate punctuation, avoiding run-on sentences, paragraphing, and combining simple sentences to make compound and complex sentences are other possible lessons on editing skills.

** Good resources to use for teaching writing are *What a Writer Needs* by Ralph Fletcher (Stenhouse Publishers) and *Craft Lessons: Teaching Writing K–8* by Ralph Fletcher and JoAnn Portalupi (Stenhouse Publishers).

Publishing, or "Going Public": There are several ways in which to help students develop a sense of authorship.

- Highlight authors and illustrators at every opportunity.

- Celebrate an Author of the Month/Student Author of the Week.

- Share writing using an Author's Chair.

- Share models of different ways to publish.

- Publish in a variety of formats. Options range from accordion books, banners, and flip books to peek-a-boo books, pop-up books, and wheel books.

** Good resources to use for helping students to "go public" are *The Ultimate Guide to Classroom Publishing* by Judy Green (Pembroke Publishers) and the companion book, *Making Books: Over 30 Practical Book-Making Projects for Children*, by Paul Johnson (Pembroke Publishers).

See **BLM S-55-T-59** for five samples of complete lesson plans that you might do with your students to introduce and reinforce the phases of the writing process.

✦ Ensure that your students see writing as purposeful and for an intended audience. When students understand that the intention of writing is to share thoughts, ideas, information, and feelings with an audience, they see the purpose for what they are doing.

** An excellent resource to refer to is *Writing: Resource Book*, in the *First Steps* series researched and developed by the Education Department of Western Australia, Longman Publishing, and Irwin Publishing in Canada.

✦ Introduce your students to different purposes for writing:

- *to entertain*, as in a narrative story, a script, poetry, a joke, a riddle, or a puzzle
- *to express feelings and thoughts*, as in a journal entry, a diary, poetry, or a personal letter
- *to obtain information*, as in a questionnaire, a survey, or an interview
- *to clarify thoughts*, as in making notes or explaining
- *to inform*, as in a poster, an invitation, a program, a report, a speech, a research project, or a presentation
- *to describe*, as in a description, a story, a characterization, a sequence of events, an advertisement, a label, or a sign
- *to explain*, as in instructions, directions, recipes, rules, or a science experiment
- *to state opinions and/or persuade*, as in an editorial, a letter to the editor, a debate, or cartoon

✦ Conduct mini-lessons to large groups, small groups, or individual students based on particular needs that you notice in their writing and to highlight specific concepts, skills, or strategies arising from the learning expectations of the curriculum.

✦ Make flexible writing conferences an integral part of your writing time. You and small groups of students can discuss, share, revise, edit, and celebrate writing at these meetings. You can also address specific learning expectations.

✦ Keep records of your writing conferences that document what was discussed and what was planned for follow-up. Figure 7.25 provides a model.

Writing Conference Record

Student Name: _Rena_   Date: _Nov. 10_

Form of Writing: _Narrative writing_

Subject/Title of Writing: _Julie on "The Price Is Right"_

Issues Discussed: _use of quotation marks_

Follow-up: _point out books using dialogue and note quotation marks, observe further writing to see if any transfer occurs_

BLM T-60 **Figure 7.25** *Writing conference form*

✦ Encourage peer and group interaction by establishing with the students routines and expectations for peer writing conferences. You might want to establish a routine where students choose partners during the pre-writing stage: they talk out their writing to their partners and answer any questions they may be asked before they begin their draft. Another practice is to allow students to talk to someone about their writing-in-progress, but at a designated talking area (on the carpet or at a table) where they won't disturb others who are working quietly.

✦ You might want to introduce a planning board to help focus and organize students as they move through the various phases of writing. (See Figure 7.26.) When students finish a phase, they move their name cards to the appropriate pocket on the planning board. Upon completion of one piece of writing, they begin another. They decide whether or not to publish and share. They write one piece of writing after another and come to understand that writing is a continuous, ongoing process.

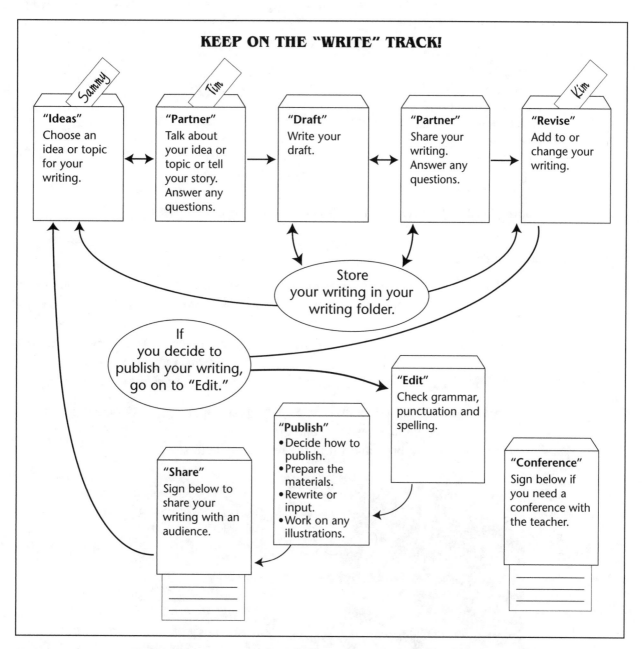

Figure 7.26 *Writing planning board*

See **BLM T-61** for writing planning board cards.

NOTE: *The arrows on the planning board indicate that this is not a linear process. Rather, students move back and forth among all the phases of the process.*

◆ Encourage and accept all attempts at writing based on the developmental stages of your students. See Figure 7.27, which shows the stages of learning to spell.

Stages of Spelling	
Scribble stage	*elmem*
Random letter stage	x L t d z d
Consonants stage	t b w d t s
Phonetic spelling stage	the bo wt dn the sttt
Conventional spelling stage	the boy went down the street

Figure 7.27 *Stages of spelling*

> **NOTE:** *The use of scribble or approximate spelling allows even very young children to believe that they are writers. When they are encouraged to try to spell the words they need, they use approximations and come as close as they can to conventional spelling, bringing together all the knowledge and skills they already possess. They become risk takers, experimenting with letters and sounds. Their spelling skills will develop as they write and mature.*

✦ If students are reluctant to use approximate spelling, encourage them to write the initial consonant and draw a line for the rest of the word. They can later go back and fill in the remaining letters.

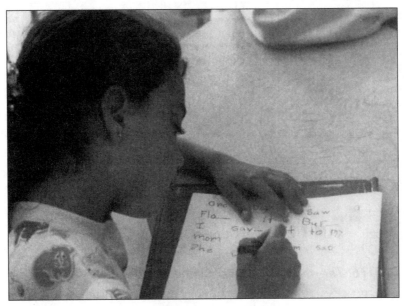

Figure 7.28 *Here, a student is using the "magic line" for a word she finds hard to spell.*

✦ Encourage students to write down all the sounds that they hear and to try to spell the words on a separate spelling notepad or sheet of paper. Figure 7.29 shows an example of a spelling notepad.

First Try	Second Try	Third Try
mistree	misteree	mistery
sudnlee	suddenly	

BLM S-62 Figure 7.29 *A spelling notepad*

✦ Teach strategies that students can use to spell words that they do not know how to spell. "Look, say, think, print, check" is one example, outlined in Figure 7.30.

Look, Say, Think, Print, Check

Look   Look at the word with a partner.

Say   Say the word carefully.
Your partner listens carefully.

Think   Cover the word and get a picture of the word in your head.

Print   Your partner gives you the word.
Repeat the word out loud and print it from memory.

Check   With your partner, check to see if you wrote the word correctly.

BLM T-63 Figure 7.30 *Spelling strategies chart*

✦ Teach your students spelling and grammar concepts in a variety of ways. Spelling and grammar lessons should be meaningful, stem from genuine writing samples, and correspond to the expectations of each grade level and to the developmental stages of the students in your classroom.

NOTE: Skill-building mini-lessons during the editing phase of writing provide an alternative to the traditional spelling and grammar lessons, which were customarily followed by fill-in-the-blank worksheet assignments. These busy work types of exercises produced little transfer of learning into daily work.

✦ If your school or district requires you to use a formal spelling program calling for the use of commercially produced spelling textbooks, incorporate variety into such a program by adding theme words or words that students need to spell to the list words in the text. Keep in mind that it is not always necessary to follow a spelling textbook program in a lockstep manner.

Be creative! Giving students a pre-test of the list words in the speller and seeing what words they *need* to know will meet the needs of individual students and can justify to parents and administrators why you are deviating from the text. If appropriate, you may also want to send the speller home as homework.

✦ Consider involving your students in a home spelling program so that they can practise and reinforce at home the concepts they have learned in class. (See Chapter 10, Homework: A Window into the Classroom.)

✦ If you decide to introduce a home spelling program, send a letter home to parents informing them about the routines. (See Figure 7.31.)

Dear Parents,

The Grade 6 classes will begin a home spelling program on Monday, September 26, which will run every second week. For this program, students will be learning standard spelling rules and common patterns that are intended to improve their overall writing progress. The program will run as follows:

Every other Monday, we will be discussing in class one or more spelling rules or patterns. Students will choose 20 spelling words from a list that follows that pattern. At times, this list may include words that are associated with our theme or unit of study, or words that students are using in their personal writing. At all times, students will select words that they need to learn to spell. As a result, each student's list of words may be different.

For homework, students must write each of the spelling words in a sentence to show its meaning. Using the words, they must also complete three tasks (from a choice of 12) from their spelling task sheet. This sheet is attached to their spelling notebooks.

On Friday, spelling homework is due and a spelling dictation will be given. Students will work in pairs to administer the Friday dictation to each other.

We are looking forward to starting this home spelling program and request that you encourage your child to complete the requirements.

Sincerely,

J. Hargraves
Ms. J. Hargraves

Please sign below and have your child return this form as soon as possible.
- -
I will check that my child has completed his/her spelling homework regularly.

Parent's Signature:_____

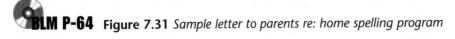

BLM P-64 **Figure 7.31** *Sample letter to parents re: home spelling program*

** Acknowledgements to Joan Hargraves formerly with the York Region District School Board, for contributing some of these spelling ideas

◆ Explain to your students their roles and responsibilities in this home spelling program.

◆ Ensure that your students understand the spelling tasks that they will be completing at home before you begin this program. For example, if one of the tasks asks the students to create an acrostic poem using their spelling words, then you need to have already taught your students what an acrostic poem is. Figure 7.32 outlines several spelling tasks.

Spelling Tasks

For every new list of words, you must complete a task from the following. Choose three different tasks each week until you have completed all of the tasks once. These tasks are to be done in your spelling workbooks. Your books will be collected every other Friday.

1. Syllabication
Write your words in one column.
Write your words in syllables in column two.
Check the dictionary to see if you are correct.
In column three, write the dictionary page number where you found each word.

Example:

Word	Syllable	Page Number
Sister	*sis-ter*	*507*
Rotate	*ro-tate*	*319*

2. Smaller Words
Choose five of the longest words from your list.
For each of these words, create as many small words as possible.
You can scramble the letters to create the words.

Example:
environment – men, iron, on, mint, vet

3. Magazine Search
Find and cut out each word from a magazine. Paste these words into your notebook.

4. Acrostic Poems
Create an acrostic poem for five of your words.

Example:

Snow

Soft and fluffy
Never warm
Open the door
Wade into the cold . . .

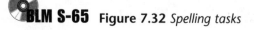 **BLM S-65** **Figure 7.32** *Spelling tasks*

As you strive to create a balanced literacy program that meets the needs and interests of your students, you will integrate language into all areas of the curriculum. When reading, writing, listening, speaking, viewing, and representing are included in all areas of your program in an integrated, interconnected way, you will be . . .

- *immersing* your students in rich, purposeful literacy opportunities,
- setting appropriate *expectations* for success,
- *demonstrating* what language looks like and sounds like,
- *modelling* appropriate literacy practices,
- providing *time* for them to *practise* their skills and demonstrate their knowledge,
- giving them *feedback* on how they are progressing, and
- *celebrating* what they produce!

In this way, you will be creating a dynamic classroom that fosters independent, self-motivated literate learners.

8 Technology and Learning

In a world of advanced technologies, teachers stand on the brink of a new way of teaching and learning. Computers have revolutionized what you do in the classroom and how you do it. The advent of computers into education in the seventies and early eighties paved the way for the multitude of technological tools you have at your disposal. In addition to cassette tape recorders, televisions and VCRs, overhead projectors, and cameras, you now have access to laptop computers, digital cameras, DVD players, laser printers, computer-generated synthesizers, scanners, laser-disc technology, the Internet, CD players, and more.

Keeping up with the rapidly changing technological landscape is an exciting and challenging task for teachers, but it is absolutely essential that you maintain a high degree of proficiency. By the time children are ready to begin Kindergarten, many have already been exposed to multimedia that have kept them entertained, taught them new concepts, and equipped them with valuable technological tools. As more and more computer-literate students arrive in your classroom, you need to know how to prepare them adequately for the future. Students need to learn how to create electronic books, collect and analyze information using databases, use spreadsheets to document and calculate data, and gather research using electronic encyclopedias and the Internet. Your students need to communicate through and with others as they read, write, calculate, explore, and create using the computer as a tool.

No matter what career your students will eventually have, they are almost certain to require computer skills. You must prepare your students to be literate in whatever environment they will eventually face, print, technological, or virtual reality. Today, everyone seems to have an e-mail address and wherever you are, you are bombarded with Web sites to refer to and services available by "logging on." Soon, most commercial and financial transactions will be conducted using e-mail and the Internet. The prospect can often be mind-boggling, but you, as a teacher, must be prepared for it.

The challenge for teachers has been the speed at which change has occurred. For experienced teachers, it has been difficult to keep up with the changes while still delivering a full and meaningful program. The answer is not to look at computers as a separate subject, but rather, to see technology as a tool that can make teaching and learning in all subject areas easier, at times more efficient, and often more interesting and exciting. As technology assists in so many different ways, it will free you up to become more of a facilitator of learning rather than an imparter of knowledge.

The first thing you will need to do as a professional is to ensure that your own computer skills are as proficient as possible. The more you integrate the computer into your own lifestyle, the easier it will be to integrate it into your classroom and your program. As you use the computer to research information on the Internet, record your lesson plans, prepare your report cards, or pay your bills by electronic banking, you will see how it can become integral to your own life, and you will be more willing to tackle the inclusion of technology into all aspects of your program. You will be better able to see the worthwhile possibilities of what technology can do for your students. You will see how access to the Internet will open up new paths for students to find important information and to research relevant topics. You can also use the Internet to foster excellent dialogue in your classroom on censorship, freedom of speech, and media literacy, as you teach students to become critical readers, watchers, and thinkers.

Computer literacy is usually not as pressing an issue for teachers new to the profession, as you are the first generation brought up with computers as part of your everyday life. Most university or college students graduating today could not have made it through their courses without the use of a computer. Your task, therefore, is to become proficient with what technology can offer a classroom environment and how you can maximize the benefits for your students. Knowing what software is available and which is appropriate for your students, understanding how to teach keyboarding skills to young students, and being well versed in Internet capabilities and limitations are some of the skills that new teachers must possess beyond their own comfort with the actual hardware and software.

When you become computer literate and comfortable in today's technological classroom, you will have to deal with issues that require reflective thought and critical decisions. From the important decision of having computers in the classroom versus a well-equipped lab in the school, to the much deeper issue of equity between genders and within diverse learning communities, it is clear that issues about technology need to be discussed, debated, and resolved in order for all students to have the best, most current, and relevant education possible. That is a tall order to fill, but one that *must* be filled!

Creating a Technology-Rich Classroom

✦ Ensure that you are as technologically literate as possible. Look into courses and workshops that you might attend to upgrade your skills, if necessary.

✦ Become familiar with the computer terminology that is being used in your school, district, or board.

✦ Become familiar with the hardware available to you in your school.

✦ Find out whether you will use classroom-based computers or a computer lab.

*NOTE: Whether to have computers in the classroom or to use a computer lab is a much debated issue that usually requires a whole school decision, and will depend on the number of computers available in the school. The ideal situation is to have **both** available in your school so that students can learn skills such as keyboarding as a large group in a lab, but can also use the one or more computers in your classroom for integration possibilities throughout your total program.*

✦ Decide where the one or more computers will be situated in your classroom. You will want to put them near ample electrical outlets or purchase the proper power bars so that you can plug in all the pieces of equipment necessary. You should always allow for extra outlets for future expansion of your equipment. You should also situate the computers in an area where other students are not attracted to what is happening on the monitor and away from any sand, water, food, paints, and window glare.

✦ Examine available resources, documents, and guidelines to determine what you expect your students to be able to know, do, and value in technology. Make sure that these expectations are appropriate to the age and stage of development of your students. (Refer to Chapter 5, Planning an Integrated Curriculum.)

✦ Decide how you will know when your students have achieved the desired expectations and what assessment tools you will use. Chapter 11, Assessing, Evaluating, and Reporting, provides some guidance.

✦ Consider how the computer can assist your students with special needs, including students new to the country. See the following examples for possible strategies to use.

Example 1:	Students with small muscle coordination difficulties can find handwriting a challenge and often find a keyboard easier to manipulate than a pen or pencil.

Example 2:	Students with visual impairments can use the computer to enlarge the print so that they are better able to read the text.

Example 3:	Students who are new to the country and language can use software programs that highlight specific language patterns, allow them to repeat words and phrases, and record attempts at speaking the new language. Other software programs use visuals to generate oral and written language. Having students work in pairs also stimulates second language development as they discuss what they are doing at the computer.

- ✦ Become familiar with the software available to you in your school and board or district. Many boards or districts have procedures to loan software for a period of time.

- ✦ Take time to evaluate new software before you use it with your students. Bear in mind that most boards or districts have policies and procedures for the selection and evaluation of computer software. Some schools will also have established priorities for specific software to be used.

- ✦ Make limited use of skill-and-drill software and any games that might require little depth of understanding or critical thinking on the part of the student.

- ✦ Ensure that word processing is a vital aspect of your program and is integrated into all subject areas, especially in the revision and editing stages of the writing process. The cut-and-paste features allow students to move and rearrange text with ease. The search and find features allow students to substitute words and look for inconsistencies. Spell checks encourage students to use their knowledge of how words are spelled to choose the correct one from a list. Grammar checks require students to know how to recognize and understand appropriate structures. Using word-processing programs encourages students to create and save multiple drafts without having to rewrite, and helps them feel like real authors as they revise, edit, and publish their work.

- ✦ Integrate other computer software programs into your program, such as graphic arts, desktop publishing, databases, spreadsheets, presentation software, multimedia, hypermedia, and simulations.

✦ Train at least two students to act as peer tutors who will teach other students in your class. It's advisable to choose students who have more extensive experience working with computers.

✦ Ensure that your students help each other and know where to go when they need assistance. You might do this by setting up a peer tutor or experts list in the classroom or school so that students know who to go to for help, depending on the problem. In some schools, a staff member (not necessarily a teacher) is hired to support the computer technology and maintenance.

✦ Use your peer tutors to ensure that all students in your class have the necessary background skills in place, such as how to turn on the computer, click and drag, save, and print.

✦ Choose student monitors to maintain the computers in your classroom. Monitors may be responsible for turning the computers on and off each day, checking the connections, dusting the computer monitors, and keeping the computer area neat and tidy.

✦ Provide training in keyboarding to any students — even Grade 1 students — who do not already have these skills.

NOTE: If most of your students need training in keyboarding, it is advisable to use a computer lab for this purpose.

✦ Obtain an unformatted disk which can be initialized for either an IBM or a Mac platform, for each student in your classroom. Doing so is just as important as providing students with notebooks for their math work. They need to be able to save, organize, and manage their own work.

✦ Demonstrate for your students how to handle the disks before they are distributed. Remind them to check that they have clean hands before handling disks or working on a keyboard.

✦ Examine your themes, topics, or units of study to see where computers can integrate well. The following examples will give you some ideas of how you might integrate computers into your units of study.

Example 1: For a study of weather in Science and Technology, you could have your students create a graph or table detailing the weather for a prolonged period of time. They might be required to use a database to gather and organize the data as they collect it, and the computer could create a pie chart from the information received through the database.

Example 2: For a study of drug awareness in Health Education, students can use the Internet to research information on the uses and misuses of drugs, and find the statistics on drug use and their implications. They can learn how to record their references from Web sites and may be required to present their information using technology as a tool, perhaps in the form of a computer slide show presentation, overhead presentation, or video.

Example 3: In your primary grade mathematics program, students can sort objects represented on the screen or that they have drawn using a graphics program. They can then classify the groups and graph the results. See Figure 8.1 for an example.

Figure 8.1 *Sorting chart*

Example 4: To encourage primary students to write stories, students can use a simple word-processing program that includes graphic arts to create accompanying illustrations. They can also use these programs to create cooperative stories or a page for a class big book, to make journal entries, and to write poems, letters, cards, or invitations.

✦ Decide how you will organize who works on the computer(s) at what time and for how long. Your decision may depend on how you have integrated the computer into your units of study.

- *Scheduled Time*

  If your students need access to the Internet to research a topic, you may want to schedule specific times for each student.

- *Sign-in System*

  If your students are expected to use the computer for story writing, you may want to introduce a sign-in system for students to have access to the computer for an extended period of time, as needed.

NOTE: You will want to make sure that the one or more computers that you have in your classroom will be used to their full potential and that they are not sitting idle during the day. At the same time, you should ensure that the use of computers is equitable among your students, and that one or two students do not monopolize the computer.

✦ Discuss rules for use of the computer, and decide what other students can and cannot do when someone else is on the computer.

✦ With your students, talk about the pros and cons of use of the Internet. Discuss the misuse of the Internet and the existence of inappropriate Web sites, and ensure that you have a system in place that will block access to these inappropriate sites.

✦ Obtain permission from your students' parents before you allow students to access the Internet. See Figure 8.2.

Dear Parents,

The use of technology in schools today is a vital part of the curriculum and a very important life skill for all students to learn. The computer will be integrated into all aspects of our program this year. Students will write using word processing, create databases and spreadsheets, collect, sort, and calculate data, and collect information using electronic encyclopedias. We will also use the Internet for a variety of purposes, including searching for and collecting information.

In our classroom, school, and district, we have strict guidelines for the use of the Internet with students and we would like to make you aware of those guidelines. Students will

- access the Internet only with prior approval by the teacher;
- visit only those sites that have been predetermined by the teacher;
- never give out their names or any other distinguishing information to anyone else while using the Internet;
- properly reference all material taken from the Internet (plagiarism remains a serious offence whether from print materials or the Internet).

Please discuss the above guidelines with your child, sign the attached permission slip, and return it to the school as soon as possible.

Thank you for your support.

Sincerely,

M. Pollishuke
Mindy Pollishuke

| I have discussed the guidelines above with my child and give permission for him/her to use the Internet in class. | I have read and agree to abide by the guidelines outlined in the letter above. |

| *Kate Sangelle* | *Linda Sangelle* |
| Parent's signature | Student's signature |

BLM P-66 **Figure 8.2** *Letter to parents re: use of the Internet*

◆ Involve your students in e-mail communication and bulletin board conferencing with one another and with others, such as penpals and authors.

◆ Consider creating a class Web site. You might want to post information about your school and classroom events, student work, homework, and interactive activities based on your classroom units of study.

NOTE: *Inviting parents to access the class Web site provides you with another format for keeping your parents informed and involved. You might have a student volunteer post the daily homework assignments on your site so that parents can check it each evening.*

◆ Invite your students' parents to take part in information sessions about the use of technology in your program. You might want to offer a series of family computer evenings where parents and students attend sessions together.

◆ Keep abreast of new resources, including guidelines, software programs, and appropriate educational Web sites.

◆ Consider creating a technology centre or a take-it-apart centre where students will be engaged in looking at different aspects of technology such as inventions and kitchen gadgets. (See Chapter 6, A Learning Centre Approach.) Consider sending home a letter to parents highlighting the use of technology in your program. You could also ask parents for materials for the technology centre. See Figure 8.3.

Dear Parents,

This year the students in our class will be exploring many aspects of technology in order to understand the impact that technology has on our world. Along with our work with the computer, they will also look at other aspects of technology.

Through the use of problem solving and experimentation, students will explore how technology helps us in our daily life, how new technologies are invented, and what future possibilities exist. At our technology centre, they will examine a variety of kitchen gadgets, look at how things work, and design their own inventions.

It would be appreciated if you and your child could find materials for our centre. The following are examples of what you might consider contributing:

- broken toys, clocks
- flashlights
- knobs
- magnets
- nails, nuts, and bolts
- tubing
- wire
- yarn

Thank you for your interest and support.

Sincerely,

Mrs. Pollishuke

Mrs. Pollishuke

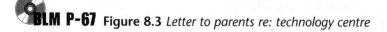

BLM P-67 **Figure 8.3** *Letter to parents re: technology centre*

As you become comfortable with the use of technology in all aspects of your program, you will be more confident in saying that your students will achieve the necessary skills for today and tomorrow's technological environment. Incorporating technology into all aspects of your classroom program will ensure that your students are well prepared for the future that awaits them.

Out-of-Classroom Excursions

Taking students out of the regular classroom and school environment into the larger community generates interest and enthusiasm, helps to motivate students, creates positive attitudes towards learning, and provides students with meaningful and relevant experiences. Out-of-classroom excursions or field trips enhance the classroom program and encompass all facets of learning. Although field trips can be physically demanding, requiring supplementary funding and extra time for preparation, they should be valued and considered as an integral part of your program.

Field trips can be organized to familiar places such as the neighbourhood park or local mall, or to special locations, such as a space exploration centre, a museum, or an art gallery. As you begin to plan your out-of-classroom excursions, take into consideration the field trips your students have already experienced. Their prior knowledge plays a role in the planning and organization of your out-of-classroom experiences for them.

Each out-of-classroom excursion should have curriculum relevance for the students involved. It should also be based on clearly defined learning expectations and should be within the level of understanding and maturity appropriate for your students. Be sure to consider what you will do *before*, *during*, and *after* each excursion. Doing so will help to ensure the success of the field trip and will also enrich the total experience.

Out-of-classroom excursions provide first-hand experiences from which much learning occurs in all areas of the curriculum. Field trips are a genuine form of integration. Students learn to appreciate and respect nature and the outdoors, which often stimulates an awareness of and an interest in environmental issues. They experience real-life situations, view artifacts from the past, and discover the realm of scientific exploration and experimentation. They see, hear, smell, taste, and touch, using all their senses to make meaning from these relevant excursions.

As a teacher, you need to be aware of all your official responsibilities as you take your students away from the security of the classroom and school environment and into the wider community. Ensure that you have signed parental permission for each and every trip, know your legal obligations, and always provide safe and secure supervision. By doing so, you will make any out-of-classroom excursion a valuable, exciting, productive, and safe addition to your classroom program and to your students' experiences. Field trips allow your students to think, explore, wonder, and investigate people, places, and things in new and exciting ways.

Planning Out-of-Classroom Excursions

✦ Investigate all the possible out-of-classroom excursions that correspond with the unit of study you are planning. Some types of appropriate and effective field trips to plan for students of a variety of ages are as follows:

- explorations of the schoolyard, neighbourhood, community, or city
- tours of historical buildings and sites
- visits to museums, zoos, farms, factories
- trips to plays, musical performances, art galleries
- travels to new cities and tours of the exciting highlights
- overnight field trips to outdoor education centres or campgrounds

✦ Choose the field trip that is most appropriate in terms of your students' needs and interests and the overall learning expectations for your unit.

✦ Ensure that you have some familiarity with the place to be visited, especially the itinerary of things to do and see, and knowledge of the facilities, such as washrooms, cafeteria, telephones, and shelter. If at all possible, visit the site ahead of time.

✦ Find out the cost of the trip per student and adult, including all taxes and transportation costs, if applicable. Also, think about how this cost will be paid, either from school funds, fundraising, or family contributions.

NOTE: Ensure that no student is excluded from the field trip because of an inability to pay. Usually, the school has procedures in place to accommodate students who are unable to pay the fee.

✦ Book your out-of-classroom excursion well before you begin your unit.

✦ Arrange for your transportation and confirm details. You may need to review school bus, private vehicle, or public transportation procedures for students.

✦ Decide and record the learning expectations for this out-of-classroom excursion.

✦ Plan the learning experiences that the students will do *before*, *during*, and *after* the trip, and determine the materials needed.

NOTE: *Any out-of-classroom excursion lends itself to the teaching of mapping skills. For example, distribute a map showing the route from the school to the field trip's destination. Encourage the students to observe the route while travelling to and from the site. Consider incorporating mathematics skills as well by asking students to calculate the distance they will travel or the time it will take to arrive.*

✦ Decide on the assessment strategies you will use, for example, observation, self-assessment, reflection, portfolio entry, and work samples such as sketches, notes taken, tally sheets, or charts.

✦ Consider bringing along a camera, video camera, or tape recorder to document the field trip experience. The recording could be useful as data for assessment purposes, as well as serve as a form of communication about your trip and as an impetus for discussion and writing. Be sure to decide who will be responsible for the equipment and how you will organize its use.

✦ Prepare for the inclusion of students with special needs. For example, arrange for volunteers or teaching assistants to supervise certain students, arrange for a special van to transport a student in a wheelchair, or confirm special funding, if necessary.

✦ Ensure that you have your principal's approval and signed permission for all out-of-classroom excursions. When the trip is unusual or potentially risky (e.g., a swimming or boating trip), you may also need to have signed permission and approval from your director of education or a designate, such as a supervisory officer.

✦ Ensure that you are familiar with the school emergency plan while on a field trip and all the potential safety issues pertaining to the particular field trip you are planning. You have a legal **duty of care** which involves appropriate and effective supervision, inspection, protection, and instruction. Providing that avoids any charge of **negligence** (e.g., failing to find out about student allergies when providing lunch for students in an outdoor education centre, or not arranging adequate supervision). It is recommended that you take first aid courses every few years to be prepared for possible emergency situations.

** Good resources to refer to for information about the legal responsibilities of teachers are *Teachers and the Law: A Practical Guide for Educators* by A. Wayne Mackay and Lyle I. Sutherland (Emond Montgomery Publications Limited), and *The Law Primer: A Guide for Teachers, Second Edition* by John McNaughton (Tartan Publishing).

✦ At least two weeks before the trip, write a letter to parents, asking for signed permission and funding if required. In some jurisdictions, a district or board form letter must be used for all out-of-classroom excursions. Specific details such as the following should be outlined in the letter to parents:

- purpose of the field trip
- connection to the program
- intended follow-up
- time and place of departure
- time and place of return to school
- lunch arrangements
- type of transportation to be used and cost if applicable
- suggested clothing to wear
- funds needed

Figure 9.1 shows a sample letter to parents about an upcoming field trip.

NOTE: *In most school districts, a blanket permission form signed at the beginning of the year is not adequate: parents need to know what their children are doing and where they are each day.*

✦ Decide where and how you will collect and store the money that the students bring in for the trip. You may want to have a checkoff system or enlist the help of one or two students to count the money. Never leave money unattended or in an unlocked desk. It is best if it is kept in an envelope and stored in the office for safekeeping.

✦ Follow up with students for whom you believe the cost will be a concern and make funding arrangements on their behalf. Be sensitive to these students' feelings.

Dear Parents,

On Monday, March 20, our class will be going on a field trip to the Royal Ontario Museum. We will be travelling by school bus, leaving at 9:00 a.m. and returning by 3:30 p.m. Students are asked to bring a bag lunch and $1.00 on the day of the trip if they wish to purchase a drink. Also, please have your child bring in $4.00 to cover the cost of the entrance fee. It would be appreciated if this money is brought in by March 10.

This field trip reinforces our unit on early civilizations and addresses the learning expectations in the Social Studies curriculum at the Grade 5 level. We plan to visit the Egyptian exhibit to gain a better concrete understanding of the history and life of ancient Egyptians. Students will do research activities in the upcoming weeks to extend their learning in this area.

If you are able to accompany our class on this field trip, we would appreciate your assistance. Please indicate on the form below if you would like to join us.

Please sign the attached form and return it to me by Friday, March 20. Students will not be permitted to go on this trip without the permission form signed and returned.

Thank you for your support and interest.

Sincerely,

Mrs. Pollishuke

Mrs. Pollishuke

PARENT PERMISSION FORM

☐   Yes, I give permission for my child _____ to go on the trip to the
     Royal Ontario Museum on Monday, March 20.

☐   No, I do not give permission for my child _____ to go on the trip
     to the Royal Ontario Museum on Monday, March 20.

☐   Yes, count me in as a helper on this field trip.

Please contact me at _____ .

Parent/Guardian Signature: _____   Date:_____

BLM P-68   **Figure 9.1** *Sample letter to parents re: upcoming field trip*

◆ Decide how you will organize your groups during the field trip and how many adult volunteers you will need.

◆ If adult volunteers accompany you on the field trip, ensure that they have clear guidelines and expectations as to their responsibilities. You may wish to write them a letter outlining their responsibilities on the field trip. Figure 9.2 provides an example.

Dear Volunteer,

Thank you for volunteering to accompany us on our upcoming field trip to the museum. I welcome your offer of assistance. I'm sure that the students will enjoy a richer, more productive day because of it.

Please meet me at 8:30 a.m. on Monday, March __, in Room 212. I am calling all the volunteers together then to answer questions, clarify expectations, and explain how you can help on this day. In the meantime, here is some information about our school expectations and your role as a volunteer.

RESPONSIBILITIES

- Teachers are responsible for the conduct and manners of the class at all times. Refer any situation requiring discipline to me immediately.
- You will be asked to supervise a small number of students. Please keep a record of their names and use the materials I will provide such as a clipboard, paper, and a pencil.
- While you are on your own with your group of students, please review the rules for taking washroom breaks and water fountain drinks, not running, being respectful, and cooperating with others.
- Please do not purchase treats for your group of students. Other students in the class whose volunteer may decide not to treat them might see this as inequitable. Students have been invited to bring their own money, and will have some time in the gift shop to purchase souvenirs if they wish.
- Please ensure that you are on time to meet the bus at the end of our day.

BUS SAFETY

- The bus driver is responsible for the safety of the bus and its passengers.
- Students must not leave their seats while the bus is in motion.
- Students must sit properly at all times (no leaning in the aisles).
- Students' behaviour shall be the same as in a classroom setting.
- Activities that might distract the driver or other users of the road are not permitted. Singing while the bus is in motion is permitted only with the prior consent of the driver and teacher.
- Windows may be adjusted only with the consent of the driver or adult-in-charge.
- Students must not put their hands, head, or objects out of the window.
- Students' lunch bags, books, parcels, etc. must be placed on the floor or held on laps.
- Eating and drinking are not permitted on the bus unless prior arrangements have been made with the bus driver.
- While the bus is in motion, students and adults must not talk to the driver except in case of an emergency.

SEATING ARRANGEMENTS FOR ADULTS ON THE BUS

1. If there is only one adult, please sit at the back of the bus.
2. If there are two adults present, one should sit at the back and one at the front.
3. If there are three (or more) adults, sit at the back, centre, and front, please.

Buses should be loaded from the rear forward. If there is not a full load, an equal number of front and rear seats should be left vacant with equal distribution on both sides of the bus.

Thank you again for offering your assistance.

Sincerely,

S. Schwartz
Susan Schwartz

BLM P-69 **Figure 9.2** *Sample letter to field trip volunteers*

◆ Prepare your students for a successful field trip by reviewing safety rules, appropriate social skills, and code of behaviour expectations, as well as academic expectations.

◆ If you have access to a cellular phone, it is advisable to take it with you in case of an emergency. Keep school and emergency numbers handy.

◆ File the itinerary for the field trip with the school office, and include a list of your students, the staff, and the adult volunteers accompanying you on the field trip. Keep a copy for yourself.

◆ Inform the office about the whereabouts of the students who will not be attending the trip, namely, those who are absent or who will stay with another teacher for the day. Ensure that you leave appropriate work assignments with the students who will stay with another teacher.

◆ If some or all students are being transported by private vehicle, keep a copy of the list of students in each vehicle and leave a copy with the school office. In your letter to parents, notify them that their children are being transported by private vehicle. At no time should students be transported by other students during school trips.

◆ For any overnight field trip, ensure that at least one adult has a car on-site in case of emergencies.

◆ For an overnight field trip or a trip which involves serving a meal, ensure that you have recent medical information about each student, as well as parental permission to seek medical attention in case of an emergency.

◆ For students with severe allergies, ensure that you know the procedures regarding anaphylactic shock and how to administer epipens in crisis situations. You may require a first aid session by a public health nurse or trained professional early in the school year.

◆ Ensure that all student information is kept confidential, but is easily accessible if needed in an emergency.

◆ Prepare a variety of follow-up experiences as part of your classroom program and unit of study. Consider writing thank-you letters to the staff at the site you have visited.

◆ Plan to feature highlights of your field trip as part of your ongoing communication with parents. You might decide to send home a newsletter, create a class newspaper in which students write articles about different aspects of the trip, create a class scrapbook of photos and writing and send it home with individual students on a sign-out basis over a period of time, or invite parents to an after-school meeting or an Open House evening where related work samples are displayed or a video is shown. (Refer to Chapter 12, Partnerships with Parents.)

Out-of-classroom excursions are excellent opportunities for students to experience the greater community. Adequate preparation and planning and careful consideration of safety and supervision issues will ensure the success of your field trips. Familiarizing yourself with school emergency plans and your students' medical histories will prepare you for any emergency that may arise so that your students are safe and secure in the wider classroom environment. Check that you have made all the necessary preparations for the field trip and that you have planned appropriate before, during, and after learning experiences for your students. Preparation equals success!

10 Homework: A Window into the Classroom

Homework is often seen as a window into the classroom as it acquaints parents with their children's in-school learning experiences. When your students do their homework, parents see concrete examples of your classroom program. It is important that parents realize the significance and relevance of homework assignments to their children's overall educational experience. Homework has the potential of involving parents as partners in the teaching/learning process. It is a shared commitment among teachers, students, and parents, who all have an important role to play in making the experience positive and productive. Homework is a powerful tool to use to connect and communicate with parents. It can also be used as a vehicle to educate parents on how to help their children at home.

Homework needs to be relevant, meaningful, appropriate to the needs and interests of each student, and closely connected to your program. Every time you assign homework, you need to determine and be able to articulate the purpose of the homework and its type, as well as the specific learning expectations that it is addressing.

Homework assignments should reflect a variety of tasks that are appropriate to the age, academic needs, learning styles, and maturity of individual students. These should be varied and clearly focused. Homework does not take the place of remedial teaching, and under no circumstances should it be assigned as a punishment for misbehaviour or for failure to perform as expected. Involving students in the planning and organizing of their homework assignments when appropriate and within their ability range is an effective way to build ownership and provide meaningful experiences.

Timely feedback on homework experiences is most beneficial to students' learning and attitudes. You need to find the time to check, assess, and address in some way the homework you assign. To emphasize the relevancy and importance of homework, make comments on report cards about each student's success with homework completion, accuracy, and quality of work.

Homework supplements and supports in-school experiences as students are provided with opportunities to practise, integrate, and apply their learning. Regular and meaningful homework experiences encourage students' development of responsibility, self-discipline, time management, and work habits, and can help to develop positive and enthusiastic attitudes towards independent study and lifelong learning. With careful planning and thought, and when all partners are involved and valued, homework can contribute positively to educational growth.

Creating Effective Homework Experiences

◆ Find out if your school or district has a formal homework policy, and if so, refer to it as you plan homework experiences for your students. It should provide you with homework goals and objectives, address the amount, frequency, and scheduling of assignments, and articulate the responsibilities of all partners.

◆ Ensure that all partners are aware of their responsibilities in the homework process. The following checklist may be beneficial in clarifying these responsibilities.

Responsibilities Re: Homework Process

Students
- ❑ complete assignments on time and in an acceptable form
- ❑ manage their time and work
- ❑ ask teachers for help if they do not understand something

Teachers
- ❑ ensure homework is meaningful, relevant, and geared to each student's needs, intellectual abilities, and interests
- ❑ clearly communicate homework expectations, purpose, method, and requirements to students and parents
- ❑ ensure that students understand how to do assignments
- ❑ notice any learning concerns
- ❑ communicate with parents regularly
- ❑ provide follow-up, and identify areas that require further work
- ❑ check and assess homework regularly and in a timely fashion
- ❑ provide appropriate feedback to students and to parents
- ❑ include comments on report cards about each student's success with homework

Parents
- ❑ ensure that children carry out their responsibilities re: homework
- ❑ create a suitable environment at home for children to work
- ❑ set aside time and oversee that work is completed
- ❑ monitor children's stress levels in relation to homework assignments and report to the teacher if there is a concern
- ❑ take children to the library, answer questions, show support of homework, and help relate homework to their children's world
- ❑ read to children and talk about homework and school events

---

 **BLM P-70**   **Figure 10.1** *Responsibilities for homework*

♦ Ensure that your parents are aware of your classroom homework expectations and requirements through notes sent home, weekly newsletters, or monthly calendars that highlight school and classroom events. (See Chapter 12, Partnerships with Parents.) If district or school homework policies stipulate specific amounts of time to be spent on homework, emphasize to parents that these are to be used as a guide only and will vary depending on the program as well as on the developmental levels, learning styles, and individual needs and interests of the students.

♦ Ask your students to record their after-school activities and commitments for your information and planning and for the fostering of their own planning and time management skills.

♦ When you assign homework, pay due consideration to student involvement in co-curricular activities and to the assignments that may be given by other teachers.

♦ Include information about your homework expectations at curriculum nights and parent-teacher conferences. Indicate clearly when and how you wish parents to be involved.

♦ To avoid student frustration, always ensure that students have the prerequisite skills to complete the homework assignment independently. If you wish to involve parents, communicate this clearly to the parents and students and be flexible with the results in case some parents cannot participate fully.

♦ Provide appropriate feedback for homework and do so within a reasonable time period. Marking and providing positive and constructive comments validates the homework and reinforces work habits and work completion.

NOTE: *Remember that when parents are aware of and share in the learning experience, they are often just as excited as their children to receive your feedback.*

♦ For major homework assignments or projects, identify in advance the criteria for assessment. You may wish to share or develop a rubric that outlines the criteria and levels of achievement with the students. (See Chapter 11, Assessing, Evaluating, and Reporting.)

♦ Track students' work completion and accuracy of homework assignments, and monitor carefully those students who may be struggling.

♦ Monitor students with special needs, including those new to the country, who may require modification of homework expectations.

◆ Work together with resource staff to monitor certain students re: their homework and in-class work completion.

◆ Have your students use a student homework planner to regularly record assignments, commitments, and events. These weekly agendas, or day timers, are most appropriate for students in Grade 2 and up.

◆ Communicate with parents about the importance of student planners. Ensure that your students and parents understand their responsibilities regarding the homework planner. Figure 10.2 provides a sample letter to parents about their use.

Dear Parents,

This year, the students in our school will be using student planners designed to help them develop the important life skills of responsibility, organization, and time management. These planners encourage students to become more reflective about their learning process and progress, and at the same time, invite sharing and positive interaction with family members. We highly recommend the use of these planners as a continuing link between home and school and as part of our school's homework initiatives.

In these planners, the following expectations will be reinforced:

- Students will bring their planners back and forth to school and home daily.
- Students will use the allotted class time daily to record homework assignments, responsibilities, and events.
- Teachers will monitor the planners on a regular basis and provide support as needed.
- Parents will ask to see the child's planner, will review progress, and will sign the planner each day or week (to be determined in consultation with the teacher).
- Parents are invited to ask questions, express concerns, and make positive comments in the planner.
- Growth in skills developed through the use of the planner will be reflected on each child's report card.

Please sign the commitment contract found below and have your child return it to the school as soon as possible. We welcome your input, and if you have any questions, concerns, or ideas to share, please call the school.

Sincerely,

S. Schwartz
Susan Schwartz

- -

Please complete this part of the form and return it to the school at your earliest convenience.

We agree to commit to the use of the student planner for the academic year 2001–2002. We also agree to contribute towards the replacement cost of any lost planner.

_____
Student

_____   _____
Parent   Date

BLM P-71 Figure 10.2 *Sample letter to parents re: student planners*

◆ Include a time for students to write in their planners each day, for example, the last ten minutes before dismissal from school.

◆ Check to ensure that students are recording their homework assignments in their planners each day and initial the planners before they go home. Doing this is especially important at the beginning of the year when you are establishing routines. Later on, you may wish to initial only the planners of certain students each night, or to choose a student monitor to initial planners.

◆ Communicate your expectations to parents regarding when they should sign the student planners (every day, week, or month depending on the student).

◆ Contact parents immediately when you have a concern. Involve resource staff, or inform your principal if you anticipate problems. Be proactive.

◆ Consider brainstorming with students, and sometimes with parents, appropriate consequences for not completing homework. For example:

- Insist that students complete the assignment even after the due date.
- Negotiate a new due date with students.
- Arrange for students to finish their homework during class time.
- Involve parents by sending a note home.
- Have a telephone discussion.
- Meet with all partners.

◆ For students who have difficulty in using the homework planner consistently, consider taking any of the following measures:

- Acknowledge students who remember their planners each day and provide positive recognition.
- Give out group points or use a reward system, such as entering tickets for a weekly draw, when planners are brought back and forth.
- Brainstorm with the specific student or with the whole class possible consequences when planners are forgotten or lost.

◆ Include a home reading program as part of your homework expectations. Use the following suggestions:

- Have a wide variety of reading materials available in your classroom.
- Create a quick and easy-to-use sign-out system. For example, write students' names on library book pockets, and display on a poster. Students place their book borrowing cards into their name pockets each night and return them to their books the next morning.

- Have book bags available for students to take their books home.
- Provide support to students when they select books to read independently at school and at home. Figure 10.3 provides tips for students on selecting books to read.

Tips for Selecting Books to Read

- Listen to what other people say about this book.
- Look at the cover, title, and illustrations and predict what the story might be about.
- Look at the table of contents, index, pictures, and captions for information about the book.
- Read the outline on the book jacket to find out what the book might be about.
- Read the first page of the book, and then flip through the book to see if it interests you.
- If you become "stuck" on five words on one page, you may want to consider looking for an easier book.
- Look for familiar authors and illustrators.

BLM S-72 **Figure 10.3** *Tips for students re: selecting books to read*

- Work with the librarian to teach library skills so students will know in which section of the library they will find specific books.
- Use interest inventories and surveys to assist children and their parents in choosing books.
- Provide information about authors and illustrators. Highlight an *Author of the Month*.
- Keep a list of all the books read by the class on display so that others can refer to it. Create a bulletin board "We recommend…" and include the titles of favourite books and names of authors and illustrators.
- Have students track the books read at home by recording the author's name and/or number of pages read each night. (See Chapter 7, Literacy and Language Learning, for sample reading records.)
- Schedule time in class for students to informally talk about the books they have read or are reading at home.
- Ask for book reports in a variety of interesting formats. (Refer to Chapter 7, Literacy and Language Learning, for ideas about book reports.) Provide opportunities for students to share or present what they have done.
- Send home stories or information on audiotape for students to listen to and follow along.

NOTE: *Adopting this practice is especially beneficial for students new to the English language. Consider loaning tape recorders to students who may not have these at home.*

- Inform your parents early in the year about your expectations regarding reading at home. Encourage parents to read *to* and *with* their children often, even after children are able to read for themselves. Once children are reading on their own, advise parents to talk with their children about their reading. Also, parents should be encouraged to read to and talk with their children in their first language if it's other than English. If they do so, families will continue to value and share their language, culture, background, and experiences. Figure 10.4 shows a sample letter to parents of young children about reading at home.

Dear Families,

Welcome to our **Home Reading Program**.

Research has shown that children will become better readers if they are read to regularly. By reading *to* or *with* your children, you help them to see the importance that you place on reading; you allow them to hear good literature which they may not yet be able to read on their own; and you show them in a concrete way that you care about their learning.

For our home reading program, your child will be bringing books home on a regular basis. Please read the books to him/her and discuss the stories. If the book is easy enough for your child to read, you might take turns reading the pages. Your child may ask for the same book many times — this is a part of the learning-to-read process and should be encouraged.

Happy reading together!

Sincerely,

S. Schwartz
Susan Schwartz

BLM P-73 **Figure 10.4** *Sample letter to parents re: home reading program*

- Consider extending your home reading program to other areas of the curriculum, such as mathematics, science, and social studies. These theme-based homework activities can become part of a *Homework in a Bag* program, such as is outlined in *Retelling, Relating, Reflecting: Beyond the 3R's* by Susan Schwartz and Maxine Bone. You can send home fiction and non-fiction books centred around different themes in a bag or backpack once a week with a number of students. In each homework bag is a journal in which students and parents read and write responses to the resources provided. Materials to write on and to write with, samples of previous students' work, and directions are included in the bag.
- Value the work done for *Homework in a Bag* by setting aside class time each week for the students to talk about and show what they have learned, written, and created at home.

✦ Along with your home reading program (and possibly a *Homework in a Bag* program), ensure that you vary the types of homework you assign. Below are some examples of different types of homework:

Example 1: Practice and Review Homework

Such homework reinforces skills previously taught in class and assists in improving speed of recall and accuracy of skills and concepts. With this type of homework, you need to guard against overuse of worksheets. Vary the tasks or provide an active component such as a game or an activity to reinforce skills and concepts. Examples of practice and review homework include the following:

- Learn the spelling of new vocabulary by doing activities with a list of words.
- Study for an upcoming test.
- Learn the lines for a play, poem, riddle, or song.
- Play a game to reinforce a skill or concept.
- Choose five questions on this page and complete.
- Complete the odd numbered questions, from 1 to the end.
- Ask someone to time you for one minute, and see how many questions you can answer.
- Make up five questions of your own, using two dice. Roll and multiply two numbers together. Write the number story and answer.
- Answer the questions and check your answers with a calculator.

Example 2: Finish-up Homework

When students do not finish their work in class, they are often asked to complete it for homework. The expectation that class work is to be completed helps students develop personal responsibility, time management skills, and self-motivation. However, if a student has finish-up homework every night, it may indicate that the classroom program is not meeting his or her needs. An overwhelming amount of finish-up homework can cause a decrease in students' self-concept. They may feel inundated with the workload and resent having to finish up at home when they see others who complete work easily and quickly. Thus, it is important to monitor the amount of finish-up homework your students are doing and their rate of accuracy and completion. If a student is spending an inordinate amount of time on homework each night, you may need to modify the homework, and possibly the classroom program, for that child.

Parents can provide the input necessary to highlight that a student is experiencing difficulty with homework or with your classroom program. Encourage parents, through letters, newsletters, phone calls, or conferences, to let you know if students are experiencing stress or concerns. You may want to ask the parents of students with a great deal of finish-up homework to record the amount of time spent on homework each night. Work with parents to monitor the time spent at home and establish an appropriate schedule for homework. Set up a system where the student is checked regularly, reinforced, or praised when classroom work is completed in class.

Example 3: Preparation Homework

This type of homework helps students to prepare for an upcoming assignment or to contribute during the next day's lesson. It is usually followed by related lessons in class and can serve to stimulate interest in a new theme or topic. You can assign this type of homework through a letter to parents which can describe the homework as well as provide information about your upcoming theme or topic. Here are some examples:

- Interview someone at home on what they know about . . .
- Ask three people to explain their understanding of . . .
- Find an article about . . . in the newspaper or magazine and be prepared to share.
- Watch the program on TV and be prepared to discuss.
- Read this article/chapter/poem and be prepared to discuss . . .

Example 4: Extension or Application Homework

This type of homework helps students to extend and apply the concepts and skills they have learned in class. Here are some sample homework suggestions:

- Measure your bedroom, and calculate the area in square metres.
- Develop a food budget for a week for your family by collecting newspaper ads to verify prices.
- Complete a problem using the problem-solving strategies we have practised.

Example 5: Projects as Homework

Projects are examples of the extension and application type of homework, but are completed over a longer time period. In projects, students integrate, extend, or apply a variety of skills or concepts learned in class to new situations. Projects can be as varied as the imagination, and need to be meaningful and tied to the learning expectations of your program. Completing projects at home usually calls for much independence, critical thinking, planning, and problem solving. It involves organization, time management, and responsibility in meeting due dates. Projects can also permit an expansion of personal interests and creativity. For example, students could be asked to paraphrase, summarize, and organize information; to interview, take notes, and do research; or to employ creative and artistic skills. A project can be the culminating task for a unit of study, as well as an example of performance-based assessment where students demonstrate their learning in authentic ways. (Refer to Chapter 11,

Assessing, Evaluating, and Reporting.) Some examples of project types are as follows: research assignments, reports, presentations, speeches, commercials, plays, dioramas, structures, artistic creations, slide shows, HyperStudio presentations, and video. Projects requiring technology are becoming more common as technology becomes increasingly integrated with and important in classroom programs. (Refer to Chapter 8, Technology and Learning.)

✦ For any project or major assignment, establish realistic timelines and due dates. Keep in mind that students need to practise and learn how to budget their time. Assignments with a short due date (e.g., two weeks) help to teach time management, while lengthy assignments with due dates scheduled sometime in the future create frustration. Throughout the year, all students should do many mini-assignments or mini-projects which involve teaching and application of specific skills, such as labelling, taking jot notes, summarizing, recording footnotes, or creating a table of contents.

NOTE: Major projects of considerable length should be assigned only after students have done many mini-projects and should be monitored at intervals to ensure success, with check points and feedback along the way. You may want to divide the assignment or project into parts and ask to see proposals, plans, and ongoing work. Doing this safeguards the student with few time management skills and helps all students be more successful in meeting the appropriate expectations.

✦ For projects or major homework assignments, send home a letter to parents outlining expectations, criteria for assessment, the purpose, timelines, due dates, and so on. Suggest how parents can be involved in positive ways. See Figure 10.5.

Dear Parents,

April will be an exciting month as we will be working on a new integrated unit, Inventions, which covers expectations in Science, Social Studies, Language Arts, and Mathematics. During this time, we will be researching many different inventions.

For homework, your child is expected to choose a piece of technology in the home, such as a lightbulb, refrigerator, television, or computer, and to research how it was invented and how it has changed people's lives. A project outline, noting timelines for your child's work completion, is due on April 14. The first part of the project, which includes research jot notes, any illustrations, and a bibliography of references used, is due on April 20. The completed written project, including all drafts, as well as the completed invention, is due on April 29.

The students have a chart which outlines how the project will be assessed. This chart has been developed in consultation with the students in the class so your child should be well aware of the criteria.

We would appreciate your support in these ways:

- Talk with your child about his/her topic.
- Discuss the chart with your child to ensure that he/she is aware of the criteria.
- Help your child by taking him/her to the library to find supplementary books about the topic.
- If you have access to a computer and the Internet, help your child search for appropriate sites that might elicit information.

If you have any questions, please call me at (416) 777-8888.

Sincerely,

S. Schwartz
Susan Schwartz

BLM P-74 **Figure 10.5** *Sample letter to parents re: upcoming project*

✦ When students go on a holiday and parents ask for homework, give the following suggestions:

- Keep a journal or log of the people you see, the places you go, and the activities you do. Encourage other members of your family to make journal entries.
- Take photographs and write captions describing what is happening in the photos. Present this as a report of your trip.
- Take slides or videotape, and be prepared to talk or write about exciting parts.
- Collect souvenirs (menus, plane tickets, artifacts, postcards) and organize them in some way to be shared with classmates on your return.
- Collect bags on your trip and tape them together as a *Bookful of Bags* which serves as a recount or story about your trip. Postcards and photographs can be put into specific bags to help tell the story (Schwartz and Bone).

◆ Survey your students and parents to learn about your students' homework habits as well as to find out about the effectiveness of your homework program. The following questionnaire, Figure 10.6, may prove helpful.

Homework Questionnaire

Home Reading

• How much time do you usually spend reading at home each night? _____

• When do you usually read at home? _____

• Where do you usually read at home? _____

• How many books did you read this month? _____

• How many books did you read last month? _____

• How many books did you read the first month of school? _____

• Comparing your reading this month with that of the first month of school, what can you say about your reading progress? _____

• What book did you enjoy reading the most this year? Why? _____

Homework Assignments

• Where do you usually do your homework? Why? _____

• What time do you usually do your homework? _____

• How much time do you usually spend doing homework each night? _____

• Who helps you most often with your homework?_____

• What was your favourite homework assignment this month?_____

• What was your hardest homework assignment this month? _____

• What was your easiest homework assignment this month?_____

Homework Planner

• Do you remember to take your planner home at the end of each day? _____

• Do you remember to bring it back to school every morning? _____

• If you answered no to one or both of the above questions, what strategies can you think of to help you improve? _____

• When do you look at and use the planner? _____

• How does using this planner help you with organization and time management?_____

• How has feedback from your teacher helped you to improve? _____

• How have comments from your parents helped you to improve? _____

• Other comments? _____

_____

BLM S-75 Figure 10.6 *Homework questionnaire*

✦ Brainstorm with your colleagues, students, and parents for other ideas about homework, the use of the homework planner, and ways to involve all partners in the process.

Homework is an integral part of your overall classroom program and can provide parents with a clear understanding of your goals, expectations, and educational beliefs. Careful planning of your homework assignments ensures ongoing communication between home and school, as well as benefits the academic achievements of your students as they practise, review, reinforce, extend, and apply their learning in their home environments.

11 Assessing, Evaluating, and Reporting

Assessment and evaluation are the foundations upon which you build your classroom program. They are integral components of the teaching/learning process. Essentially, assessment and evaluation are what drive your program, setting the direction and flow of your curriculum and actions.

In today's educational context, teachers are pulled in different ways. They are often faced with a prescribed curriculum, sometimes content laden and outlined for specific grade levels. "The pressure to cover the curriculum is perhaps the most direct and immediate pressure that teachers feel . . . one tends to focus on teaching content instead of teaching students" (Strickland and Strickland, p.10). However, as a teacher, you need to maintain a commitment to teaching to the strengths, needs, and interests of your students based on your knowledge of how children develop and learn, while at the same time adhering to the stated expectations. You need to compare what you know about your students to what you are required to teach. The place to begin is where your students are in relation to what the curriculum expectations state; you can then move your students towards meeting those expectations.

Your assessment and evaluation practices must be grounded in what you know and value about education and how children develop and learn. It is important that you find out as much as you can about your students and what they know, can do, and feel. Knowing your students as individuals means recognizing and building on their strengths, and acknowledging and addressing their needs, thoughts, and feelings. The knowledge that you gain through assessment and evaluation practices provides you with the essential information you need to analyze, in order to program effectively and appropriately.

Assessment is the gathering and analysis of data collected about your students' performance, abilities, and progress. Knowing and understanding where your students are coming from helps you to plan where they are going. Assessment goes hand in hand with instruction. The initial data you collect on students' needs and interests, or the **diagnostic assessment** you do, helps you to make decisions about what and how to teach. The ongoing collection of information about your students as learners is referred to as **formative assessment**. Observation, daily classroom procedures, performance-based tasks, and formal and informal testing all provide you with a window into your students' learning process and progress. As you analyze the data that you're gathering, you make decisions about your program and about the modifications necessary to meet the individual needs of students in your classroom. For **summative assessment**, you consider what the students have produced at the end of a unit, term, or year. This cumulative collection of data ultimately forms the basis for evaluative judgments.

In planning what assessment strategies to use, remember to adopt a variety of *alternative* assessment strategies in addition to the more traditional paper/pencil tasks. The more *authentic* and *performance-based* the assessment is, the more students will see the relevancy to their own world, and they will be better able to apply the learning they have achieved.

The terms *assessment* and *evaluation* are often used synonymously, but there are distinct differences. **Evaluation** differs from assessment in that it is the application of a value, or judgment, about student performance and ability at certain end points during the learning process. It puts a value on the sum total of all that students have demonstrated through the assessment strategies used. Evaluation forms the basis for reporting student progress and achievement. It can be expressed in a variety of formats ranging from anecdotal comments to the assignment of specific grades.

The use of diagnostic, formative, and summative measures help to determine where your students are, where they should be going, and how to get them there. These measures increase your confidence and competence in articulating your program to parents, students, colleagues, and administrators, and in programming appropriately and effectively to meet the needs and interests of your students and the curriculum.

Collecting Assessment Data

✦ Examine your long-range and unit plans to determine the expectations that you will be addressing in all curriculum areas. (See Chapter 5, Planning an Integrated Curriculum.)

✦ Looking at the expectations you have chosen to address, decide which diagnostic assessment strategies you will use to collect initial data about what your students already know, can do, and feel in relation to those expectations.

✦ Collect formative assessment data while your students are engaged in ongoing learning experiences.

◆ At the end of a unit, term, or year, collect summative assessment data that will help you determine your students' level of progress and achievement.

◆ Strive to make your assessment tasks as authentic as possible so that your students will see the relevancy of what they are doing in relationship to real-life situations. For example, if a class is studying water pollution in science and discovers that a pond behind their school has been polluted through the dumping of waste by a nearby company, you might ask your students to write letters to the company president and to the appropriate government agency expressing their concern and their ideas about what should be done about the pollution. Through this letter-writing task, students would demonstrate what they have learned about pollution as well as show growth in citizenship and environmental awareness.

◆ Ensure that you use a variety of the many *alternative assessment* strategies available. This broad term, popularized by Grant Wiggins, refers to "any type of assessment that deviates from the traditional model exemplified by locally created tests and standardized examinations with their multiple-choice, one-answer format" (Strickland and Strickland, p. 9).

◆ Observe your students at intervals and record objective statements about specific students or groups of students.

◆ Make sure your observations are objective and non-judgmental and record noteworthy behaviour, interactions, performances, challenges, and successes.

◆ Observe your students at scheduled times and spontaneously, during each day, in a variety of settings and situations. Observation allows you to hear and see exactly what students are saying and doing.

◆ Use some of the introductory, team/community-building or getting-to-know-you tasks and learning experiences that you include in your planning as opportunities for observation. (See Chapter 4, Classroom Atmosphere.) These important learning experiences serve the dual purpose of providing you with vital diagnostic assessment data while building a community of learners.

◆ You may find the following chart, Figure 11.1, helpful in focusing on what to observe. (Although it notes some important aspects related to child development, it is not intended to be an all-inclusive list.)

Student Observation Chart

Physical Development

- ❏ appearance
- ❏ large and small muscle coordination
- ❏ fine-motor skills
- ❏ health and hygiene
- ❏ hearing development
- ❏ sight development
- ❏ speech development
- ❏

Cognitive Development

- ❏ thinking skills
- ❏ decision making
- ❏ problem solving
- ❏ predicting and inferring abilities
- ❏ understanding of cause-and-effect relationships
- ❏ imaginative thinking
- ❏ acquisition of specific skills in all curriculum areas
- ❏ multiple intelligences
- ❏ learning styles
- ❏

Emotional Development

- ❏ self-image
- ❏ self-confidence
- ❏ responsibility
- ❏ independence
- ❏ coping skills
- ❏ organization
- ❏ work habits
- ❏

Social Development

- ❏ interactions with peers and with adults
- ❏ communication skills
- ❏ cooperation
- ❏ problem solving
- ❏ decision making
- ❏ trust of others
- ❏ respect towards others
- ❏

Figure 11.1 *Student observation checklist*

✦ Prepare observation record sheets using one square for each student. Write brief and objective comments directly onto a paper divided into squares, or use Post-it notes that fit into the squares. If you use Post-it notes, you can place them one on top of the other in the squares as you make additional observations throughout the day or week. In this way, an accumulation of observations about many students can be easily stored on one page. With this page, you can see at a glance if you have missed observing any particular students. (This At-a-Glance system of observation and record keeping was first introduced in *Look! Hear!* published by the North York Board of Education.)

OBSERVATION RECORD SHEET			
Selena	*Karen*	*Sam*	*Mike*
Sept. 12 • Worked with 3 others on cooperative project • Built 3-D tower	Sept. 12 • Keyboarded by herself	Sept. 15 • Wouldn't leave centre until tasks completed the way he wanted	

BLM T-76 **Figure 11.2** *Observation record sheet*

✦ Prepare a summary record sheet for each student. See Figure 11.3 as a model. At the end of the week or month, Post-it notes from the observation record sheets can be transferred to these one-page summaries which make evaluation and report card writing easier.

Student Summary Sheet

Student Name: _____*Lisa Docherty*_____ (Fall,)Winter or Spring Term (circle)

Social and Emotional Development	Work Habits
	Sept. 16 • Needed 3 reminders to settle down to work
Language Sept. 15 • Used descriptive words in space story	Mathematics

Drama	Visual Arts	Music	Health and Physical Education

Social Studies	Science and Technology
	Sept. 24 • Built 3-D structure
French	Computers Sept. 20 • Able to use Word Processing program to compose story

BLM T-77 **Figure 11.3** *Student summary sheet*

✦ Based on your observations, write in-depth anecdotal notes about each student on a regular basis. These notes for reference could be written in a spiral-bound book, a looseleaf binder, or on individual file cards.

✦ Collect further information using interviews and conferences, which are face-to-face interactions with students.

NOTE: *It is a good idea to prepare for an interview or conference by having a set list of questions, but you should also be ready to ask questions spontaneously during the conversation. Remember to* **use** *the information from the interview or conference to program more effectively to meet students' needs. A good idea is to re-interview students later in the year to determine growth over time.*

◆ Continue to collect information in all curriculum areas by using question-naires, surveys, and inventories. These sometimes consist of checklists or sentence completion exercises that elicit information from students, serving as concrete evidence of students' attitudes, interests, perceptions, and learn-ings. Using them with parents can yield important information about their children's backgrounds and experiences and allow you to develop a more complete picture of your students. In addition, these written tools can be used to elicit parent and student opinions and perceptions about your program or school events. See Figures 11.4 and 11.5.

Reading Interview

Name: _____   Date: _____

Grade: _____   Interview Setting: _____

1. When you are reading and come to a word you don't know, what do you do?
   _____
   _____

   Do you do anything else?
   _____
   _____

2. Who do you know who is a good reader?
   _____

3. What makes _____ a good reader?
   _____

4. Do you think _____ ever comes to a word she or he doesn't know? _____

5. If your answer to question 4 is No: Suppose _____ comes to a word she/he doesn't know, what do you think she or he would do?
   _____
   _____

6. If you knew someone was having trouble reading, how would you help that person?
   _____
   _____

7. What do you think a teacher would do to help that person?
   _____
   _____

8. How did you learn to read?
   _____
   _____

9. What would you like to do better as a reader?
   _____
   _____

10. Do you think you are a good reader? Why?
   _____
   _____

BLM T-78 **Figure 11.4** *Reading interview*

Source: "Reading Interview" by Carolyn L. Burke in *Reading Miscue Inventory: Alternative Procedures* by Yetta Goodman, Dorothy Watson, and Carolyn Burke (Richard C. Owen Publishers). Reprinted with permission of the publisher.

BLM S-79   **Figure 11.5** *Mathematics attitude survey*

✦ Assess your students in literacy using a variety of assessment tools and strategies. For example, a **running record**, along with an oral retell, assesses a beginning reader's ability to decode and comprehend text, while a **miscue analysis** assesses a more proficient reader's ability to do the same thing.

** A good resource on running records is *An Observation Survey of Early Literacy Achievement* by Marie Clay (Heinemann); a good resource on miscue analysis is *Reading Miscue Inventory: Alternative Procedures* by Yetta Goodman, Dorothy Watson, and Carolyn Burke (Richard C. Owen Publishers).

✦ Collect and store dated samples of your students' work in all curriculum areas, either in progress or completed. Work samples might include task sheets, artwork, writing samples, journal entries, reading response logs, science experiments, mathematics worksheets, and maps, graphs, and charts. Dated work samples provide concrete evidence of growth over time.

✦ File or store these work samples so that you and your students have easy access to them when needed. Types of individual filing systems include theme folders, writing folders, art folders, hanging files, a file box, a scrapbook, envelopes, a logbook, a notebook, and portfolios.

✦ Create checklists as needed to record and track your students' progress, completion of tasks, and achievement. When used as a summative assessment tool, where a summary of achievement levels can be recorded or a grade entered beside each student's name, checklists let you see at a glance which students are progressing well and which may still need some intervention. See Figure 11.6. You can also create a checklist for individual students, as is found in Figure 11.7, Observing Student Writing, to check off evidence of specific skills or concepts observed.

CHECKLIST Re: COMPLETED TASKS				
Names of Students	Learning Experiences			Comments
	Science Experiment # 1	Graph	Create a Structure	
Marie	✓	✓	✓	Very task-oriented
John	✓		✓	Needed support in graphing
Matthew		✓	✓	Absent for science experiment

BLM T-80 Figure 11.6 *Checklist re: completed tasks*

✦ When appropriate, design tests, quizzes, and formal exams that correlate specifically to the curriculum being taught. Paper/pencil tests, the traditional method of assessing students' retention of facts and knowledge, can provide objective assessment data *when used for a specific purpose*. They measure material taught and are commonly used for pre and post purposes. They can sometimes assist you in finding out what students already know about a topic, theme, or unit of study. Similarly, summative tests can help you find out what students have learned at the end of a topic, theme, or unit of study. When designing tests, be sure to include a variety of questions that represent different levels of thinking. (Refer to Chapter 5, Planning an Integrated Curriculum, which outlines Bloom's Taxonomy, and Chapter 7, Literacy and Language Learning, which presents the 3 R's framework, for information on the different levels.)

✦ Involve your students in keeping learning logs, which document what students plan to do during the day and what they accomplish. Learning logs, which can be workbooks, spiral-bound notebooks, looseleaf binders, or folders, permit reflection on what students have learned, what they may still need to work on, and how well they believe they have done.

✦ Involve your students in keeping personal or response journals. A **personal journal** can feature a student's recollection of events, personal or imaginative stories and poems, or other personal writings; a **response journal** can contain student reflections on something experienced, on material read, on movies or videos seen, on music heard, or on a trip taken. (For more information on journals, turn to Chapter 7, Literacy and Language Learning.)

OBSERVING STUDENT WRITING

Student: _Kimberly_

Title of Writing: _The Mystery of the Trap Door_

CONTENT

Form of Writing
- ☑ Narrative story writing
- ☐ Poetry
- ☐ Report
- ☐ Recount/Retelling
- ☐ Procedure
- ☐ Explanation
- ☐ Exposition/Persuasive writing/Point of view
- ☐ Letter
   - ☐ Formal
   - ☐ Informal
- ☐ Other

Development of Writing
- ☑ Beginning/Introduction
- ☑ Middle/Body of text
- ☑ End/Summary/Closure
- ☑ Appropriate features re: the form selected
- ☐ Sufficient information
- ☐ Well developed
- ☑ Unity of thought
- ☑ Smooth flow of ideas
- ☑ Awareness of audience
- ☐ Sense of voice
- ☐ Stylistic devices
- ☐ Other

Organization
- ☑ Coherent
- ☑ Logical
- ☑ Sequential
- ☑ Suits the purpose of the writing
- ☐ Other

Language
- ☑ Appropriate to the writing
- ☐ Descriptive words
- ☑ Conversation/Dialogue
- ☐ Metaphors
- ☐ Similes
- ☐ Other

MECHANICS

Grammar and Usage
- ☐ Sentence fragments
- ☑ Complete sentences
- ☐ Run-on sentences
- ☑ Short sentences
- ☐ Compound sentences
- ☐ Complex sentences
- ☐ Compound-complex sentences
- ☑ Subject-verb agreement
- ☐ Conjunctions
- ☐ Adjectives
- ☐ Adverbs
- ☐ Clauses
- ☐ Adverbial clauses
- ☐ Other

Capitalization
- ☑ Beginning of sentences
- ☑ Proper names
- ☐ Places
- ☐ Titles
- ☐ Other

Punctuation
- ☑ Periods
- ☑ Question marks
- ☐ Exclamation marks
- ☑ Quotation marks
- ☐ Commas
- ☐ Colons
- ☐ Semi-colons
- ☐ Other

Spelling
- ☐ Scribble
- ☐ Random letters
- ☐ Initial consonants
- ☐ Phonetic spelling
- ☑ Conventional spelling with few errors
- ☑ Plurals
- ☑ Endings (-ed, -ing, -tion)
- ☐ Other

BLM T-81 **Figure 11.7** *Checklist re: observing student writing*

> The mistery of
> The Trap Door!
> chapter 1
> The trap door
>
> Once apoun atime there were two girls named Kim and Hila. One day they went to the park. When they got there they started to play. Just then Hila saw something. "Come here Kim." said Hila "What do you want"? said Kim "I found a trap door right here."

◆ Provide many opportunities for your students to self-assess as they begin to take ownership of their own learning and reflect on their progress and performance. Be sure to provide a set of criteria by which students assess their own work. Also, it is important to provide samples of exemplary performance or products so that students have models from which to work and examples to emulate. By involving your students in self-assessment, you increase their motivation to improve and grow. They begin to set realistic and attainable goals for themselves.

◆ Provide opportunities for your students to do peer assessment, where they help to critically assess each other's progress and achievement. This type of assessment, for which it is important to provide students with a format, puts into practice the cooperative skills that students have learned. Figure 11.8 shows an example of a record sheet that students can use for self and peer assessment.

Science Experiment #_____

Self and Peer Assessment

Student: _____   *Date:* _____

*Topic of Experiment:*_____

Use the scale below to assess your work.
Share with a peer and have him/her assess your accomplishments.

Needs to improve	1
Okay/Satisfactory	2
Good	3
Excellent	4

	Self	Peer
1. The purpose was clearly stated.	____	____
2. The hypothesis was original and thought-provoking.	____	____
3. Materials were used effectively.	____	____
4. The procedures outlined were sequential and detailed.	____	____
5. Observations were objective and thorough.	____	____
6. Conclusions were relevant to the hypothesis.	____	____
7. Diagram(s) complemented the written portion of the experiment.	____	____
8. The write-up was neat and clearly stated.	____	____
9. Safety was adhered to throughout.	____	____
10. Sharing of work accomplished was well stated.	____	____

BLM S-82 **Figure 11.8** *Checklist re: self- and peer assessment*

** A good resource for more information on self- and peer assessment is *Self-Evaluation . . . Helping Students Get Better at It*, edited by Carol Rolheiser (The Clear Group, Ontario Institute for Studies in Education, and the Durham Board of Education, Ontario).

✦ As you plan your integrated program, incorporate tasks such as projects, simulations, performances, and audio/video/technological presentations which call for performance-based assessment. Bear in mind that performance-based tasks should have clearly defined criteria so that students are well aware of what they are expected to produce in order to demonstrate what they have learned.

✦ Create *rubrics* that correspond with the curriculum planned and that clearly outline the criteria and levels of achievement that students are expected to attain. Rubrics can be used to assess a performance task, a unit of study, or achievement throughout the year. Rubrics help to identify the quality and quantity of what is expected of students, making explicit for students what they should know, be able to do, and value. They are useful for self-assessment as students can see how they are progressing and what they need to do to improve their performance or increase their knowledge. As a result, rubrics help students set goals for their own improvement and progress.

✦ Involve your students as much as possible in the creation of rubrics so that they gain ownership and clearly know what is expected of them. As students work collaboratively with the teacher to articulate the criteria for exemplary performance, they are able to see clearly what they need to do in order to reach that level.

✦ In order to create a rubric with your students, you will want to do the following:

- Determine the task or performance for which you will need to create a rubric.
- Show the students models of expected products or performances.
- Brainstorm with your students the criteria necessary to create that exemplary product or performance. Add your own ideas to this list.
- Prioritize the criteria you and your students believe are most essential.
- If possible, sort these criteria into identifiable categories.
- Taking each category and the criteria, write qualifying statements of varying degrees.

✦ Use the following words as qualifiers to help you develop statements for rubrics:
- rarely, sometimes, frequently, consistently;
- no variety, some variety, a wide variety;
- little use, some use, regular use, excellent use;
- not, somewhat, extremely;

- few, some, many;
- quite a few errors, hardly any errors, error free;
- limited, partial, comprehensive;
- none, some, many.

NOTE: *These qualities are also useful when combined with report card statements. See Appendix 2: Sample Comments for Report Card Writing.*

◆ When introducing rubrics to primary students, you might read aloud the picture book *Moira's Birthday* by Robert Munsch and involve them in creating a rubric about what makes an outstanding party, a good party, an average or okay party, and a not-so-good party. Develop statements that represent the qualities in each of these parties. For example, if food at a party is an essential component or category, then an outstanding party would have a great amount of pizza, cake, chips, pop, and so on. A good party might have pizza and cake, an average party might have just cake, and a not-so-good party would have cookies and not enough for all the guests. Continue to develop statements that represent the categories for an outstanding party and the descriptive statements for each level. Figure 11.9 illustrates what a completed rubric for a party might look like.

Rubric for a Party

Category	Outstanding	Good	Okay	Not-so-good
Food	Pizza, cake, chips, pop	Pizza, cake	Cake	Cookies
Entertainment	Planned activities Games Performances Active involvement by guests	Games Active involvement by guests	Guests watch a movie	No entertainment
Decorations	Streamers, balloons, posters, flashing lights Theme-based, including napkins, plates, cups, and tablecloths	Theme-based, including napkins, plates, and cups Some balloons Some streamers	Few balloons	No decorations
Loot bags	Filled to the brim with all different toys and candy	Five different items in the loot bags	One or two things in the loot bags	No loot bags

BLM T-83 **Figure 11.9** *Rubric for a party. See BLM T-83 for a sample blank rubric template.*

◆ When involving older students in creating rubrics, you might ask small groups of students to work on defining the levels of achievement for each category. Each group would be responsible for working through one category and then sharing ideas with the whole class for feedback. As students work with and use the rubrics, you might discuss how their created rubrics could be further revised and improved.

◆ Consider implementing portfolio assessment into your program on an ongoing basis. **Portfolios** are collections of student work that exemplify, through the inclusion of work samples, products, artifacts and reflections, what students have accomplished and what they have learned during a specific time. There are two major types of portfolios: *growth* portfolios demonstrate how students have grown in their learning process and should contain meaningful artifacts and reflections about what they have done and learned; *showcase* portfolios, on the other hand, contain reflections and demonstrations of best work. They can be seen as precursors to career or employment portfolios, which are increasingly expected in the job market.

◆ Decide on the type of portfolio your students will create: growth or showcase.

◆ Decide which area or areas of the curriculum the portfolio will represent. For example, decide whether the portfolio will include items from mathematics, writing, or the arts, or if it will contain selections from all curriculum areas.

◆ Decide appropriate timelines for using portfolios. For example, will your students use portfolios for a two-week period, a month, a term, or all year?

◆ Determine the type of container your students will use for their portfolios. A box, file folders, binders, or a scrapbook are some options.

◆ Make decisions about how the portfolios will be organized. For example, the contents of portfolios can be organized in chronological order, by themes, topics, or categories, or according to specific criteria or expectations. Depending on the age of the students and their experience with portfolios, you might choose to involve students in making these decisions or leave the organization of the portfolios entirely to them. You could ask them to develop a table of contents to identify what is in their portfolios. This page could clearly identify the organization used.

◆ Decide who will choose the materials to be featured in the portfolio. Consider that involving students in the selection of portfolio entries promotes a sense of ownership and increases motivation. Students make decisions and solve problems as they choose appropriate artifacts, work samples, and demonstrations of learning.

✦ Send a letter home to parents explaining the portfolio process. Figure 11.10 provides a sample.

Dear Parents,

During this year, our students will use portfolios to assess their learning and achievement. Portfolios allow students to reflect on the work they have done and make thoughtful decisions about goals for future learning. We will introduce the portfolio process by inviting an artist to visit our class to share his portfolio with us. We too have portfolios which we will use to demonstrate the process. If you have a portfolio and are able to join us to share it, please let us know and we will schedule a time for you to visit our class.

At specific intervals throughout the year, students will be required to select pieces of work for inclusion in their portfolios. Work will be collected from all subject areas and will represent best work, most creative work, most improved work, most challenging work, and so on. These collections will enable us to assess and evaluate aspects of your child's growth over time. Students will be required to write about the artifacts they have chosen, why they have selected each one for inclusion, what they have learned, and what goals they need to set for the future. They will share the contents of their portfolios with their peers throughout the year, in addition to using their portfolios at our upcoming parent-teacher conferences to show you what they have learned.

If you have any questions or suggestions, please call us at 416-395-2222.

Sincerely,

S. Schwartz   M. Pollishuke

S. Schwartz and M. Pollishuke

BLM P-84 **Figure 11.10** *Sample letter to parents re: portfolios*

✦ Decide how you will *introduce* portfolios to your students. The following ideas may prove useful.

- Create your own portfolio and share it with your class.

- Invite a photographer, artist, or writer into your class to share his/her portfolio.

- Ask students' parents if they have personal or professional portfolios that they could share with the class.

- Discuss collections of various sorts with your students, and make comparisons to the portfolio as a collection of their work.

- Ask your students to bring in an artifact from home to share with the class. This artifact and an accompanying reflection can then become the first entry for their portfolio.

- Have your students create a finished product, such as a work of art, a report, or a published book. This product and an accompanying reflection can also become the first entry for their portfolio.

◆ Explicitly teach students how to make decisions about what to include in a portfolio. For example, at the end of a month or term, have them review a collection of their work on a particular theme, topic, or unit of study. Ask them to choose their best work, the work that shows the most growth, the work that they found the most challenging, the work that they enjoyed the most.

◆ Model the process of reflection and sharing for the students, and have individual students share reflections with the whole class as well as in small groups.

◆ Invite your students to reflect on each artifact included in the portfolio by providing them with prompts that spark their thinking. Here are a few examples: "This is about… (retell); This is significant to me because… (relate); I learned… (reflect)" (Schwartz and Bone).

◆ Provide time for students to share some of the entries in their portfolios with their peers and adults. Sharing with others helps to push thinking to higher levels and provides an authentic audience for the writing. The use of prompts to encourage response also proves helpful. Examples include the following: "An idea that captured my interest was…"; "That made me think about…"; "A question that was raised for me was…."

◆ Consider how you will assess the portfolio. You might consider creating a rubric that outlines the categories to be assessed, including organization, presentation, quantity and quality of entries, and reflective practice.

◆ Consider having students share their portfolios with their parents, as happens in student-led conferences which are discussed later in this chapter under "Reporting Student Achievement."

◆ Pass the portfolios on to students' teachers for next year, or encourage students to share their portfolios with their teacher in the next grade.

** *The Portfolio Organizer: Succeeding with Portfolios in Your Classroom*, by Carol Rolheiser, Barbara Bower, and Laurie Stevahn (ASCD), is an outstanding resource to use to help with the implementation of portfolios with students of all ages and with the implementation of professional portfolios. Many of the above activities are adapted from it.

Evaluating Student Progress

✦ Examine all the relevant data that you have collected about each student. Look for patterns of behaviour and evidence of growth.

✦ Make inferences and judgments based on a student's progress and behaviour patterns.

✦ Adjust your program to ensure that you are meeting the needs of individual students.

✦ If your district or board requires you to give each student a numerical or letter grade, be sure to use a full range of assessment data to generate the grade. Do not rely on an individual assignment or performance task to form the basis of the grade.

✦ When assigning grades, you could attach a numerical or letter grade to each level of achievement identified on a rubric. For example, an outstanding level on a rubric could represent a grade of A to A+.

NOTE: Grades should never come as a surprise to students. Students should be well aware of how they are doing so they are able to take ownership to improve their performance. The assigning of grades can be detrimental to students' self-esteem and prove counterproductive to their progress. Grades should be reserved for knowledge and skill and not for effort. You don't want students to think that they can even fail at trying.

Reporting Student Achievement

✦ Using the collected data, write clear, concise evaluative statements for reporting purposes. (See Appendix 2 for sample comments for report card writing.)

✦ If at all possible, have the report cards translated for parents whose first language is not English. For reporting purposes, a translator could be a relative or an educator, such as another teacher, a bilingual assistant, or a multicultural consultant. For confidentiality reasons, you should avoid asking another parent in the school or an older student to act as a translator.

✦ During interviews or conferences with parents, reinforce the idea of a team effort between home and school. Discuss the child's progress, examine and discuss dated work samples, and informal and formal test results, and share daily observations and your interpretations. Answer questions about your program, report card comments, and grading system used. Be positive and encouraging while also being straightforward.

✦ Begin a conference with positive statements about the student's strengths and interests.

✦ When discussing a student's areas of challenge, always note how you plan to assist the student in improving his/her performance, and discuss next steps for your focus of instruction. Invite parents to also suggest next steps that they can take. Consider developing an action plan with parents and student.

✦ During parent-teacher conferences, provide parents with concrete examples of how they can help their children at home. (Refer to Chapter 12, Partnerships with Parents, for sample letters to parents.)

✦ Consider using the following checklist, Figure 11.11, as a guide to successful parent-teacher conferences.

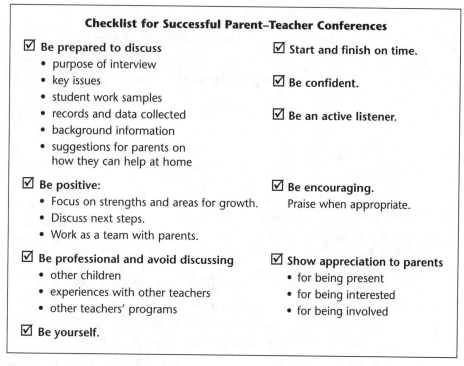

Checklist for Successful Parent–Teacher Conferences

☑ **Be prepared to discuss**
- purpose of interview
- key issues
- student work samples
- records and data collected
- background information
- suggestions for parents on how they can help at home

☑ **Be positive:**
- Focus on strengths and areas for growth.
- Discuss next steps.
- Work as a team with parents.

☑ **Be professional and avoid discussing**
- other children
- experiences with other teachers
- other teachers' programs

☑ **Be yourself.**

☑ **Start and finish on time.**

☑ **Be confident.**

☑ **Be an active listener.**

☑ **Be encouraging.**
Praise when appropriate.

☑ **Show appreciation to parents**
- for being present
- for being interested
- for being involved

(Acknowledgments to Brian Care)

Figure 11.11 *Checklist for successful parent–teacher conferences*

✦ Consider including students in conferences with you and their parents. Prepare them for what to expect and advise them on how they can participate actively.

✦ Consider initiating **student-led conferences**, which place the students at the centre and give them the responsibility of presenting to their parents what they have learned, the goals they have set, and the actions they plan to take. Such conferences allow parents and students alike to become more relaxed and confident as they engage in a dialogue about progress and achievement. Portfolios can be easily presented.

✦ Introduce the idea of student-led conferences early in the year so students and parents will be fully prepared for the process and know what to expect. You can do this at the same time as you introduce your portfolios.

✦ Model a conference with your students, walking them through every step of the process, from greeting their parents until they say goodbye.

✦ Ensure that your students have had significant rehearsal time to practise articulating their learnings and identifying their goals. Having them rehearse in pairs or groups of four prepares them for the big day and alleviates any anxiety.

✦ Provide students with a structure to help them organize their time during the conference. Figure 11.12 may prove helpful.

Checklist for Your Conference

- Introduce your parents to your teacher.
- Take your parents on a tour of your classroom.
- Highlight the work you see on display.
- Demonstrate for your parents something you enjoy doing in the classroom, for example, how to do a spreadsheet or construct a model.
- Share your work with your parents. Do one or more of the following:
  - Walk your parents through your portfolio, folder, or collection of work.
  - Highlight your best work and explain why it is your best.
  - Highlight your most significant learning.
  - Show your parents something that was difficult for you to do, and explain why you think so and what you did about it.
  - Share a sample of your favourite writing.
- Discuss with your parents the goals you have set for next term.
- Thank your parents for coming and looking at your work.
- Say goodbye to your teacher.

 **BLM S-85** **Figure 11.12** *Checklist re: student-led conferences*

> ***NOTE:*** *Once you, your students, and their parents become comfortable with this process, you might want to schedule multiple conferences at the same time. While you are circulating as a facilitator and are available to answer*

questions and offer support, four conferences might be taking place at the same time at four different tables in the room. Students and parents are so focused on what they are doing that they are usually not distracted by the numbers of people talking at the same time.

✦ Reassure your parents that they can schedule a traditional parent conference if needed. However, usually parents' questions are answered and their concerns alleviated during a student-led conference.

✦ Prior to using student-led conferencing, ensure that you have the support of your administrators. They may receive questions about the process from concerned parents, and you will want your administrators to be well informed and supportive. Invite them to join you in facilitating a practice session with the students or the actual student-led conferences with parents.

✦ Reflect on the process with your students, parents, and administrators by asking for feedback either orally or in writing. For example, you might have conversations about student-led conferences or ask for an open-ended evaluation form, such as Figure 11.13, to be completed.

Reflections on Student-led Conferences
Student Name: *Kimberly*
Parent Name: *Jennifer Craighton*
Date of Conference: *Nov. 10*
Highlights of Conference: *My daughter has done so much work this term.*
Next Steps: *Kimberly needs to read more at home.*
Other Reflections: *I was so impressed with Kimberly's confidence and the way she talked about her work. Wow!*
Signature of Parent: *Jennifer Craighton*

BLM P-86 Figure 11.13 *Parent reflections on student-led conferences*

** For more information about student-led conferences, see *Student-led Conferences: Using Portfolios to Share Learning with Parents*, by Janet Millar Grant, Barbara Heffler, and Kadri Mereweather (Pembroke Publishers).

Final Thoughts

Assessment forms the foundation upon which your program is built. As you discover what your students already know and can do and base your programming decisions on that knowledge, you will be tailoring your instruction to their unique needs and interests. As assessment is interwoven with instruction, your program becomes more meaningful and relevant. When you begin the process of evaluation, you are forming the judgments that will be shared with students, as well as with parents to keep them abreast of how their children are progressing. Successful interactions with parents pave the way for positive partnerships between the home, school, and community.

12 Partnerships with Parents

Establishing strong partnerships with parents* and ensuring that parents are consistently and positively involved in their children's progress at school and at home will reap many rewards. As parents become an integral part of your classroom and school community, they will become more knowledgeable about and supportive of your program. In today's political climate, many parents are critically attuned to the education of their children and many participate actively. In some communities, however, it continues to be a challenge to involve parents in the school experience. Nonetheless, it is essential that you continue to reach out to all families.

There are many ways to keep all parents informed about your classroom program. Sending home classroom and school newsletters, notes, or communication outlines, and inviting parents to attend curriculum nights and information sessions will keep parents up-to-date.

Parent-teacher interviews or conferences, reporting procedures, daily agenda or homework planners, and regular homework assignments help parents to keep abreast of how their children are progressing. When parents are well informed about their children's educational program and progress, they become better able to assist their children at home. They can participate to a much greater extent in their children's physical, social, emotional, and cognitive development.

Inviting parents to school and classroom events, such as assemblies, musical or drama presentations, open house evenings, or curriculum fairs, encourages them to take part in the celebrations and successes of your students and classroom program. When children accompany their families to these events, they all share in the pride and ownership of these successes.

When parents become volunteers in the classroom or school, not only do they serve as a beneficial support to students and teachers alike, they gain a better understanding of what school is all about and how children learn. With

* As previously stated, the term "parent" represents parents, guardians, and appropriate caregivers.

189

the many budget cuts today, teachers and administrators need to take a serious look at how volunteers can contribute to the learning process. Volunteer programs can be initiated as a school project where educators, parents, and community members work together to make it successful.

As a teacher, you need to know your community and understand the socioeconomic, religious, cultural, and linguistic backgrounds of your students, parents, and community members in order to better appreciate and support their needs. Parents from diverse cultures need to be consciously considered and programs should be put into place to ease them into the school environment. When providing programming information, newsletters, reports, and invitations to classroom and school meetings and events, you should offer translations, translators, and materials in various languages to meet the needs of the whole community. You need to continuously plan how to involve all parents in positive ways.

Creating Partnerships with Parents

✦ Greet your parents at the door or in the schoolyard as they drop off or pick up their children.

✦ Make an initial contact with all parents early in the school year by telephoning or writing a letter or postcard. (See Figure 12.1.)

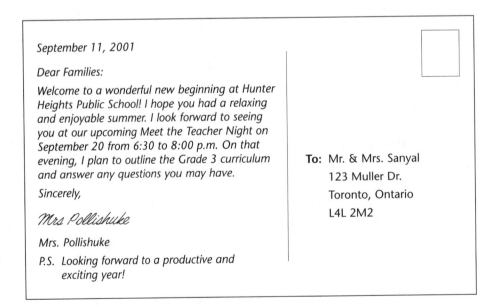

September 11, 2001

Dear Families:

Welcome to a wonderful new beginning at Hunter Heights Public School! I hope you had a relaxing and enjoyable summer. I look forward to seeing you at our upcoming Meet the Teacher Night on September 20 from 6:30 to 8:00 p.m. On that evening, I plan to outline the Grade 3 curriculum and answer any questions you may have.

Sincerely,

Mrs Pollishuke

Mrs. Pollishuke

P.S. Looking forward to a productive and exciting year!

To: Mr. & Mrs. Sanyal
    123 Muller Dr.
    Toronto, Ontario
    L4L 2M2

Figure 12.1 *September postcard to families*

> **NOTE:** *You might want to send postcards or letters to your new students before September. Students love receiving mail addressed to them and a postcard or letter is a great way to introduce yourself and welcome them to your class.*

Early in the school year, send home information about your program, rules, routines, special events, and timetable, so parents are well informed about their children's program. You may decide to use newsletter or letter format. Figures 12.2 and 12.3 provide examples.

NEWS FROM ROOM 203!

WELCOME TO OUR ROOM!

I would like to welcome you to Room 203. This is going to be an exciting and productive year for all of us. We are all looking forward to learning new things, trying out new ideas and celebrating our successes in Grade 5 this year. If you have any questions or concerns, please do not hesitate to call me at 905-974-6661.

Sincerely,

Mrs M. Pollishuke

AGENDAS

We will be using the **homework agendas** to plan our days and reflect on our achievements. These agendas will be coming home each night and will provide you with a good idea of what your children have done for each day. Please discuss the homework agenda with your children, highlighting what they have accomplished and in what areas they may need to spend more time.

GYM SCHEDULE

Our class is scheduled for the use of the **gym** every Monday and Wednesday morning. It is essential that all children wear appropriate clothes in order to participate fully in the gym program. Please ensure that your children bring shorts and running shoes to school on gym day or if you wish, they may leave a gym bag at school. It is important that all clothing and materials from home be clearly marked with your children's names.

TRIPS

We hope to be able to offer our students many **out-of-classroom excursions** throughout the year in order to broaden the scope of our program. Please ensure that all permission forms are returned promptly to the school so that your children do not miss out on these important learning opportunities.

If you would like to volunteer to help on any of these trips, please fill out the request for volunteers form when it is sent home.

LUNCH PROGRAM

As you may be aware, Hunter Heights does have a **school lunch program** for those children who cannot go home for lunch. Please make sure that you have returned the forms to allow your children to remain in school for lunch and that they are aware that they may not leave school property if they are part of the program.

INFORMATION SHEET

I will be sending home a **student information sheet** in the next few days and hope that you will fill out all the pertinent information and return it promptly to the school. The more information I have on your children, the better able I will be to program for their specific needs.

BLM P-87 Figure 12.2 *Class newsletter*

Dear Parents,

Please join us at our Curriculum Night on Wednesday, September 20, to find out what we have planned for this year. At that time, I will give you an overview of the upcoming program and answer any questions you may have.

As the year progresses, I plan to be in constant communication with all the homes of the students in my class. I want to keep you well informed about what we are doing and learning throughout the year. In the meantime, I would like to outline some initial routines that you need to be aware of immediately.

- We will be using **homework planners** to plan our days and reflect on our achievements. These planners will be coming home with your children each night and will provide you with a good idea of what they have done each day. Please discuss the homework planners with your children, highlighting what they have accomplished and what areas may need more time and attention.

- Our class is scheduled for the use of the **gym** every Monday and Wednesday morning. It is essential that all children wear appropriate clothes in order to participate fully in the gym program. Please ensure that your children bring shorts, t-shirts, and running shoes to school on gym days, or, if you wish, they may leave gym bags at school. It is important that all clothing and materials from your home be clearly marked with your children's names.

- Hunter Heights has a **school lunch program** for those children who are unable to go home for lunch. Please make sure that you have returned the forms to allow your children to remain in school for lunch and that they know that it is inappropriate to leave school property if registered in the lunch program.

- Please complete the **student information form** attached and return it promptly to the school. The more information I have about each child, the better able I will be to program for students' specific needs.

Welcome to our classroom. I look forward to getting to know both you and your children throughout this school year. Please do not hesitate to contact me if you have any questions or concerns.

Sincerely,

M. Pollishuke

Mrs. M. Pollishuke

BLM P-88   **Figure 12.3** *Sample letter to parents re: beginning of the year*

✦ At the beginning of the year, collect background information about your students and parents including the family structure, the languages spoken at home, medical history, the way the child travels to and from school, and any other information pertinent to the child's time in school. If your school does not already have a set procedure, you might consider sending home a form such as in Figure 12.4 (which is referred to in Figure 12.2 and Figure 12.3).

BLM P-89 **Figure 12.4** *Student information form*

Throughout the year, communicate with your parents on a regular basis to keep them informed and aware. You may decide to use a newsletter format (see Figure 12.2), a calendar format (see Figure 12.5), "Ask Me About" newsletters (see Figures 12.6 and 12.7), or a Friday File (see Figure 12.8).

SEPTEMBER

Sunday	Monday	Tuesday	Wednesday	Thursday	Friday	Saturday
	Welcome Back to School				1	2
3	Labour Day 4	First Day of School 5	6	Gym Day Bring your shorts 7	8	Happy Birthday Jennifer 9
10	11	12	Library Day Pick a great book! 13	14	15	16
17	18	Computer Lab 19	20	Curriculum Night Bring your parents! 21	22	23
24	25	26	27	28	29	Rosh Hashanah 30

BLM P-90 **Figure 12.5** *Class calendar*

Dear Families,

This **Ask Me About** newsletter is intended to let you know about some of the things we are doing in class. When you ask your children "What did you do in school today?" they often answer "nothing" even though much learning has occurred. The format of this newsletter encourages you to ask the questions that will spark your child to talk about his/her day and the learning that took place. These prompts can help to focus your conversations about school happenings. They are built on the premise that if parents ask the right questions based on a bit of knowledge, the children will carry the rest and a flood of talk can result. We hope you will find this newsletter informative and useful.

Please take the time to ask your child about some of the things listed below.

Sincerely,

S. Smith
Mrs. Smith

ASK ME ABOUT

- ❑ one math activity I did this week
- ❑ one of the books my teacher read to us
- ❑ the book I am reading for my novel study
- ❑ what I am writing
- ❑ my art project
- ❑ the new song I learned this week in choir
- ❑ the visitor that came to our school this week
- ❑ the trip we went on today

BLM P-91 **Figure 12.6** *"Ask me about" newsletter*

Ask Me About...

Kindergarten Newsletter
Park View Heights Public School

Friday, June 12

On Monday, our Painted Lady butterflies emerged. One emerged in the morning before we came to class. The other emerged in the afternoon when we went to the library. Ask me to tell you about the Painted Lady butterfly. They were in a terrarium. We kept them for four days. We released them yesterday. I'll tell you how we did that. Ask me to tell you why we let them go.

We read more books about butterflies and moths. Ask me to tell you what I found interesting.

We have other objects about insects. We have a paper wasp home, a dead Monarch butterfly, the empty chrysalides of Painted Lady butterflies and some models of insects. Ask me to tell you about them.

Mrs. Hartman has read many stories this week. I'll tell you what I liked about one of them.

Ask me to tell you what I have been writing in my writing book.

On Monday, Mrs. Garden, a volunteer, showed us how to drip paint on paper to make butterflies. I'll tell you about my butterfly.

I have been making letters in a new printing book. Ask me to tell you what letters I have been practising. I am also printing words.

Ask me to tell you what mathematics activities I have been doing this week. We can do a shape activity at the paint centre.

(Acknowledgments to Elizabeth Hartman)

BLM P-92 **Figure 12.7** *"Ask me about" newsletter for Kindergarten*

NOTE: *You may want to identify one or two learning expectations that you have addressed during that week on the back of your Ask Me About newsletter. Doing this will give your parents insights into the curriculum expectations for the grade.*

Dear Parents,

Every Friday, your child will be bringing home a file folder containing work accomplished during the week and/or letters or notes for you to see. The purpose of this **Friday File** is to inform you about our classroom program and the progress that your child is making. Please review with your child the work in this folder and ask him/her questions about specific items. Your child should be able to tell you about the things that he/she has learned.

Please sign the front of the folder and send it and the work to school with your child each Monday morning.

Thank you for your cooperation.

Sincerely,

M. Pollishuke

Mrs. M. Pollishuke

BLM P-93 **Figure 12.8** *Sample parent letter re: Friday File*

◆ Consider creating a classroom and/or school Web site, and post important information about your program for your students' parents to access. (See Chapter 8, Technology and Learning.)

◆ Make contact with all parents on a regular basis. Discuss each child's program and progress, outline concerns, and celebrate successes. You also gain an excellent opportunity to gather information about your students' backgrounds and experiences.

◆ If some of your families are new to the country and do not speak English, ensure that you send home translations of your important letters in the appropriate languages.

◆ Line up translators for your families whose first language is not English. A translator might be a bilingual assistant, another teacher, a parent in the school who speaks the same language, or an older student.

◆ If you are concerned about a particular student and you know his/her family's first language is not English, connect with a multicultural consultant that might be affiliated with your school or district or with an appropriate community agency.

◆ At a scheduled curriculum night or information meeting, introduce yourself and outline clear program objectives and expectations as well as information about your routines, timetable, special events, and so on.

◆ During a curriculum evening where students accompany their parents to the school (or during an Open House), plan a scavenger hunt through your classroom or school, ensuring that families visit all important areas. In this scenario, the child provides a walking tour and talks to family members about the learning that is taking place in the classroom and school. Figure 12.9 is an example of a scavenger hunt page, which you may want to modify for your own classroom and school.

Let's go on a Harbour Woods HUNT...

Please check after you visit each one.

OUR CLASSROOM:

____ The table where I sit

____ Timetable (on board)

____ Computer centre

____ Book corner

____ Mathematics area

____ Science corner

____ Social Studies area

____ Painting centre

____ Current events

____ Word wall

____ Parent news bulletin board

____ Homework folders (on round table)

____ Information about homework (Please pick up.)

LIBRARY RESOURCE CENTRE:

____ Say hello to Mr. Sturnick, our teacher-librarian.

____ Say hello to Mrs. Brown, our Special Education resource teacher.

____ See the new books on display.

____ View the new IBM computers.

____ See how fast you can type using the "All the Right Type" keyboarding program.

MUSIC:

____ Meet Ms. Taylor, our new music teacher, in Room 5.

____ Name and play some of the instruments we've used.

COMMUNITY CHILD CARE:

____ Meet some of our child-care staff.

SCHOOL ADVISORY COUNCIL:

____ Meet some of the members of our School Council.

____ Enjoy some refreshments (provided by the Council).

BLM P-94 **Figure 12.9** *Sample scavenger hunt*

✦ Provide interested parents with professional reading, such as educational documents and resources, to promote a better understanding of current philosophy and practices. Set up a lending library for parents to borrow your resource books and educational videotapes.

✦ Provide parents with concrete examples of how they can help their children at home. You may find the following three letters, shown as Figures 12.10, 12.11, and 12.12, helpful.

Dear Families,

Keep in mind that your interest, involvement, and support will help to improve your child's achievement and success. The following are suggestions of activities that you and your child can do at home.

- Have your child see you read and write.

- Relate reading to everyday life, for example, billboards, traffic signs, store signs, menus, TV guides, catalogues, magazines, comics, labels, maps, and crossword puzzles.

- Share experiences, work samples, and anecdotes.

- Take your child on outings — to shopping malls, museums, planetariums, art displays, concerts, sporting events, airports, farms, zoos, amusement parks, family vacations. Enjoy spending time together!

- Leave notes for your child, for example, in a lunchbox, under a pillow, on the refrigerator door, and encourage writing back.

- Write letters, shopping lists, invitations, things-to-do lists, and more together.

- Help your child find a penpal.

- Keep a diary, journal, or log and share with your child. Think about having everyone write and draw in a family journal when on a holiday together or at the cottage.

BLM P-95 Figure 12.10 *Sample letter to parents re: home-initiated activities*

Dear Parents,

Here are some tips for helping your young child with reading. I hope you find them useful.

- Read to your child as often as you can.

- Talk about the cover, title, author, and illustrator. Predict what the story might be about.

- Draw attention to the illustrations when reading to your child.

- Make connections, telling your child what you are reminded of. Ask a few *why* questions as you read.

- Encourage your child to choose the books you read together and help your child to tell the story from the pictures in the book.

BLM P-96 Figure 12.11 *Sample letter to parents re: helping young children with reading*

Dear Parents,

Here are some helpful hints on how you can help your child with reading. I hope you find them useful.

- Continue to read to your child every day. Vary the type of books read, for example, humorous stories, jokes/riddles, short stories, poems, chapter books, newspapers, magazines, recipes, and puzzle books.

- Encourage your child to go to the local library regularly, continue to visit bookstores together, and use the Internet to find information.

- Emphasize with your child the importance of *making sense* when they read. Encourage them to take risks and "have-a-go" at a word.

- De-emphasize the need to get 100 percent accuracy and try strategies such as reading ahead, rereading, looking at the word parts, and sounding out the word.

- Accept your child's efforts with praise and concentrate on all the things he/she does right, not on any errors.

- If your child makes a mistake when he/she is reading aloud, allow time for self-correction. If the mistake makes sense, ignore it.

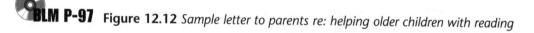

BLM P-97 **Figure 12.12** *Sample letter to parents re: helping older children with reading*

Source: Figures 12.11 and 12.12 are adapted from *Parents as Partners: Helping Your Child's Literacy and Language Development*, part of the *First Steps* series developed by the Education Department of Western Australia. Distributed in Canada by Pearson Education Canada Inc.

✦ Provide opportunities for parents to take part in school or classroom events. For example, parents may be able to help supervise class trips; listen to children read; type student stories; help with the editing and publishing of students' writing; present topics about which they know a lot; answer interview questions about their occupations, experiences, and interests; organize fun fairs, fundraising events, and conferences for young authors; participate in the work of the School Council or parent teacher association; and act as parent volunteers in the classroom and library.

✦ Actively enlist the help of your parents to work in your classroom or school as regular volunteers. At a curriculum night, community event, or Open House, post on a chart, board, or door specific ways parents can help in your classroom. Invite them to sign up, and at the same time, ask them to indicate the times they are available or send home a letter inviting parents to work as volunteers in your classroom. (See Figure 12.13.)

Dear Parents,

Would you be interested in volunteering in my classroom? If yes, please indicate the days you may be available and the time of day that would best suit you. Also, be sure to let me know the types of activities you might be interested in doing. Please note that you may need to participate in some training sessions to prepare you for this role. If you are interested, I encourage you to complete the form below and return it to me at your earliest convenience.

Sincerely,

Mrs. Schwartz

Mrs. Schwartz

- -

Yes, I am interested in volunteering in the classroom.

Name: _____

Phone Number: _____

Days Available: _____

Time of Day: _____

Type of Activities: _____

BLM P-98 **Figure 12.13** *Sample letter to parents re: asking for volunteers*

> **NOTE:** *You may also find it an asset to encourage others in your school community to become involved in your classroom or school. Caregivers, seniors, older students from neighbouring schools, and business community members may have something to contribute.*

> ✦ Follow up later with another letter or phone call finalizing the times, list of responsibilities, and expectations.

> ✦ Ensure that you provide your volunteers with a timeline for their involvement, perhaps a month, and check with them at intervals to see how they are enjoying their work. Give them options and, if you can, rotate the tasks to create interest.

> ✦ Ensure that you plan ahead so volunteers always have something to do in your classroom. Volunteers need to feel useful and valued when they give their time.

> **NOTE:** *Before volunteers begin working in your classroom or school, hold an input session to encourage them to share their strengths, interests, and talents and to allow you to clarify expectations and provide training in specific areas, such as computers and reading.*

- ✦ Encourage your volunteers to ask questions if they are unsure about what you are asking them to do.

- ✦ Ensure that your volunteers are aware that what they do and learn about other students and teachers in the school and in your classroom is strictly confidential. A letter such as the following would be useful in clarifying expectations and the seriousness of the confidentiality issue. It is often best if the letter is signed by the principal and seen as part of school policy. See Figure 12.14.

Dear Volunteer,

Once you begin to work in a school setting, you will have access to knowledge about children's behaviour patterns, academic ability, emotional maturity, and relationships with others. In some cases, information of this nature is imparted in order that you might work more effectively with an individual child. In other cases, it is simply acquired in the course of frequent contact in the school. You, as a school volunteer, are also in a position to know more about staff members than most parents. However, it is essential that you recognize the confidential nature of any such information. Under no circumstances should such knowledge or opinions be shared in the community or with anyone who has no legitimate need to know. Similarly, care must be taken to refrain from expressing comments harmful to the reputation of a pupil or professional. If any questions or concerns develop, first approach the staff member involved, and then, if necessary, go to the principal. A volunteer has every right to expect that his or her participation will be treated with the same confidentiality and respect.

Thank you for your time, interest, and participation as a volunteer in our school.

Sincerely,

Susan Schwartz

Susan Schwartz

BLM P-99 **Figure 12.14** *Sample letter to volunteers re: confidentiality*

- ✦ Ensure that your volunteers are aware of the school code of behaviour, consequences for inappropriate behaviour, and expectations for their role. The following letter, Figure 12.15, is useful as clarification. You may also need to make sure that your volunteers have a copy of the school or district code of behaviour. (See Chapter 4, Classroom Atmosphere.)

Dear Volunteer,

Classroom teachers are responsible for establishing and maintaining classroom routines. If, in your role as a volunteer, you encounter any situation requiring discipline, please refer it to one of us.

When dealing with inappropriate behaviour by students in our classroom and school, the focus is always on providing logical consequences (versus punishments), encouraging students to take responsibility for their own actions, and creating opportunities for growth and learning.

As a volunteer, you need to be aware of our Student Code of Behaviour and the consequences for any inappropriate behaviour.

We hope that, with a better understanding of our goals for student discipline, you will find working in our classroom a positive experience.

Sincerely,

Mrs. Schwartz   Mrs. Pollishuke

Mrs. Schwartz and Mrs. Pollishuke

BLM P-100 **Figure 12.15** *Sample letter to volunteers re: discipline.*

BLM P-101 *See BLM P-101 information for volunteers re: fire drills and emergency procedures.*

✦ Provide information to your volunteers about the developmental characteristics of children, multiple intelligences, and theories about how children learn. Figures 12.16, 12.17, and 12.18 provide a quick summary of each and may prove useful.

DEVELOPMENTAL CHARACTERISTICS OF CHILDREN

As a volunteer, you will find that a knowledge of the developmental characteristics of children can provide you with greater understandings as you interact with students of different ages.

CHILDREN AGES 5–7
(SK to Grade 2)

- starting to develop small muscle and eye-hand coordination (cutting and pasting)

- possess a high energy level (unable to sit still for long)

- learning physical skills that will let them play games (tossing a ball)

- learning to recognize words

- memory is developing

- enjoy telling stories

- beginning to make judgments and decisions

- beginning to accept that rules apply, but do not yet understand the underlying principles

- subject to extreme expressions of emotions

- learning to control aggression

- believe adult approval is very important

- learning to share and take turns

- have frequent but short-lived arguments with peers

CHILDREN AGES 8–10
(Grades 3 to 5)

- possess high energy level (need lots of physical activity)

- able to look after personal hygiene

- show great variety in reading levels

- like to talk and discuss

- understand money and how to make change

- developing logical thinking (rules and consequences)

- experimenting with abstract words (slang common)

- becoming independent

- wanting to belong or be with others

- sensitive to criticism and ridicule

- demonstrating heightened competitiveness

- interested in hobbies

CHILDREN AGES 11–14
(Grades 6 to 9)

- subject to growth spurts (awkward times, clumsiness)

- increasing in strength

- developing refined physical skills (sports)

- beginning puberty

- capable of thinking independently and critically

- beginning to question rules and authority

- showing some under-standing of ethics (honesty, justice)

- prone to a lack of self-confidence

- finding peer acceptance important

- prone to loud, boisterous behaviour

- showing interest in the opposite sex

Source: Adapted from *Observing Children*, published by the Toronto Board of Education

BLM P-102 **Figure 12.16** *Information for volunteers re: developmental characteristics of children*

AN INTRODUCTION TO MULTIPLE INTELLIGENCES

Harvard psychologist Howard Gardner, in his book *Frames of Mind*, concludes that all individuals possess distinct intelligences, though one or more may be stronger than others. This tendency towards greater strengths in certain types of intelligences over others can make a difference in many areas of our lives: from preferred learning styles, to the things that interest us both in school and out, to our career choices later in life. Here's how to recognize the characteristics of each form of intelligence.

1. THE LINGUISTIC LEARNER:
"The Word Player"

- loves to read books, write, and tell stories
- is good at memorizing names, places, dates, and trivia information
- learns best by saying, hearing, and seeing words

2. THE LOGICAL-MATHEMATICAL LEARNER:
"The Questioner"

- likes to do experiments, figure things out, work with numbers, ask questions, and explore patterns and relationships
- is good at math, reasoning, logic, and problem solving
- learns best by categorizing, classifying, and working with abstract patterns/relationships

3. THE SPATIAL LEARNER:
"The Visualizer"

- likes to draw, build, design, and create things, look at pictures/slides, watch movies, play with machines
- is good at imagining things, sensing changes, doing mazes/puzzles, and reading maps and charts
- learns best by visualizing, dreaming, using the mind's eye, working with colours/pictures

4. THE MUSICAL LEARNER:
"The Music Lover"

- likes to sing, hum tunes, listen to music, play an instrument, respond to music
- is good at picking up sounds, remembering melodies, noticing pitches/rhythms, keeping time
- learns best by rhythm, melody, music

5. THE BODILY/KINESTHETIC LEARNER:
"The Mover"

- likes to move around, touch, and use body language
- is good at physical activities (sports, dance, acting), and crafts
- learns best by touching, moving, interacting with space, processing knowledge through body sensations

6. THE INTERPERSONAL LEARNER:
"The Socializer"

- likes to have lots of friends, talk to people, join groups
- is good at understanding people, leading others, organizing, communicating, manipulating, and mediating conflicts
- learns best by sharing, comparing, relating, cooperating, and interviewing

7. THE INTRAPERSONAL LEARNER:
"The Individual"

- likes to work alone, pursue own interests
- is good at understanding self, focusing inward on feelings/dreams, following instincts, pursuing interests/goals, being original
- learns best by working alone, doing individualized projects, self-pacing instruction, having own space

8. THE NATURALIST LEARNER:
"The Nature Lover"

- likes to be outdoors, shows an interest in nature (plants and animals)
- is good at scientific exploration in the outdoors
- learns best by being outdoors, exploring, and experimenting

BLM P-103   **Figure 12.17** *Information for volunteers re: multiple intelligences*

HOW CHILDREN LEARN

Dr. Brian Cambourne, in *The Whole Story*, outlines seven conditions that must be evident in order for children to learn.

Immersion: to be immersed in a wide variety and number of resources, concrete materials, books, and experiences

Demonstrations: to be exposed to direct teaching, seeing concrete examples, instructing, modelling

Expectations: to be provided with clear, appropriate expectations and messages; to have consistency

Responsibility: to be able to make choices, have ownership, show responsibility

Approximations: to experiment, guess, become risk takers

Practice: to use, reinforce, and have adequate time on task

Feedback: to receive constructive support and feedback from others

Keeping in mind the above conditions of learning, how can you, as a volunteer, reinforce students' learning? Here are some of the ways:

- *Immerse* the students in a book or experience.

- Provide *demonstrations* and model enthusiasm.

- Have clear *expectations* and be consistent.

- Allow the students to make choices and be *responsible*.

- Encourage the students to *approximate*, guess, become risk takers. Reinforce the idea that "it's okay to make a mistake — we learn from and through our mistakes."

- Help the students *practise* and encourage them to stay on task.

- Provide positive *feedback* in any one-on-one situation and celebrate the learning that occurs.

BLM P-104 **Figure 12.18** *Information for volunteers re: how children learn*

✦ Give your volunteers a greater understanding of what they will see while in your classroom, in terms of groupings and learning centres. The following fact sheet, Figure 12.19, may prove helpful.

CLASSROOM GROUPINGS

As a volunteer, you may find that an understanding of classroom groupings will serve you well as you see students and teachers engaged in a variety of activities and experiences in the classroom or school.

- *Large-group experiences with a teacher*
  Students may participate in read-aloud experiences, discussions, input sessions, direct instruction, chanting, choral reading, dramatic reading, and singing.

- *Small-group experiences with a teacher, volunteer, or other students*
  In these learning experiences, students practise cooperating, working together in active/interactive ways. They are encouraged to become problem solvers, decision makers, and independent workers. The teacher may work with one group or an individual, or may be seen circulating among the many groups, asking questions, encouraging, and facilitating the learning.

  Students may say they are doing "centres," or "tubs." These usually include a variety of small-group tasks about a specific theme or unit of study (e.g., fairy tales, the environment, place value). Students may use tracking sheets which show when and what they have accomplished and help them move from one task to another. These tracking sheets often include self-assessments where students think about how well they have done or how well they have worked with others on a certain task.

- *Individual students*
  Students may be seen working one-on-one with a teacher or volunteer, or working independently without assistance.

A balance of large-group, small-group, and individual learning experiences is important in every program across the grade levels.

BLM P-105   **Figure 12.19** *Information for volunteers re: classroom groupings*

✦ Provide some training for your volunteers. For example, you may want to do so before students and volunteers engage in paired reading. Figure 12.20 may prove helpful in this instance.

PAIRED READING GUIDE

The following procedure will provide you with a guide to follow when reading one-on-one with a student. The focus of this interaction is for you and the student to have an enjoyable experience reading together. We hope that the student will develop a positive attitude towards reading, as well as reinforce and extend comprehension and oral language skills. We encourage you to have as natural a conversation as possible about the text. Please refrain from correcting the student if it seems that he/she understands the meaning of the passage.

BEFORE YOU READ

Retell • Talk about the title, author, illustrator, picture, diagrams, characters, setting...

Relate • Make connections: "This reminds me of...;" "This makes me think of...."

Reflect • Predict what will happen.

• Ask questions: "I wonder why...?"

STRATEGIES TO USE WHILE READING TOGETHER

• Listen and stop to make comments about the content of the reading.

Retell • "I notice that..."

Relate • "This reminds me of..."; "This makes me think of..."

Reflect • "I wonder why..."; "What will happen next?"

• Encourage the child to talk about the reading.

• Point and follow along (or encourage the child to follow along with his/her finger).

• When the student cannot read a word, encourage him/her to use a variety of reading strategies :

  - skip the word
  - look at the pictures or diagrams
  - think about what went before and what might happen next
  - read ahead
  - reread
  - sound out using phonics
  - look at the root words or word parts
  - guess

• When the student is still unable to read the word, then give the word.

• If you have given the word a number of times, this material may be too difficult. Try the following:

  - read together with the student
  - read and the student reads the last word of each sentence
  - read one line and the student reads the next
  - read the first paragraph, poem, or line, and the student reads the same again: "Repeat after me."

DURING/AFTER THE READING

RETELL:	RELATE:	REFLECT:
This is about...	This reminds me of...	I wonder if...?
I notice that...	This makes me think of...	I wonder why...?
I especially like...	This makes me feel...	Now I understand...

Source: *Retelling, Relating, Reflecting: Beyond the 3R's*, by Susan Schwartz and Maxine Bone (Irwin Publishing).

BLM P-106 **Figure 12.20** *Information for volunteers re: paired reading guide*

- ✦ Ensure that you show your parents and other volunteers that they are appreciated. Thank them for their contributions to your program or school. Possible appreciation events include special breakfasts, lunches, or after-school barbecues; thank-you gatherings involving singing, reciting poems, and sharing pictures or cards made by your students for the volunteers; or the presentation of a book for the library in honour of the volunteers.

Establishing and maintaining strong partnerships with parents will ensure that they feel valued and involved in their children's educational life and knowledgeable about the school environment, your program, and their children's progress. A sincere commitment to parental involvement can only benefit you and your students as parents become important participants in the learning process.

Final Thoughts: "Your Mountain Is Waiting"

Teaching is one of the most noble and rewarding professions. It allows you to make a significant impact on the lives of others as you contribute to the future generation by sharing your skill and knowledge. When you interact with students daily, you are giving of yourself in innumerable ways. Your enthusiasm, your positive attitude, and your passion for learning will influence each and every student with whom you will come into contact. As you share yourself with the learners in your care, they, too, will experience that exhilaration, that optimism, and that love of learning. Nothing quite compares to seeing a small child's face light up upon first realizing that the squiggles on the page have meaning or when a student cries out, "Aha, now I understand!" When this happens, you will know for sure that you are making a difference in the lives of children!

As a beginning teacher, you need to keep these thoughts in mind because entering the teaching profession can be a formidable undertaking. You have so many new things to consider, so many plans to make, and so many processes to master that you may feel overwhelmed. Careful planning will set your mind at ease and ensure that you have everything you need to have. It will allow you to gracefully begin that wonderful professional journey.

Often, teachers new to the profession, as well as experienced teachers new to a school, ask, "What do I do first? Where should I begin?" These can be daunting questions, but ones that require clear and concise answers. Each chapter in this book is intended to assist you in answering those questions. As you set up your first classroom, we hope you will use the ideas in many of the chapters to establish the learning environment and classroom atmosphere and to plan a stimulating program for your students. We believe that all of the concepts noted in the various chapters will work together to help you create your very own dynamic classroom. However, those two short questions may still remain: "What do I do first? Where should I begin?" We hope that the checklist in Appendix 1, Beginning Teacher's Checklist, will help you address these particular concerns. Successful teachers grow in their effectiveness throughout their careers.

Just as planning a program for your students helps you to chart their course, considering your own needs helps you to succeed in a seemingly challenging situation. We encourage you to strive for balance in your life, as you juggle the needs of your students, parents, and community; the requirements of your school, district, and board; and your desire for fulfillment in your personal life. Our best advice is to look to others for support. A good mentor, coach, or administrator can help you to reflect on your growth as an educator and set realistic goals, organize your professional priorities, and establish balance between your personal and professional life.

We encourage you to take a deep breath, gather all the energy and reserve you have, and jump in! Never again in your professional career will you experience a year like your first year of teaching, where everything that you do, say, and feel will be experienced for the first time. And never again will you experience the same apprehension, exhilaration, and wonderment as you will with your first class!

As Dr. Seuss once said:

...
You're off to Great Places!
Today is your day!
Your mountain is waiting.
So... get on your way!

Source: *Oh, the Places You'll Go!* (New York: Random House, 1990)

You are on your way to start a great journey.

Appendix 1:
Beginning Teacher's Checklist

Once you are hired...

- ❑ Celebrate! Call all the people you care about!

- ❑ Check out the district or school Web site if available.

- ❑ Find out about your new school, the neighbouring schools, the neighbourhood, and its clientele.

- ❑ Obtain a map of the school and surrounding area.

- ❑ Drive or walk through the neighbourhood and note the housing, stores, restaurants, post office, bank, malls, community centre, parks, etc.

- ❑ Visit the school, and have someone take you on a guided tour, if possible.

- ❑ Meet all the staff in your school:
    - ☐ the teachers in your grade/division/team
    - ☐ secretaries
    - ☐ custodial staff
    - ☐ librarian
    - ☐ Special Education teacher
    - ☐ ESL teacher
    - ☐ guidance teacher
    - ☐ classroom assistants
    - ☐ child-care staff, if applicable

- ❑ Find out about the resource staff who are in the district or at the school board and how you can access them.

❑ Collect resource documents and materials you will need:

  ❑ Ministry or state curriculum documents and guidelines
  ❑ district policy statements and documents
  ❑ commercial resources, guidelines, and texts available in the school

❑ Obtain a copy of the following and review them:

  ❑ school handbook
  ❑ school and district mission statement
  ❑ fire drill and emergency procedures
  ❑ occasional teacher procedures
  ❑ district and/or school code of behaviour (discipline, procedures for office support)
  ❑ district and/or school homework policy
  ❑ schedules for yard duty, gym, music, French, library, computer lab, preparation time
  ❑ list of school committees
  ❑ list of co-curricular responsibilities
  ❑ confidential staff phone number list
  ❑ useful board phone numbers
  ❑ parent-teacher groups or School Council information

❑ Find out the policy and procedures for your school:

  ❑ school hours
  ❑ significant dates such as holidays, reporting, and professional development days
  ❑ opening day procedures
  ❑ school entry and dismissal routines
  ❑ bussing procedures
  ❑ early dismissal and late arrivals
  ❑ recess and yard duty schedule and procedures
  ❑ lunch schedule and procedures
  ❑ staff meeting schedule and procedures
  ❑ assembly procedures
  ❑ students staying after school
  ❑ student movement in the halls
  ❑ assistance from the office for emergencies, illness, or discipline concerns

- ☐ Special Education and remedial or support procedures
- ☐ safety patrol
- ☐ AV and technology equipment distribution and procedures
- ☐ teacher and student dress code

❑ Research and create a list of acronyms that are used in your district or school, or in education generally. For example: I.P.R.C. (Identification Placement Review Committee), L.D. (Learning Disabilities), S.O. (Supervisory Officer)

❑ Find out your legal responsibilities and the rules, regulations, and procedures for
- ☐ supervision
- ☐ Special Education
- ☐ student records and official files
- ☐ student attendance registers
- ☐ report cards and reporting to parents

❑ Find out the procedures for out-of-classroom excursions or field trips. (Refer to Chapter 9, Out-of-Classroom Excursions.) Consider the following:
- ☐ permission forms
- ☐ ordering busses or other forms of transportation
- ☐ supervision

❑ Find out if there are any required field trips for your specific grade level.

❑ Find out about the budgeting procedures for your school:
- ☐ Do you have a specific amount to spend for your classroom budget?
- ☐ How much can you allocate for consumables, texts, petty cash?
- ☐ Does the cost of photocopying and paper come out of your total classroom budget?
- ☐ Do you order materials as part of a grade team, division, or school?
- ☐ Do you store your own stock, or is there a general school stockroom?
- ☐ How do you order books and other resources?

❑ Find out how to order films, videos, and software, and how to borrow a digital camera or video camera, if available.

- ❏ Find out if there is an audiovisual or computer technician available for assistance in your school or district.

- ❏ Find out about available storage areas, stockrooms, and meeting rooms.

- ❏ Locate important areas and equipment in the school:
  - ☐ photocopier(s)
  - ☐ telephone for confidential phone calls
  - ☐ gym equipment

Once you know your teaching assignment and have access to your classroom...

- ❏ Clarify what subjects you are required to teach and if there are any rotary requirements.

- ❏ Find out what preparation time you might have, and if you are required to provide preparation time for others.

- ❏ Obtain keys to your classroom, and any other keys for cupboards, desks, or other rooms to which you may need access.

- ❏ Survey your classroom and note the entrances, windows, chalkboards, bulletin boards, electrical outlets, sink, and security measures in place.

- ❏ Determine what you will need in terms of materials, resources, and equipment.

- ❏ Plan your classroom environment. (Refer to Chapter 2, The Physical Set-up of the Classroom.)

- ❏ Decide on a tentative initial seating arrangement for your students.

- ❏ Gather any technological equipment you will need for your classroom:
  - ☐ an overhead projector
  - ☐ a tape recorder and/or CD player
  - ☐ headphones and listening bar
  - ☐ computers

❏ Find out how you can access other equipment and if there are procedures for use. This equipment might include a

- ☐ television
- ☐ VCR
- ☐ camera
- ☐ video camera
- ☐ digital camera

❏ Try out any technological equipment you plan to use. Be sure you know how to use it before you need it.

❏ Collect and organize some materials and resources you will need to begin. (Refer to Chapter 7, Literacy and Language Learning.) Include the following:

- ☐ picture books, novels, non-fiction, magazines
- ☐ books for a classroom library
- ☐ textbooks at your grade level
- ☐ dictionaries, atlases, thesauruses
- ☐ globes, maps, atlases
- ☐ mathematics manipulatives, science and technology equipment
- ☐ consumables, such as paper, pencils, markers, notebooks, and art supplies

❏ Order any other supplies you will need for September as early as possible. You might need to meet with other teachers at your grade or division level to put in a group order.

❏ Begin to collect found materials for classroom use. Visit garage sales.

❏ Create a prioritized wish list. Peruse company catalogues for wish list materials and keep all ordering information. It is always a good idea to have a wish list available in case you are asked what you need but given a short timeline for ordering materials.

❏ Decide on routines and procedures for your class:

- ☐ washroom
- ☐ entry and dismissal
- ☐ pencil sharpening
- ☐ lost supplies
- ☐ toys and personal items (cards, games) brought to school

- ☐ library visits, book exchange
- ☐ dress for gym class
- ☐ learning centres
- ☐ computers
- ☐ monitors (door, pencil sharpening, boards, distribution of materials)

☐ Cover your bulletin boards, and decide how you will highlight your door and display areas. (Refer to Chapter 2, The Physical Set-up of the Classroom.)

☐ Set up your own filing system.

Once you have your class list...

☐ Find out about the students in your class by

- ☐ looking at student records and previous work files, if available
- ☐ talking to previous teachers
- ☐ talking to administrators and resource teachers

☐ Note important information about your students such as

- ☐ special needs
- ☐ medical information
- ☐ custody concerns
- ☐ total numbers and the gender balance in your class
- ☐ how your students travel to and from school

☐ Find out the procedures to use for recording attendance.

Once you are ready to begin planning your program...

☐ Find out the dates of any significant school events including

- ☐ curriculum nights
- ☐ open houses
- ☐ concerts
- ☐ play day

☐ Establish a long-range plan for the year in collaboration with teaching partners if possible. (Refer to Chapter 5, Planning an Integrated Curriculum.)

- ❑ Set up an initial timetable for the first few weeks. (Refer to Chapter 3, Timetabling.)

- ❑ Plan your first week of school and your first day in detail, being sure to include some "getting-to-know-you" tasks such as are outlined in Chapter 4, Classroom Atmosphere.

- ❑ Plan lessons in which you can incorporate the teaching of routines, safety, and respect.

- ❑ Decide on the daily routines that will be followed.

- ❑ Plan your first unit in detail.

- ❑ Meet with the librarian and ask for help in collecting additional resources for your unit.

- ❑ Plan how you will assess, evaluate, monitor, and track student work. (Refer to Chapter 11, Assessing, Evaluating, and Reporting.)

- ❑ Set priorities, create a "to-do" or "must-do" list, and check off tasks as they are completed.

- ❑ Find out about volunteers (parents, older students, seniors), the procedures for inviting them into your classroom, and the tasks you might want them to do. (Refer to Chapter 12, Partnerships with Parents.)

- ❑ Find out what an occasional teacher package should include and be prepared to forward one to the office.

Once you begin setting goals for your professional growth...

- ❑ Create a personal time management schedule.

- ❑ Consider how you might contribute to the total school environment. Be sure to set realistic expectations for your time and energy in your first year of teaching.

- ❑ Find out if your district or school has a special support program for new teachers. If a formal method of mentoring has not been set up, find your own mentor. This should be someone who

  - ❑ has the same or a similar teaching assignment, if possible
  - ❑ has a classroom that is close to yours, if possible

- ☐ will answer your questions no matter how small
- ☐ will support you when the going gets rough
- ☐ knows their way around the school and board
- ☐ is trustworthy and supportive

☐ Let your mentor and principal know your areas of interest for professional growth.

☐ Continue to read professionally and dialogue with others. Find out if your school has professional resources available.

☐ Consider attending workshops and conferences, and taking additional qualification courses to further your professional growth.

☐ Establish and continue to maintain a professional portfolio highlighting your accomplishments, successes, and learnings.

☐ Build in social and family time, and continue to work at balancing your personal and professional life.

Wishing you all the best in your career as an educator!

Appendix 2:
Sample Comments for Report Card Writing

Work Habits/General Comments

- is gaining steadily in self-confidence
- aspires to higher levels of sophistication
- produces high calibre work
- responds well to reassurances and constructive criticisms
- derives enjoyment from
- continues to apply himself/herself to
- shows increased self-confidence in
- enjoys a challenge in
- rises to the challenges presented
- contributes many original ideas
- displays creativity and imagination in
- her/his enthusiasm is a noteworthy attribute
- her/his leadership qualities are an asset
- is developing good work habits both in directed and independent situations
- functions extremely well in group situations
- is aware of the importance of
- is aware of the benefits of
- is quick to grasp new ideas
- assumes a responsible approach to
- participates well in
- consistently demonstrates an ability to
- demonstrates an understanding of
- has a thorough understanding of
- an encouraging sign lately has been

- is improving in his/her ability to
- it would be most beneficial for _____ to
- has not yet realized his/her potential in
- has developed some better work habits but is not always consistent in their application
- a more consistent effort is necessary
- at times, forgets the importance of good independent work habits
- needs encouragement and reinforcement in
- is easily discouraged
- is experiencing difficulty in working in group situations
- is slow to begin assignments
- needs encouragement to complete assignments
- is less comfortable in creative situations
- rarely becomes voluntarily involved in discussions
- is easily distracted
- needs many reminders to stay on task and not disturb others around him/her
- is being encouraged to pay close attention to instructions
- is working on
- is being encouraged to put more thought and effort into his/her daily assignments

Language

- is aware of the benefits of independent reading
- chooses books to look at and practises reading behaviours (turns pages, talks about the pictures, tells a story)
- readily/frequently chooses reading as an independent activity
- participates well in shared reading experiences
- enjoys reading orally
- oral reading displays fluency and good expression
- selects stories by author
- is able to identify beginning, middle, and end of stories read
- is able to retell events in sequence
- expresses personal opinions about what is read
- demonstrates some recall of letter names and rhyming patterns
- is developing a good sight vocabulary
- makes use of phonetic skills and picture clues

- is beginning to use a variety of strategies to read unfamiliar words or passages
- can use all cueing systems when faced with unfamiliar words or passages
- is able to identify the main idea
- is able to identify the main idea and points out some supporting detail
- is able to set a purpose for his/her reading
- is able to predict and infer
- is able to reread, predict, and read on to make sense of what she/he has read
- is able to extract information and meaning from what she/he reads
- understands the elements of story, including plot, characterization, setting
- uses appropriate strategies when reading non-fiction, such as reading subheadings, looking for key ideas, adjusting speed of reading
- is able to decode words but is experiencing some difficulty in understanding the meaning of passages
- does not readily choose reading as an independent activity
- is beginning to write a few letters and words about pictures and drawings
- enjoys choosing own topics for story writing
- bases writing on personal experiences
- enjoys writing in a variety of formats, including stories, poems, directions
- uses familiar words in her/his writing
- is beginning to use correct punctuation and spelling in writing
- is able to revise (add or change ideas) a piece of writing
- has a good awareness of audience
- is able to share writing with a partner and accepts feedback well
- is able to organize his/her thoughts in a clear and concise manner
- shows clarity of thought in written work
- is beginning to write using complete sentences and paragraphs
- paragraphs are organized and include main idea and supporting details
- spelling of familiar words is accurate but still has difficulty with unfamiliar words
- uses humour in stories written
- is able to use an editing checklist to proofread his/her writing
- creative attempts at writing are enjoyable

- enjoys taking written work to published form
- shows pride in his/her published efforts
- needs encouragement and reassurance in choosing own topics for story writing
- has a great many stories to tell but has difficulty putting them into written form
- contributions to oral discussions are worthwhile and well expressed
- can originate ideas which he/she readily shares with others
- shows confidence in oral presentations
- participates enthusiastically in oral presentations, such as plays, puppet shows, concerts
- responds appropriately during class discussions
- shares experiences and opinions in small-group settings
- listens carefully and is considerate of others
- is encouraged to take turns when speaking and not interrupt the speaker
- oral contributions are often unrelated to the topic being discussed
- needs many reminders to listen carefully while others are speaking
- does not readily participate in group discussions
- needs to listen more carefully and ask appropriate questions

Mathematics

- grasps mathematical concepts easily
- has a good grasp of the concepts in math this term, including
- enjoys a challenge in this area
- applies the operations she/he has learned in solving problems
- is competent in reasoning things out to a logical conclusion
- has difficulty grasping new concepts
- displays uncertainty when faced with new concepts, but overcomes it with time and encouragement
- needs much reinforcement in grasping new concepts
- has the ability to retain information and recall it when needed
- uses mathematical language appropriately
- illustrates new learning in a variety of ways
- is working at improving the speed and accuracy of her/his number work
- can represent numbers in pictures

- reads and prints numbers to
- is able to group numbers
- is able to count by 2s/5s/10s
- is able to easily add and subtract two-digit numbers
- is able to add three-digit numbers with regrouping
- does not fully understand the relationship between addition and multiplication
- understands the relationship between addition and subtraction
- understands the relationship between division and multiplication
- has a good grasp of estimation strategies
- can round off numbers to nearest 100s/10s
- is able to represent answers in numbers, words, and pictures
- uses fractions, integers, and decimals with confidence
- is able to apply operations using fractions/integers/decimals
- understands and can apply percentages accurately
- is able to predict using probability and record results accurately
- can create and extend patterns
- is able to identify, create, and extend patterns using concrete materials and numbers
- is able to estimate, measure, and record using everyday materials such as paperclips
- applies knowledge of number and measurement to real-life situations
- has a sound understanding of quantity and measurement
- understands length, width, height, and depth
- applies measurement skills when working with length, time, money
- is able to tell time to the hour/minute/second
- understands concepts of area, perimeter, circumference, and volume
- is able to describe clearly steps taken to solve a problem
- is able to explain her/his thinking when solving problems
- is able to recognize and name solid shapes
- can describe and name two- and three-dimensional objects
- shows good understanding of geometric concepts
- understands flips, slides, and turns
- has a thorough understanding of transformational geometry
- is able to use a ruler to successfully construct angles and line segments
- has difficulty understanding the relationship between units of time
- experiences difficulties in selecting appropriate problem-solving strategies

Social Studies

- demonstrates a good background knowledge in
- has a good understanding of
- is able to conduct investigations into
- is able to observe and make predictions
- is able to recognize
- is able to compare and contrast
- is able to show similarities and differences in
- asks simple questions
- participates enthusiastically in all tasks
- participates well in all group investigations
- has satisfactorily completed all of the assigned tasks for our unit on
- is able to locate information
- uses a variety of methods to gather information
- is able to organize information clearly
- is to be commended for his/her efforts in our study of
- is very aware and interested in
- is curious and observes the world around him/her
- discusses intelligently
- uses charts, maps, and diagrams to
- needs encouragement to complete assignments in
- experiences difficulty in organizing information
- needed assistance to
- did not fully understand the significance of

Science

- uses equipment and tools appropriately, for example, microscope, audiovisual materials
- selects appropriate tools
- demonstrates an awareness of
- is able to compare and contrast
- is able to show similarities and differences in
- asks simple questions
- is able to observe and make predictions
- participates enthusiastically in all tasks
- participates well in all group investigations

- is aware of the characteristics of
- is able to design and construct
- is able to clearly explain and describe
- has a good understanding of
- has satisfactorily completed all of the assigned tasks for our unit on
- is to be commended for his/her efforts in our study of
- is very aware and interested in
- is curious and observes the world around him/her
- discusses intelligently
- needs encouragement to complete assignments in
- experiences some difficulty when asked to use equipment for
- needs to exhibit more care when working with equipment
- experiences difficulty in organizing information
- needs to develop better recording skills

The Arts

- enjoys participating in all areas of the arts
- expresses feelings and thoughts through artistic attempts
- artwork shows good small-muscle coordination
- makes good choices in use of materials
- uses texture/shape/colour for
- experiments with many different materials
- is able to produce detailed drawings and paintings
- uses appropriate art vocabulary to describe
- pays attention to detail
- is encouraged to put more thought into her/his artistic endeavours
- puts a minimum amount of effort into his/her artistic work
- is aware of body, space, and time
- uses a wide variety of materials in creative attempts
- demonstrates a particular flare for dramatics
- is able to interpret
- is able to demonstrate, through role playing, an understanding of character
- is able to use tableaux, role-play, and movement to express ideas/ feelings
- uses appropriate dramatic vocabulary

- requires encouragement to participate fully in dramatic/dance activities
- sings with enthusiasm
- enjoys musical activities
- is able to keep a steady beat
- is able to distinguish between
- is able to identify
- experiments with different sounds to
- shows an awareness of rhythm and beat in musical tasks
- can correctly use…
- describes her/his response using appropriate musical terms such as
- needs to listen more carefully and consistently
- shows originality and creativity in

Health and Physical Education

- participates fully/enthusiastically in all aspects of our gym program
- demonstrates good large-muscle coordination
- is flexible and agile
- demonstrates flexibility, skill, and coordination
- is well coordinated
- incorporates most movement skills into
- is able to work cooperatively with a partner
- is able to work cooperatively with a small group
- follows instructions well and plays safely
- uses equipment with skill and coordination
- follows the rules and listens attentively to instructions
- participated actively and enthusiastically in
- strives to improve in athletic performance
- requires continued encouragement to cooperate in gym class
- has some difficulty with flexibility and coordination
- must remember to bring gym clothes every day

Appendix 3: Favourite Children's Literature

Classroom Atmosphere

Self-concept

Cannon, Janell. 1997. *Verdi*. San Diego, CA: Harcourt Brace.

Castle, Caroline. 2000. *For every child: UNICEF — the rights of the child in words and pictures*. London, UK: Hutchinson Children's Books.

Cazet, Denys. 1987. *Frosted glass*. New York: Bradbury Press.

Cohen, Miriam. 1986. *No good in art*. New York: Bantam Doubleday Dell.

DePaola, Tomie. 1990. *The art lesson*. New York: G.P. Putnam's Sons.

Howe, James. 1987. *I wish I were a butterfly*. San Diego, CA: Harcourt Brace Jovanovich.

Moss, Thylias. 1993. *I want to be…* New York: Dial Books for Young Readers.

Shannon, David. 1998. *A bad case of stripes*. New York: The Blue Sky Press.

Wyeth, Sharon Dennis. 1998. *Something beautiful*. New York: Bantam Doubleday Dell.

Bullying and Relationships

Agassi, Martine. 2000. *Hands are not for hitting*. New York: Free Spirit.

Blume, Judy. 1984. *Pain and the great one*. New York: Simon & Schuster Children's.

Burningham, John. 2000. *John Patrick Norman McHennessy — The boy who was always late*. London, UK: Random House.

Browne, Anthony. 1991. *Willy and Hugh*. Vancouver: Douglas & McIntyre.

Cannon, Janell. 2000. *Crickwing*. San Diego, CA: Harcourt Brace.

Caple, Kathy. 1994. *The wimp*. Boston: Houghton Mifflin.

Cohen, Miriam. 1985. *Liar, Liar, pants on fire*. New York: Greenwillow Books.

Cosby, Bill. 1997. *The meanest thing to say*. New York: Scholastic.

Couric, Katie. 2000. *The brand new kid*. New York: Doubleday Random House.

Goffe, Toni. 1992. *Bully for you*. Auburn, ME: Childs Play.

Gotlib, Alan, Alice Brass, and Brenda Hall. 1997. *"B" is for bully: An innovative approach to increase awareness about bullying. Play and study guide*. Toronto, ON: Gotlib.

Henkes, Kevin. 1991. *Chrysanthemum*. New York: Greenwillow Books.

Howe, James. 1996. *Pinky and Rex and the bully*. New York: Atheneum Books for Young Readers.

Johnson, Julie. 1998. *How do I feel about: Bullies and gangs*. Brookfield, CT: Millbrook Press.

Konzak, Burt. 1994. *Noguchi the samurai*. North York, ON: Stoddart.

Lester, Helen. 1999. *Hooway for Wodney Wat*. Boston: Houghton Mifflin.

Love, Ann. 1992. *The prince who wrote a letter*. Auburn, ME: Childs Play.

Masters, Anthony. 1995. *Bullies don't hurt*. London, UK: Puffin Books.

Morgan, Nicola. 1988. *Temper, temper*. Markham, ON: Fitzhenry & Whiteside.

Nickle, John. 1999. *The ant bully*. New York: Scholastic.

Polacco, Patricia. 1994. *My rotten red-headed brother*. New York: Simon & Schuster.

Sadu, Itah. 1994. *Name calling*. Toronto, ON: Women's Press.

_____. 1993. *Christopher, please clean up your room!* Richmond Hill, ON: Scholastic.

Slater, Teddy. 1995. *Who's afraid of the big bad bully?* New York: Scholastic.

_____. 1993. *N-O spells no*. New York: Scholastic.

Stolz, Mary. 1985. *The bully of Barkham Street*. Madison, WI: Demco.

Stones, Rosemary. 1998. *No more bullying*. Essex, UK: Happy Cat Books.

Wood, Audrey. 1988. *Elbert's bad word*. San Diego, CA: Harcourt Brace Jovanovich.

Feeling Different, Seeking Peace and Friendship

Cannon, Janell. 1993. *Stellaluna*. San Diego, CA: Harcourt Brace.

Clements, Andrew. 1988. *Big Al*. New York: Picture Book Studio.

Cohn, Janice. 1995. *Christmas menorahs: How a town fought hate*. Morton Grove, IL: Albert Whitman.

Crease, Skid. 1994. *In the great meadow*. Toronto, ON: Annick Press.

Fox, Mem. 1988. *Koala Lou*. San Diego, CA: Harcourt Brace.

Geoheagen, Gareth. 1994. *Six perfectly different pigs*. Milwaukee, WI: Gareth Stevens.

Golanbock, Peter. 1990. *Teammates*. San Diego, CA: Harcourt Brace Jovanovich.

Horstman, Lisa. 1994. *Fast friends: A tail and tongue tale*. New York: Alfred A. Knopf.

Knight, Mary Burns. 1993. *Talking walls*. Kingston, ON: Quarry Press.

Lacoe, Addie. 1992. *Just not the same*. Boston: Houghton Mifflin.

Pelligrini, Nina. 1991. *Families are different*. New York: Holiday House.

Rockwell, Norman. 1997. *Willie was different: A children's story*. New York: Random House Books for Young Readers.

Scholes, K. 1989. *Peace begins with you*. San Francisco, CA: Sierra Club Books.

Usell, Martin. 1991. *Hairy Hairy*. London, UK: BBC Books.

Feeling Different in a New Land

Aliki. 1998. *Painted words, spoken memories*. New York: Greenwillow Books.

Ashley, Bernard. 1992. *Cleversticks*. London, UK: HarperCollins.

Bannatyne-Cugnet, Jo. 2000. *From far and wide: A Canadian citizenship scrapbook*. Toronto, ON: Tundra Books.

Filipovic, Zlata. 1994. *Zlata's diary: A child's life in Sarajevo*. New York: Viking Penguin.

Gray, Luis. 1997. *The long road*. Toronto, ON: Tundra Books.

Howlett, Bud. 1993. *I'm new here*. Boston: Houghton Mifflin.

Hest, Amy. 1997. *When Jessie came across the sea*. Cambridge, MA: Candlewick Press.

Levine, Ellen, and Steven Bjorkman. 1995. *I hate English*. New York: Scholastic.

McGugan, Jim. 1994. *Josepha: A prairie boy's story*. Red Deer, AB: Red Deer College Press.

Mochizuki, Ken. 1993. *Baseball saved us*. New York: Lee & Low Books.

Mollel, Tololwa M. 1990. *The orphan boy*. Don Mills, ON: Oxford University Press.

Munsch, Robert. 1995. *From far away*. Toronto, ON: Annick Press.

Oberman, Sheldon. 1994. *The always shawl*. Honesdale, PA: Boyd Mills Press.

Polacco, Patricia. 1998. *The keeping quilt*. New York: Simon & Schuster for Young Readers.

Say, Allen. 1993. *Grandfather's journey*. Boston: Houghton Mifflin.

Surat, Michelle Maria. 1983. *Angel child, dragon child*. Milwaukee: Raintree.

Uchida, Yoshiko. 1993. *The bracelet*. New York: Philomel Books.

Viorst, Judith. 1995. *Alexander, who's not (do you hear me? I mean it!) going to move*. New York: Simon & Schuster Children's.

Wallace, Ian, and Angela Wood. 1985. *The sandwich*. Toronto, ON: Kids Can Press.

Wallace, Ian. 1984. *Chin Chiang and the dragon's dance*. Toronto, ON: Douglas & McIntyre.

Willis, Jeanne. 1990. *Dr. Xargle's book of earthlings: An alien's view of earth babies*. London, UK: Red Fox.

Breaking Stereotypes

Browne, Eileen. 1993. *No problem*. Cambridge, MA: Candlewick Press.

Brott, Ardyth. 1993. *Jeremy's decision*. Don Mills, ON: Oxford University Press.

Celsi, Theresa. 1992. *The fourth little pig*. Austin, TX: Raintree Steck Vaughn.

Ernst, Lisa Campbell. 2000. *Little Red Riding Hood: A newfangled prairie tale*. New York: Aladdin Paperbacks.

Fox, Mem. 1997. *Whoever you are*. San Diego, CA: Harcourt Brace.

Munsch, Robert. 1980. *The paper bag princess*. Toronto, ON: Annick Press.

Schoop, Janice. 1986. *Boys don't knit*. Toronto, ON: Women's Press.

Zolotow, Charlotte. 1972. *William's doll*. New York: Harper & Row.

Taking Charge of Your Life

Baylor, Byrd. 1986. *I'm in charge of celebrations*. New York: Simon & Schuster Children's.

Browne, Anthony. 1990. *Changes*. London, UK: Julia MacRae Books, Division of Walker Books.

Charlip, Remy. 1993. *Fortunately*. New York: Simon & Schuster Children's.

Cooney, Barbara. 1985. *Miss Rumphius*. New York: Puffin Books.

Evans, Richard Paul. 2000. *The spyglass*. New York: Simon & Schuster Books for Young Readers.

Fernandes, Eugenie. 1999. *A difficult day*. Toronto, ON: Kids Can Press.

George, Jean Craighead. 1995. *To climb a waterfall*. New York: Philomel Books.

Munsch, Robert. 1987. *Moira's birthday*. Toronto, ON: Annick Press.

Ringgold, Faith. 1995. *My Dream of Martin Luther King*. New York: Crown.

Rylant, Cynthia. 1998. *All I see*. New York: Dutton Children's Books.

Seuss, Dr. 1990. *Oh, the places you'll go!* New York: Random House.

Stewart, Sarah. 1997. *The gardener*. New York: Farrar Straus Giroux.

Viorst, Judith. 1981. *If I were in charge of the world and other worries: Poems for children and their parents*. New York: Atheneum.

Young, Ed. 1995. *Donkey trouble*. New York: Aladdin Paperbacks.

Planning an Integrated Curriculum

Teaching and Learning Connections

Condra, Estelle. 1994. *See the ocean*. Nashville, TN: Ideals Children's Books.

Finchler, Judy. 2000. *Testing Miss Malarkey*. Markham, ON: Fitzhenry & Whiteside.

Houston, Gloria. 1992. *My great aunt Arizona*. New York: HarperCollins.

Merriam, Eve. 1991. *The wise woman and her secret*. New York: Simon & Schuster Books for Young Readers.

Morrison, Toni, with Slade Morrison. 1999. *The big box*. New York: Hyperion Books for Children.

Sollman, Carolyn. 1994. *Through the cracks*. Worcester, MA: Davis Publications.

Young, Ed. 1992. *Seven blind mice*. New York: Philomel Books.

Mathematics Connections

Anno, Mitsumasa. 1983. *Anno's mysterious multiplying jar*. New York: Philomel Books.

Barrett, Judi. 2000. *I knew two who said moo: A counting and rhyming book*. New York: Atheneum Books for Young Readers.

Edwards, Pamela Duncan. 2000. *Roar: A noisy counting book*. New York: HarperCollins.

Friedman, Aileen. 1994. *The king's commissioners*. New York: Scholastic.

Macdonald, Suse. 1994. *Sea shapes*. San Diego, CA: Harcourt Brace.

McGrath, Barbara. 1998. *More M and M's brand chocolate candies math*. Watertown, MA: Charlesbridge.

Neuschwander, Cindy, and Wayne Geehan. 1997. *Sir Cumference and the first round table: A math adventure*. Watertown, MA: Charlesbridge.

Packard, Edward. 2000. *Big numbers and pictures that show just how big they are*. Brookfield, CT: Millbrook.

Schwartz, David, M. 1985. *How much is a million?* Richmond Hill, ON: Scholastic Canada.

Scieszka, Jon, and Lane Smith. 1995. *Math curse*. New York: Viking Press.

Tompert, Ann. *Grandfather Tang's story*. New York: Crown Publishing.

Science Connections

Godkin, Celia. 1989. *Wolf Island*. Markham, ON: Fitzhenry & Whiteside.

Hooks, William H., Joanne Oppenheim, and Barbara Brenner. 1992. *How do you make a bubble?* New York: Bantam Books.

Hooper, Meredith, and Chris Coady. 1998. *The drop in my drink: The story of water on our planet*. London, UK: Frances Lincoln.

Rose, Deborah Lee. 1990. *The people who hugged the trees: An environmental folk tale*. Niwott, CO: Roberts Rinehart.

Social Studies Connections

Baker, Jeannie. 1991. *Window.* New York: Greenwillow Books.

Bunting, Eve. 1998. *So far from the sea.* New York: Clarion Books.

_____. 1994. *Terrible things: An allegory of the Holocaust.* Philadelphia, U.S., and Jerusalem, Israel: The Jewish Publication Society.

_____.1990. *The wall.* New York: Clarion Books.

Coerr, Eleanor. 1993. *Sadako.* New York: Putnam.

Dorros, Arthur. 1992. *This is my house.* New York: Scholastic.

Granfield, Linda. 1993. *Extra! Extra! The who, what, where, when, and why of newspapers.* Toronto, ON: Kids Can Press.

Hartry, Nancy. 1989. *Hold on, McGinty.* Toronto, ON: Doubleday.

Heide, Florence Parry, and Judity Heide Gilliland. 1992. *Sami and the time of troubles.* New York: Clarion Books.

_____. 1990. *The day of Ahmed's secret.* New York: Lothrop, Lee and Shepard Books.

Innocenti, Roberto. 1985. *Rose Blanche.* San Diego, CA: Harcourt Brace.

Leedy, Loreen. 1991. *The furry news: How to make a newspaper.* New York: Holiday House.

Lewis, Paul Owen. 1995. *Storm boy.* Hillsboro, OR: Beyond Words Publishing.

Moss, Marissa. 1998 *Rachel's journal: The story of a pioneer girl.* San Diego, CA: Harcourt Brace.

San Souci, Robert D. 1999. *Young Arthur.* New York: Bantam Doubleday Dell Books for Young Readers.

Sis, Peter. 1991. *Follow the dream: The story of Christopher Columbus.* New York: Alfred A. Knopf.

Van Allsburg, Chris. 1990. *Just a dream.* Boston: Houghton Mifflin.

Yolen, Jane. 1992. *Encounter.* San Diego, CA: Harcourt Brace.

Arts Connections

Anholt, Laurence. 1996. *Degas and the little dancer: A story about Edgar Degas.* New York: Barron's Educational.

_____ 1994. *Camille and the sunflowers: A story about Vincent van Gogh.* New York: Barron's Educational.

Bjork, Christina, and Lena Anderson. 1985. *Linnea in Monet's garden.* Toronto, ON: R & S Books.

Brighton, Catherine. 1990. *Mozart: Scenes from the childhood of the great composer.* New York: Doubleday.

Galli, Letizia. 1996. *Mona Lisa: The secret of the smile.* New York: Doubleday Book for Young Readers.

Lionni, Leo. 1991. *Matthew's dream.* New York: Alfred A. Knopf.

Mills, Judith Christine. 2000. *The painted chest.* Reseda, CA: Tom Porter.

Literacy and Language Learning

Reading and Writing Connections

Arnold, Tedd. 1992. *The signmaker's assistant.* New York: Penguin Putnam.

Bogart, Jo Ellen, Laura Fernandes, and Rick Jacobson. 1997. *Jeremiah learns to read.* Richmond Hill, ON: Scholastic Canada.

Bradford, Kathleen. 1996. *Write now! How to turn your ideas into great stories.* Rev. ed. Richmond Hill, ON: Scholastic Canada.

Bradley, Marie. 1995. *More than anything else.* New York: Orchard Books.

Brown, Marc. 1996. *Arthur writes a story.* New York: Little, Brown.

Bunting, Eve. 1989. *The Wednesday surprise.* New York: Clarion Books.

Caseley, Judith. 1991. *Dear Annie.* New York: Greenwillow Books.

Deedy, Carmen Agra. 1994. *The library dragon.* Atlanta, GA: Peachtree.

Duke, Kate. 1992. *Aunt Isabel tells a good one.* New York: Dutton Children's Books.

Foreman, Michael. 1994. *Grandfather's pencil and the room of stories.* San Diego, CA: Harcourt Brace.

Fox, Mem. 1989. *Wilfrid Gordon McDonald Partridge.* New York: Kane-Miller Books.

Gilman, Phoebe. 1992. *Something from nothing.* Richmond Hill, ON: Scholastic Canada.

Granfield, Linda. 1996. *Postcard talk.* Markham, ON: Pembroke.

Johnston, Tony. 1994. *Amber on the mountain.* New York: Dial Books for Young Readers.

Laskey, Kathryn. 1994. *The librarian who measured the earth*. Boston: Little Brown.

Leedy, Loreen. 1991. *Messages in the mailbox: How to write a letter*. New York: Holiday House.

Little, Jean, Maggie de Vries, and Phoebe Gilman. 1991. *Once upon a golden apple*. Toronto, ON: Penguin Books Canada.

Nixon, Joan Lowery. 1988. *If you were a writer*. New York: Four Winds Press.

Pawagi, Manjusha. 1998. *The girl who hated books*. Toronto, ON: Second Story Press.

Polacco, Patricia. 1998. *Thank you, Mr. Falker*. New York: Philomel Books.

_____. 1993. *The bee tree*. New York: Philomel Books.

San Souci, Robert D. 1997. *A weave of words*. New York: Orchard Books.

Schotter, Roni. 1997. *Nothing ever happens on 90th Street*. New York: Orchard Books.

Stevens, Janet. 1995. *From pictures to words: A book about making a book*. New York: Holiday House.

Stinson, Kathy. 1994. *Writing your best picture book ever*. Markham, ON: Pembroke.

_____. 2000. *King of the castle*. Toronto, ON: Second Story Press.

Poetry

Booth, David, ed. 1993. *Voices on the wind*. New York: Morrow Junior Books.

_____. 1989. *Til all the stars have fallen: Canadian poems for children*. Toronto, ON: Kids Can Press.

Booth, David, and Maryann Kovalski. 1993. *Doctor Knickerbocker and other rhymes: A Canadian collection*. Toronto, ON: Kids Can Press.

Fitch, Sheree. 1993. *Toes in my nose*. Toronto, ON: Doubleday.

Fleischman, Paul. 1992. *Joyful noise: Poems for two voices*. New York: HarperCollins.

Hamanaka, Sheila. 1994. *All the colors of the Earth*. New York: Morrow Junior Books.

Hoberman, Mary A., ed. 1994. *My song is beautiful: A celebration of multicultural poems and pictures*. New York: Little, Brown.

Lewis, Patrick. 1998. *Doodle dandies: Poems that take shape*. New York: Atheneum Books for Young Readers.

Little, Jean. 1986. *Hey World, here I am.* Toronto, ON: Kids Can Press.

Prelutsky, Jack. 1993. *The dragons are singing tonight.* New York: Greenwillow Books.

_____. 1983. *Random House book of poetry.* New York: Random House Books for Young Readers.

Shields, Carol Diggory. 1998. *Lunch money and other poems about school.* Madison, WI: Demco.

Silverstein, Shel. 1981. *A light in the attic.* New York: HarperCollins.

_____. 1981. *Where the sidewalk ends.* New York: HarperCollins.

Yolen, Jane. 1986. *Ring of earth: A child's book of seasons.* San Diego, CA: Harcourt Brace Jovanovich.

Alphabet Books

Base, Graeme. 1987. *Animalia.* Richmond Hill, ON: Irwin.

Harrison, Ted. 1987. *A northern alphabet.* Toronto, ON: Tundra Books.

Hepworth, Cathi. 1992. *Antics: An alphabetical anthology.* New York: G. P. Putnam's Sons.

Paul, Ann Whitford. 1991. *Eights hands round: A patchwork alphabet.* New York: HarperCollins.

Shelby, Aaron. 1991. *Potluck.* New York: Orchard Books.

Seeley, Laura. 1990. *The book of shadow boxes: A story of the ABC's.* Atlanta, GA: Peachtree.

Thornhill, Jan. 1988. *The wildlife A B C: A nature alphabet.* Toronto, ON: Owl Books.

Van Allsburg, Chris. 1987. *The Z was zapped.* Boston: Houghton Mifflin.

Wildsmith, Brian. 1981. *ABC.* Oxford, UK: Oxford University Press.

Playing with Words and Language

Delacorte, Peter, and Michael C. Witte. 1978. *Book of terns.* New York: Penguin.

Elting, Mary, and Michael Folsom. 1980. *Merry go round: A book about nouns.* New York: Clarion Books.

Golick, Margie. 1995. *Wacky word games*. Markham, ON: Pembroke.

Heller, Ruth. 1991. *Up, up, and away: A book about adverbs*. New York: Putnam Publishing Group.

_____. 1990. *Merry go round: A book about nouns*. New York: Putnam Publishing Group.

_____. 1989. *Many luscious lollipops: A book about adjectives*. New York: Putnam Publishing Group.

_____. 1988. *Kites sail high: A book about verbs*. New York: Putnam Publishing Group.

_____. 1987. *A cache of jewels and other collective nouns*. New York: Putnam Publishing Group.

Hooks, William H., Joanne Oppenheim, and Betty D. Boegehold. 1986. *Read-a-rebus: Tales and rhymes in words and pictures*. New York: Random House.

Lionni, Leo. 1990. *The alphabet tree*. New York: Alfred A. Knopf.

Maestro, Giulio. 1989. *Riddle roundup: A wild bunch to beef up your word power*. New York: Clarion Books.

Martin, Bill, Jr., and Vladimir Radunsky. 1994. *The maestro plays*. New York: Henry Holt and Company.

_____. 1991. *The happy hippopotami*. San Diego, CA: Harcourt Brace Jovanovich.

Marzollo, Jean. 1992. *I spy: A book of picture riddles*. Richmond Hill, ON: Scholastic Canada.

Most, Bernard. 1980. *There's an ant in Anthony*. New York: Mulberry Books.

Obligado, Lillian. 1986. *Faint frogs feeling feverish and other terrifically tantalizing tongue twisters*. New York: Puffin Books.

Philpot, Lorna, and Graham Philpot. 1993. *Amazing Anthony Ant*. New York: Random House.

Terban, Marvin. 1983. *In a pickle and other funny idioms*. New York: Clarion Books.

_____. 1982. *Eight ate: A feast of homonym riddles*. New York: Clarion Books.

Pattern and Predictable Books

Brown, Ruth. 1991. *The world that Jack built*. New York: Dutton Children's Books.

Brown, Margaret Wise. 1990. *The important book*. New York: HarperCollins.

Handy, Libby. 1984. *Boss for a week*. New York: Scholastic.

Campbell, Rod. 1987. *Dear Zoo*. New York: Four Winds Press.

Ahlberg, Janet, and Alan Ahlberg. 1985. *Each peach pear plum*. New York: Scholastic.

Druce, Arden. 1991. *Witch, witch, come to my party*. Auburn, ME: Childs Play.

Hoberman, Mary Ann. 1978. *A house is a house for me*. Madison, WI: Demco.

Martin, Bill, Jr. 1991. *Polar Bear, Polar Bear, what do you hear?* New York: Henry Holt and Company.

Rogers, Paul, and Emma Rogers. 1998. *The book that Jack made*. London, UK: Bodley Head.

Scieszka, Jon. 1994. *The book that Jack wrote*. New York: Viking.

Stinson, Kathy. 1995. *Those green things*. Toronto, ON: Annick Press.

_____. 1982. *Red is best*. Toronto, ON: Annick Press.

Stow, Jenny. 1992. *The house that Jack built*. New York: Dial Books for Young Readers.

Williams, Marcia. 1989. *When I was little*. London, UK: Walker Books.

Patterned Storylines

Briggs, Raymond. 1988. *Jim and the beanstalk*. London, UK: Hamish Hamilton.

Calmenson, Stephanie. 1989. *The principal's new clothes*. New York: Scholastic.

French, Fiona. 1986. *Snow White in New York*. Toronto, ON: Oxford University Press.

Gay, Marie-Louise. 1994. *The 3 little pigs*. Vancouver, BC: Douglas & McIntyre.

Kellogg, Steven. 1997. *The three little pigs*. New York: Morrow.

San Souci, Robert D. 2000. *Little Gold Star: A Spanish American Cinderella tale*. New York: HarperCollins.

_____. 2000. *Cinderella Skeleton.* San Diego, CA: Harcourt Brace.

Scieszka, Jon. 1989. *The true story of the three little pigs.* New York: Viking Kestrel.

_____. 1991. *The frog prince continued.* New York: Viking Penguin Press.

Steptoe, John. 1987. *Mufaro's beautiful daughers: An African tale.* New York: Lothrop, Lee and Shepard Books.

Tolhurst, Marilyn. 1990. *Somebody and the three Blairs.* New York: Orchard Books.

Young, Ed. 1989. *Lon Po Po: A Red-Riding Hood story from China.* New York: Philomel Books.

Appendix 4:
List of Blackline Masters on CD-ROM

Blackline Masters		Matching Text Figures

Timetabling

BLM T-1	Weekly Timetable	Figure 3.7
BLM T-2	Daily Plan	Figure 3.8

ClassroomAtmosphere

BLM T-3	Questionnaire for Establishing Classroom Routines and Procedures (2 pages)	Figure 4.1
BLM S-4	People Hunt	Figure 4.3
BLM S-5	People Search Bingo	Figure 4.4
BLM S-6	Things in Common	Figure 4.5
BLM S-7	Cooperative Group Learning Experiences (3 pages)	Figure 4.7
BLM S-8	Expectations for Successful Cooperative Learning	Figure 4.8
BLM S-9	T-Chart	Figure 4.9
BLM S-10	Cooperative Group Assessment Form	Figure 4.12
BLM S-11	Self-assessment Form	Figure 4.13
BLM S-12	Behaviour Checklist	Figure 4.14
BLM T-13	Bullying Incident Report	Figure 4.15
BLM P-14	Sample Letter to Parents Re: Bullying	Figure 4.16

Planning an Integrated Curriculum

BLM T-15	Long-range Planning Sheet	Figure 5.1
BLM T-16	Year-at-a-Glance Planning Sheet	Figure 5.2
BLM T-17	Year-at-a-Glance Monthly Planning Sheet	Figure 5.3

A Learning Centre Approach

Literacy and Language Learning

Partnerships with Parents

References

Armstrong, Thomas. 1994. Multiple intelligences: Seven ways to approach curriculum. *Educational Leadership* 52 (November): 26-28.

Aronson, E., and E. Goode. 1978. *The jigsaw classroom*. Beverly Hills, CA: Sage Publications.

Bennett, Barrie, Carol Rolheiser, and Laurie Stevahn. 1991. *Classroom management: A thinking & caring approach*. Ajax, ON: Visutronx.

_____. 1991. *Cooperative learning: Where heart meets mind*. Toronto, ON: Educational Connections.

Bezan, Tony. 1974. *Use both sides of the brain*. New York: E.P. Dutton.

Bloom, Benjamin S., and David R. Drathwohl. 1956. *Taxonomy of educational objectives: The classification of educational goals, Handbook 1: Cognitive domain*. New York: Longmans, Green.

Booth, David. 1998. *Guiding the reading process*. Markham, ON: Pembroke.

Clay, Marie M. 1993. *An observation survey of early literacy achievement*. Portsmouth, NH: Heinemann.

Colorossa, Barbara. 1999. *Kids Are Worth It*. Toronto, ON: Penguin Books Canada.

Daniels, Harvey. 1994. *Literature circles: Voice and choice in the child-centred classroom*. Markham, ON: Pembroke.

Education Department of Western Australia. 1994. *First steps: Writing resource book and the First steps: Writing developmental continuum*. Toronto, ON: Irwin.

Gardner, Howard. 1983. *Frames of mind: The theory of multiple intelligences*. New York: Harper & Row.

Gibbs, Jeanne. 1994. *Tribes: A new way of learning together*. Toronto, ON: Irwin.

Goodman, Yetta M., Dorothy J. Watson, and Carolyn L. Burke. 1996. *Reading strategies: Focus on Comprehension.* 2d ed. Katonah, NY: Richard C. Owen.

_____. 1987. *Reading miscue inventory: Alternative procedures.* Katonah, NY: Richard C. Owen.

Hunter, Madeline. 1976. *Rx improved instruction.* El Segundo, CA: T.I.P.

Johnson, David W., Roger T. Johnson, and E. J. Holubec. 1990. *Circles of learning: Cooperation in the classroom.* Edina, MN: Interaction Book Co.

Kagan, S. 1990. *Cooperative learning resources for teachers.* San Juan Capistrano, CA: Resources for Teachers.

Lazear, David. 1991. *Seven ways of teaching: The artistry of teaching with multiple intelligences.* Palatine, IL: Skylight.

Munsch, Robert. 1987. *Moira's birthday.* 1987. Toronto, ON: Annick Press.

Norris, D. and J. Bouchard. 1980. *Observing children.* Toronto, ON: Toronto Board of Education.

Ogle, D. 1986. K-W-L: A teaching model that develops active reading of expository text. *The Reading Teacher* 39: 564-670.

Opitz, Michael F., and Timothy V. Rasinsky. 1998. *Goodbye round robin: 25 effective oral reading strategies.* Portsmouth, NH: Heinemann.

Ross, J., Anne Hogaboam-Gray, and Carol Rolheiser. 1998. Skills training versus action research in-service: Impact on student research attitudes to self-evaluation. *Teaching and Teacher Education* 14(5): 463-77.

Schwartz, Susan. 1988. *All write: A teacher's guide to writing, grades K-6.* Toronto, ON: OISE Press.

Schwartz, Susan, and Maxine Bone. 1995. *Retelling, relating, reflecting: Beyond the 3 R's.* Toronto, ON: Irwin.

Seuss, Dr. 1990. *Oh, the places you'll go!* New York: Random House.

Strickland, Kathleen, and James Strickland. 2000. *Making assessment elementary.* Portsmouth, NH: Heinemann.

Wolfe, Patricia. 1987. What the "seven-step lesson plan" isn't. *Educational Leadership* (February): 70-71.

Recommended Teacher Resources

Classroom Atmosphere

Adams, Hetty. 1994. *Peace in the classroom: Practical lessons in living for elementary-age children.* Winnipeg, MB: Peguis.

Appleby, Sandra. 1999. *Survival strategies: Practical tools for educators.* Toronto, ON: Educational Services Committee, Ontario Secondary School Teachers' Federation.

Bennett, Barrie, and Peter Smilanich. 1994. *Classroom management: A thinking and caring approach.* Ajax, ON: Visutronx.

Bennett, Barrie, Carol Rolheiser, and Laurie Stevahn. 1991. *Cooperative learning: Where heart meets mind.* Ajax, ON: Visutronx.

Binder, Deanna. 1995. *Fair play for kids: A handbook of activities for teaching fair play.* Gloucester, ON: Canadian Centre for Ethics in Sports.

Collis, Mark, and Joan Dalton. 1990. *Becoming responsible learners: Strategies for positive classroom management.* Portsmouth, NH: Heinemann.

Colorossa, Barbara. 1999. *Kids Are Worth It.* Toronto, ON: Penguin Books Canada.

DiGuilio, Robert. 1995. *Positive classroom management: A step-by-step guide to successfully running the show without destroying student dignity.* California: Corwin Press.

Fine, Esther S., Ann Lacey, and Joan Baer. 1995. *Children as peacemakers.* Portsmouth, NH: Heinemann.

Gibbs, Jeanne. 1994. *Tribes: A new way of learning together.* Toronto, ON: Irwin.

Johnson, David W., and Roger T. Johnson. 1984. *Structuring cooperative learning: Lesson plans for teachers.* New Brighton, MN: Interaction Book Co.

Kaufman, Gershen, and Lev Raphael. 1990. *Stick up for yourself! Every kid's guide to personal power and positive self-esteem.* Minneapolis, MN: Free Spirit.

Kerr, Rob. 1999. *Self-discipline: Using portfolios to help students develop self-awareness, manage emotions and build relationships.* Markham, ON: Pembroke.

Kreidler, William. 1984. *Creative conflict resolution: More than 200 activities for keeping peace in the classroom.* Reading, MA: ScottForesman.

MacKay, Wayne, and Lyle I. Sutherland. 1992. *Teachers and the law: A practical guide for educators.* Toronto, ON: Edmond Montgomery Publications.

McNaughton, John. 2000. *The Law primer: A guide for teachers.* 2d ed. Toronto, ON: Tarton Publishing.

Marks-Krpan, Cathy. 2001. *The Write Math: Writing in the Math Class, Grade K-8*: Parsippany, NJ: Dale Seymour Publication.

Palmer, P. 1989. *Teen esteem: A self-direction manual for young adults.* Old Greenwich, CT: Impact.

Petovello, Laura R. 1998. *The spirit that moves us: A literature-based resource guide: Teaching about diversity, prejudice, human rights, and the Holocaust.* Gardiner, ME: Tilbury House.

Porro, Barbara. 1996. *Talk it out: Conflict resolution in the elementary classroom.* Alexandria, VA: Association for Supervision and Curriculum Development.

Rigby, Ken. 1998. *Bullying in the schools and what to do about it.* Markham, ON: Pembroke.

Ross, Peter. 1998. *Arresting violence: A resource guide for schools and their communities.* Toronto, ON: Ontario Public School Teachers' Federation.

Sharp, Sonia, and Peter Smith. 1994. *Tackling bullying in your school: A practical handbook for teachers.* New York: Routledge.

Stones, Rosemary. 1993. *Don't pick on me! How to handle bullying.* Markham, ON: Pembroke.

Webster-Doyle, T. 1991. *Why is everybody always picking on me? A guide to handling bullies.* Middlebury, VT: Atrium Society Education for Peace.

Zarzour, Kim. 1994. *Battling the school-yard bully: How to raise an assertive child in an aggressive world.* Toronto, ON: HarperCollins.

Planning an Integrated Curriculum

Armstrong, Thomas. 2000. *Multiple intelligences in the classroom*. 2d ed. Baltimore, MD: Association for Supervision & Curriculum Development.

Bennett, Barrie, and Carol Rolheiser. 2001. *Beyond Monet: The artful science of instructional integration*. Ajax, ON: Bookation.

Cullen, Louise. 1995. *Solid gold for kids: Musical energizers*. Toronto, ON: Prentice Hall Ginn.

Fogarty, Robin. 1991. *The mindful school: How to integrate the curricula*. Andover, MA: Skylight.

Gardner, Howard. 1983. *Frames of mind. The theory of multiple intelligences*. New York: Basic Books.

Lazear, David. 1991. *Seven ways of teaching: The artistry of teaching with multiple intelligences*. Palatine, IL: Skylight.

Moline, Steve. 1996. *I see what you mean: Children at work with visual information*, Markham. ON: Pembroke.

Morgan, Norah, and Juliana Saxton. 1994. *Asking better questions: Models, techniques, and classroom activities for engaging students in learning*. Markham, ON: Pembroke.

Parry, Terrence, and Gayle Gregory. 1998. *Designing brain compatible learning*. Arlington Heights, IL: Skylight Training and Publishing.

Roberts, Patricia L., and Richard B. Kellough. 1995. *A guide for developing an interdisciplinary thematic unit*. Englewood Cliffs, NJ: Prentice-Hall.

Tomlinson, Carol Ann. 1999. *The differentiated classroom: Responding to the needs of all learners*. Baltimore, MD: Association for Supervision & Curriculum Development.

Literacy and Language Learning

Allen, Janet. 2000. *It's never too late: Leading adolescents to lifelong literacy*. Portsmouth, NH: Heinemann,

Atwell, Nancie. 1998. *In the middle: New understandings about writing, reading, & learning*. 2d ed. Portsmouth, NH: Boynton Cook.

Barton, Bob. 2000. *Telling stories your way: Storytelling and reading aloud in the classroom*. Markham, ON: Pembroke.

Benedict, Susan, and Lenore Carlisle. 1992. *Beyond words: Picture books for older readers and writers*. Portsmouth, NH: Heinemann.

Booth, David. 1999. *Guiding the reading process: Techniques and strategies for successful instruction in K-8 classrooms*. Markham, ON: Pembroke.

_____. 1996. *Literacy techniques for building successful readers and writers*. Markham, ON: Pembroke.

Booth, David, and Bob Barton. 2000. *Story works: How teachers can use shared stories in the new curriculum*. Markham, ON: Pembroke.

Booth, David, and Jonathon Neelands. 1998. *Writing in role: Classroom projects connecting writing and drama*. Hamilton, ON: Caliburne Enterprise.

Burke, Eileen. M. 1994. *Using nonfiction in the classroom*. New York: Scholastic.

Daniels, Harvey. 1994. *Literature circles: Voice and choice in the student-centred classroom*. Markham, ON: Pembroke.

Deakin, David, and Gordon Moore. 1992. *Looks great: Exciting ways of presenting your projects*. Markham, ON: Pembroke.

Education Department of Western Australia. 1994. *First steps developmental continuum and resource books*. Toronto, ON: Pearson Education Canada Inc.

Fletcher, Ralph. 1993. *What a writer needs*. Portsmouth, NH: Heinemann.

Fletcher, Ralph, and JoAnn Portalupi. 1998. *Craft lessons: Teaching writing K-8*. York, ME: Stenhouse.

Fountas, Irene C., and Gay Su Pinnell. 2001. *Guiding readers and writers, grades 3-6: Teaching comprehension, genre, and content literacy*. Portsmouth, NH: Heinemann.

_____. 1999. *Word matters: Teaching phonics and spelling in the reading/writing classroom*. Portsmouth, NH: Heinemann.

_____. 1996. *Guided reading: Good first teaching for all children*. Portsmouth, NH: Heinemann.

Fry, Edward Bernard, Jacqueline E. Kressy, and Dona Lee Fountoukidis. 1993. *The reading teacher's book of lists*. 3d ed. Englewood Cliffs, NJ: Prentice-Hall.

Gentry, Richard J., and Jean Wallace Gillet. 1993. *Teaching kids to spell*. Portsmouth, NH: Heinemann.

George, Jerry. 1994. *Good grief! Good grammar! A basic and short guide to standard English*. Markham, ON: Pembroke.

Goodman, Debra. 1999. *The reading detective club: Solving the mysteries of reading*. Portsmouth, NH: Heinemann.

Goodman, Kenneth S. 1993. *Phonics phacts*. Richmond Hill, ON: Scholastic Canada.

Graves, Donald. 1993. *Explore poetry*. Toronto, ON: Irwin.

_____. 1989. *Investigate nonfiction: The reading/writing teacher's companion*. Portsmouth, NH: Heinemann.

Green, Judy. 1999. *The ultimate guide to classroom publishing*. Markham, ON: Pembroke.

Hart-Hewins, Linda, and Jan Wells. 1999. *Better books! Better readers! How to choose, use and level books for children in the primary grades*. Markham, ON: Pembroke.

Harvey, Stephanie. 1998. *Nonfiction matters: Reading, writing and research in grades 3-8*. York, ME: Stenhouse.

Harvey, Stephanie, and Anne Goudvis. 2000. *Strategies that work: Teaching comprehension to enhance understanding*. York, ME: Stenhouse.

Harwayne, Shelley. 1999. *Going public: Priorities and practice at the Manhattan New School*. Portsmouth, NH: Heinemann.

Johnson, Paul. 2000. *Making books: Over 30 practical book-making projects for children*. Markham, ON: Pembroke.

Johnson, Nancy J., and Katherine S. Noe. 1995. *Literature circles and response*. Norwood, MA: Christopher Gordon.

Keen, Ellin Oliver, Susan Zimmerman. 1997. *Mosaic of thought: Teaching comprehension in a readers' workshop*. Portsmouth, NH: Heinemann.

Kezwer, Paula. 1995. *Worlds of wonder: Resources for multicultural children's literature*. Toronto, ON: Pippin.

Luongo-Orlando, Katherine. 2001. *A project approach to language learning*: Markham, ON: Pembroke.

Marks-Krpan, Cathy. 2001. *The write math: writing in the math class, grade K–8*: Parsippany, NJ: Dale Seymour.

McCarrier, Andrea, Gay Su Pinnell, and Irene C. Fountas. 2000. *Interactive writing: How language and literacy come together, K-2*. Portsmouth, NH: Heinemann.

McCracken, Marlene J., and Robert A. McCracken. 1996. *Spelling through phonics*. 2d ed. Winnipeg, MB: Peguis.

Opitz, Michael F., and Timothy V. Rasinsky. 1998. *Good-bye round robin: 25 effective oral reading strategies*. Portsmouth, NH: Heinemann.

Phenix, Jo, and Doreen Scott-Dunne. 1991. *Spelling instruction that makes sense*. Markham, ON: Pembroke.

Routman, Regie. 2000. *Conversations: Strategies for teaching, learning, and evaluating*. Portsmouth, NH: Heinemann.

Scott, Ruth. 1993. *Spelling: Sharing the secrets*. Scarborough, ON: Gage.

Steele, Bob. 1998. *Draw me a story: An illustrated exploration of drawing as language*. Winnipeg, MB: Peguis.

Stinson, Kathy. 1994. *Writing your best picture book ever*. Markham, ON: Pembroke.

_____. 1991. *Writing picture books: What works and what doesn't*. Markham, ON: Pembroke.

Suid, Murray. 1989. *Recipes for writing: Motivations, skills and activities*. Reading, MA: Addison-Wesley.

Swartz, Larry. 1995. *Dramathemes: A practical guide for classroom teachers*. Rev. ed. Markham, ON: Pembroke.

_____. 1993. *Classroom events through poetry*. Markham, ON: Pembroke.

Taberski, Sharon. 2000. *On solid ground: Strategies for teaching reading, K to 3*. Portsmouth, NH: Heinemann.

Tarasoff, Mary. 1994. *Reading instruction that makes sense*. Victoria, BC: Active Learning Institute.

_____. 1990. *Spelling strategies you can teach*. Victoria, BC: Active Learning Institute.

Thurman, Mark. 1992. *How to plan your drawings*. Markham, ON: Pembroke.

Weaver, Constance. 1996. *Teaching grammar in context*. Portsmouth, NH: Heinemann.

Wells, Jan, and Linda Hart-Hewins. 1994. *Phonics, too! How to teach skills in a balanced language program.* Markham, ON: Pembroke.

Yopp, Ruth Helen, and Kay Yop Hallie. 1992. *Literature-based reading activities.* Needham Heights, MA: Allyn & Bacon.

Technology and Learning

Heide, Ann, and Dale Henderson. 1994. *The technological classroom: A blueprint for success.* Toronto, ON: Irwin.

Owen, Trevor, and Ron Owston. 1995. *The learning highway: The student's guide to the Internet.* 3d ed. Toronto, ON: Key Porter Books.

Webb, Colin, and Wynne Rowe. 1995. *Computers and kids: A parent's guide.* Toronto, ON: Harper Collins.

Wepner, Shelley B., William J. Valmont, and Richard Thurlow. 2000. *Linking literacy and technology: A guide for K to 8 classrooms.* Newark, DE: International Reading Association.

Out-of-Classroom Excursions

English, Barbara, and Karen Lipton-Doidge. 1997. *Creating successful field trips.* Toronto, ON: Irwin.

_____. 1997. *Fifty fascinating field trips in Metropolitan Toronto and surrounding areas.* Toronto, ON: Irwin.

Assessing, Evaluating, and Reporting

Campbell Hill, Bonnie, Cynthia Ruptic, and Lisa Norwick. 1998. *Classroom based assessment.* Norwood, MA: Christopher Gordon.

Clay, Marie M. 2000. *Concepts about print: What have children learned about the way we print language?* Portsmouth, NH: Heinemann.

_____. 2000. *Running records for classroom teachers.* Portsmouth, NH: Heinemann.

_____. 1993. *An observation survey of early literacy achievement.* Portsmouth, NH: Heinemann.

Davies, Anne, Caren Cameron, Colleen Politano, and Kathleen Gregory. 1992. *Together is better: Collaborative assessment, evaluation and reporting.* Winnipeg, MB: Peguis.

Earl, Lorna and J. Bradley Cousins. 1995. *Classroom assessment: Changing the face, facing the change.* Toronto, ON: Ontario Public School Teachers Federation (OPSTF).

Ekwall, Eldon E., and James L. Shanker. 1997. *Locating and correcting reading difficulties.* 7th ed. Englewood Cliffs, NJ: Prentice-Hall.

Everts Rogers, Sheri, and Kathy Everts Danielson. 1996. *Teacher portfolios: Literacy artifacts and themes.* Portsmouth, NH: Heinemann.

Popham, W. James. 1995. *Classroom assessment: What teachers need to know.* Needham Heights, MA: Allyn & Bacon.

Rhodes, Lynn K., ed. 1993. *Literacy assessment: A handbook of instruments.* Portsmouth, NH: Heinemann.

Rolheiser, Carol. 1996. *Self-evaluation:Helping students get better at it.* The Clear Group, Ontario Institute for Studies in Education and the Durham Board of Education., Toronto, ON.

Rolheiser-Bennett, Carol, Barbara Bower, and Laurie Stevahn. 2000. *The portfolio organizer: Succeeding with portfolios in your classroom.* Alexandria, VA: Association for Supervision & Curriculum Development.

Stiggins, Richard.J. 2001. *Student-involved classroom Assessment.* 3d ed. Upper Saddle River, NJ: Prentice-Hall Inc.

Partnerships with Parents

Botrie, Maureen, and Pat Wenger. 1992. *Teachers and parents together.* Markham, ON: Pembroke.

Davis, Bruce. 1995. *How to involve parents in a multi-cultural school.* Alexandria, VA: Association for Supervision and Curriculum Development.

Dean, Sandra. 2000. *Hearts and minds: A public school miracle.* Toronto, ON: Penguin Books Canada.

Education Department of Western Australia. 1995. *First Steps: Parents as partners — Helping your child's literacy and language development.* Western Australia: Longman.

McGilp, Jacqueline, and Maureen Michael. 1994. *The home-school connection: Guidelines for working with parents.* Portsmouth, NH: Heinemann.

Millar Grant, Janet, Barbara Heffler, and Kadri Mereweather. 1995. *Student-led conferences: Using portfolios to share learning with parents.* Markham, ON: Pembroke.

Overall, Denise. 1997. *Smart homes + smart schools = smart kids.* Richmond Hill, ON: Scholastic Canada.

Phenix, Jo, and Doreen Scott-Dunne. 1994. *Spelling for parents.* Markham, ON: Pembroke.

Scott, Ruth, and Sharon Siamon. 1994. *Sharing the secrets: Teach your child to spell.* Toronto, ON: Macmillan.

Tarasoff, Mary. 1992. *A guide to children's spelling development.* Victoria, BC: Active Learning Institute.